GOD AND LIFE
ON THE
PECOS

Father Brian Vincenzo Guerrini, ss.cc.

WESTBOW
PRESS®
A DIVISION OF THOMAS NELSON
& ZONDERVAN

This book is a work of non-fiction. Unless otherwise noted, the author and the publisher make no explicit guarantees as to the accuracy of the information contained in this book and in some cases, names of people and places have been altered to protect their privacy.

WestBow Press books may be ordered through booksellers or by contacting:

WestBow Press
A Division of Thomas Nelson & Zondervan
1663 Liberty Drive
Bloomington, IN 47403
www.westbowpress.com
844-714-3454

All images used in this book are used with the permission of:

Adobe Stock Images (stock.adobe.com)
Congregation of the Sacred Hearts of Jesus and Mary (www.ssccpicpus.com)

ISBN: 979-8-3850-1223-7 (sc)
ISBN: 979-8-3850-1224-4 (e)

Library of Congress Control Number: 2023921550

Print information available on the last page.

WestBow Press rev. date: 11/22/2023

This Book is dedicated to my

Brothers and Sisters in the Congregation of
the Sacred Hearts of Jesus and Mary

SS.CC.

Thank you for allowing me the privilege of
serving the people of New Mexico

TO THE SACRED HEARTS OF JESUS AND MARY
HONOR AND GLORY!

Contents

Foreword

God is found in the life of people, places and events of the past, present and future, even in a land referred to sometimes as *Satan's Paradise*. This book is dedicated to and has been inspired by all the people in the central Pecos River Valley of southeastern New Mexico, including my own religious community, the Congregation of the Sacred Hearts of Jesus and Mary (SS.CC.), and the people of Artesia, Dexter, Hagerman and Lake Arthur, New Mexico, whose lives have touched me tremendously and whose faith, hope, love and grit inspired me during an eleven-year period from 2002 to 2013 to compile and write this book. You have honored me and your forebearers and continued the legacy of your cultures in this land by your lives and missionary spirit. The hardiness and resiliency of a people is a product of their faith and spirit. I have been privileged to have been touched by just such spirit and faith, and I feel blessed by the presence of those memories in my heart. In this work, I wish to honor the memories of the past, present and future in this part of the Land of Enchantment.

It would be impossible for me to name every single person I have met and encountered in the eleven years I spent in this part of New Mexico, but, there are a few people who I would like to personally acknowledge, as they have been an inspiration to me in my religious life as a member of the Congregation of the Sacred Hearts and an inspiration to me in writing this book. First, I would like to thank my religious community for their love, support and encouragement as I sometimes fumbled the spiritual football passed on to me and did not truly appreciate the pearl as it truly was. Sometimes my own human ego may have hindered me in my spiritual journey, but, through it all, there was my community to stand by me, warts and all. In particular, I would like to thank my Sacred Hearts brother, Fr. Paul, SS.CC., whose selfless love and concern for others was an inspiration. As pastor of three parishes and two missions, Paul's responsibilities were tremendous, like pastors in the past in this region, but his love for others showed in his attention to detail and faithful carrying out of his duties as pastor. Next, there were Sisters Damien, SS.CC. and Marie, SS.CC., whose fighting spirits for justice and equality were indomitable. Also, there were my brothers who spent some time with our community-in-mission in New Mexico: Fr. Richard, SS.CC., God rest his soul, Fr. Ben, SS.CC., God rest his soul, and Fr. Chris, SS.CC. Without their presences, our religious community would not have been the same. And then, there was Sr. Edna, SS.CC., our ninety-year old "elk sister", who is no longer with us, but whose energy was contagious and Sr. Dominic, SS.CC., God rest her soul, whose talents in Spanish and music were invaluable.

And, of course, there were the "blessed" locals, those who made our community-in-mission lives so rich and full: our sweet Mary, secretary extraordinaire; Missy, who kept us all in line; Deacon Pablo, whose voice could wake the dead; Deacon Jesus, whose enthusiasm for tamales was incredible; Deacon Tony, our high school connection; Cecilia, whose laughter was contagious; Shellye, whose clarity was most appreciated; the three Deacon wives: Maria, Emma and Becky, who kept the Deacons in line; and Luis, whose expertise was amazing.

And, certainly, I wish to personally thank the two Bishops of Las Cruces during my time in New Mexico, Bishop *Emeritus* Ricardo Ramirez, CSB, whose guiding hands inspired us all, and Bishop Oscar Cantu, whose youthful warmth warmed our souls.

And finally, to all those who I met on a daily basis, in community, in ministry situations and on the streets. This book wouldn't exist if it wasn't for your faith, your hope and your love in good times and in bad, not unlike the pioneers who preceded you in this part of America.

I would like to say something about my religious community. I am a member of the Congregation of the Sacred Hearts of Jesus and Mary (SS.CC.), and have been since 1986. We are a religious community of men and women, religious and lay, dedicated to contemplating, living and proclaiming the compassionate love of God in the world. We are a missionary order founded on Christmas Eve in the year 1800 in France. Our founders, Fr. Pierre Coudrin and Mother Henriette Aymer de la Chevalerie, out of the chaos and violence of the French Revolution, envisioned a community of men and women, united by the compassionately loving example of Jesus and his mother, Mary, who would go out to the world and spread this compassionate love as missionaries of the Sacred Hearts. This was not easy, as our first missionaries experienced the physical demands of the missions in such remote places as the South Pacific. Members of our Congregation, like Father Damien de Veuster, SS.CC., now Saint Damien, who worked with victims of Hansen's Disease on the Hawaiian Island of Moloka'i for many years until he contracted the deadly disease and died from it, Father Eustaquio Van Lieshout, SS.CC., who worked with the poor in Brazil, five of our brothers who were martyred during the Spanish Civil War and four of our brothers who were martyred during the Commune persecution in France, now declared Blessed by the Catholic Church, have all been witnesses to this compassionate love each in their own way.

As for me, I am a product of both my childhood in the American Midwest and of my religious formation within my religious Congregation. I grew up in Indianapolis, Indiana, the first child to a first generation Italian father and a mother descended from German-Scottish roots, and, for over twenty-five years, was formed and ministered from within my religious community. I was instilled with a desire to be a missionary, to go where I could help to make a difference in the lives of others, like a Saint Damien or a Blessed Eustaquio or our five Spanish martyrs and four martyrs of the Commune. I have always had a deep compassion inside of me to help others and make things better for them. This compassion encompassed both listening to people's stories and doing whatever I could to help them on their journeys with God.

For an eleven-year period, from September of 2002 to September of 2013, I was privileged to have been a part of a renewal in our Congregation called simply "Community-in-Mission", or CIM. It was an initiative from our General Chapters to re-establish our roots as a religious community of men and women and lay people dedicated to the mission of our founders, that is, to love unconditionally, like God's love for us, and, doing this within a community that prayed, shared, reflected, and broke bread together as brothers and sisters, with a distinct "family spirit", the same spirit that our founders inspired.

The process of coming together as Sacred Hearts' brothers and sisters consisted of three months living together at our former Novitiate in southern California. This formation period consisted of talks on religious life, community life, missionary life, and life as Sacred Hearts. It was a wonderful time of discovering who we were, are, and aspired to be, as religious brothers and sisters of the Sacred Hearts, as well as looking forward to our insertion as a community-in-mission in a particular area in need.

We had a formative experience of finding out who we were as individuals, each called by God to spread compassionate love to others, as well as who we were as a community-in-mission. This proved challenging, especially in the place where we finally decided to locate our CIM, in the middle of the dry, windy, dusty plains of southeastern New Mexico, along the Pecos River, between Roswell to the north and Carlsbad to the south, centered around a small city named Artesia.

I did not originally intend this book to be a history book, but, the more I delved into the search for the existence and meaning of God and life in this part of New Mexico, the more I reflected on the search for God and life in the present, and the more I discovered that the connection between God and us comes out of the past, the land and the lives of those who inhabited and continue to inhabit this place. So, I hope that the historical milieu lends to the telling of this story.

The title of this book, *God and Life on the Pecos*, encompasses epithets for the new state of New Mexico, circa 1912, "Satan's Paradise", referring to the eternal wildness and sometimes waywardness of New Mexico, "Land of *Poco Tiempo*" and "Land of Enchantment."

Vamanos!

Fr. Brian Vincenzo Guerrini, SS.CC.
La Verne, CA, USA
2023

Introduction

A RAINBOW OVER THE LAND

While we, there were seven of us, three religious sisters, three religious priests and a religious brother, were finishing our three-month formation period in California, before embarking upon our journey into the unknown, our formators, our animators and our respective provincial governments told us that it was up to our band of seven, our "Magnificent Seven", as we liked to call ourselves, taking a movie title out of the wild west, to determine where in the great expanse of these here United States of America we felt called to be missionaries of the Sacred Hearts and share with others our call to be compassionate "lovers".

So it was that our initial seven missionaries, a diverse group of people, including two sisters and an Irish priest who had served in the Philippines, a ninety-year old sister who was the first woman to receive a Ph.D in Biology from the University of Notre Dame, a converted Jewish Buddhist priest, a rough-and-tumble New Englander priest from Massachusetts, and a meteorologist from Indiana, a rag-tag mix of ministerial and secular experience to say the least, came together to decide where we would insert ourselves as a community-in-mission in this vast country.

Initially, we decided to look at, statistically, the poorest dioceses in the country. After several weeks of intense research, we had our decision narrowed down to four dioceses along the Rio Grande border with Mexico, since they seemed to be some of the poorest dioceses per capita in the United States. They were the dioceses of El Paso, Brownsville and Laredo in Texas, and Las Cruces in New Mexico.

So, a small contingent of our group was sent out as a kind of scouting party to meet with the Bishops of these dioceses and determine where the need seemed to be the greatest. Three of us, a priest, a sister, and myself, at the time, an un-ordained brother, traveled from California like Kit Carsons to see for ourselves the "lay of the land"

We traveled to Brownsville, Texas and met with the Bishop of that Diocese at the Basilica of Our Lady of San Juan del Valle in San Juan, Texas. He was cordial and polite and we had an opportunity to explore parts of the diocese. We saw some of the *colonias*, or rural, unincorporated areas, along the Rio Grande River bordering Mexico.

Next, we traveled to the Laredo, Texas Diocese and met its Bishop in a very hot and humid parish rectory in a small city in the middle of the Diocese. He told us that the Diocese was practically brand-new, having been in existence for less than five years. We drove through some of the *colonias* upriver from Laredo, Texas along the Rio Grande and could see Mexico across the River.

We were not contacted by the El Paso Diocese, so, we did not travel there.

Finally, two of us, a priest and myself, with our Provincial, traveled to Las Cruces, New Mexico, to visit the Bishop and see parts of the Las Cruces Diocese. He pointed us to several areas in greatest need in his Diocese. The several areas included a cluster of parishes and missions in the Mesilla Valley along the Rio Grande River between Las Cruces, New Mexico and El Paso, Texas and a parish and mission around Hatch, New Mexico (the self-proclaimed "chile capital of the world") north of Las Cruces. And, finally, a cluster of three parishes and two missions running from Dexter, New Mexico, south to Artesia, New Mexico, along the Pecos River in southeast New Mexico. It seems this last area had not really had more than one priest for some time.

After our scouting party's time along the Rio Grande in south Texas and southern New Mexico, we returned to California to make a decision on where we felt we were being called to locate our "community-in-mission". Because our sisters knew very little Spanish, we felt it would be better to locate in an area where there would be enough bilingual speakers rather than an area with a lot of monolingual Spanish-speaking people. This eliminated, for us, the south Texas Dioceses of Brownsville and Laredo. Also, the State of New Mexico, was found to be, after extensive research by us, one of the poorest, if not the poorest, state per capita in the whole United States. This more or less sealed the deal for us. So, we were headed to New Mexico, the Land of Enchantment, the Land of *Poco Tiempo*, and Satan's Paradise, to be, in the footsteps of Father Damien, missionaries of the Sacred Hearts. It was time to explore what New Mexico had in store for us.

Since the Bishop felt that the area around Artesia and the southern Pecos River Valley in southeastern New Mexico seemed most in need, we decided that this was where we were being called by God. I was the first of our contingent of brothers and sisters to arrive in New Mexico, having driven all the way from Southern California to Artesia, where I pulled up to the rectory of Our Lady of Grace Catholic Church in Artesia on a bright, cloudless, typical southern New Mexico day. I was greeted by a diocesan priest, Fr. Virgilio, who was the interim pastor of the parish, who greeted me with the words, "Let's go get some food". I knew immediately that I was in a good place. I settled into the rectory awaiting the arrival of the rest of our "gang of seven" who were coming in from the East Coast, West Coast and Hawaii and I was getting used to being awoken by the soft refrain of Fr. Virgilio walking down the rectory hall saying, "Brother Briiiiiian! Let's go get some breakfast!"

After two weeks, the other members of our CIM began to arrive. There was Fr. Ben who drove all the way from Massachusetts. And Fr. Richard, who did the same. And, finally, there was Fr. Paul and the three sisters from Hawaii who all arrived in a van from California. We were now all present and accounted for! *Gracias a Dios!*

So it was that our group of seven began our lives together in the small city of Artesia, in a remote part of southeastern New Mexico, with a sense of adventure, a spirit of faith and a charism of love. Little did we know what the past, present and future had in store for us!

Once we were all together as a community, we were escorted around the eastern half of the diocese, including Artesia and the Pecos Valley, by one of the Pastoral Center staff from Las Cruces. We were taken through the deserts, plains, valleys and mountains of southeastern New Mexico, all across the vast expanse of land that made up this part of the Diocese of Las Cruces which extended all the way from Arizona to the Texas border. This was an endeavor that we all enjoyed and that thoroughly amazed us as well.

And, so it was, that we found ourselves driving through the mountains outside of Ruidoso, New Mexico when it happened. That is, the RAINBOW! There it was, staring us in the face as we drove down the highway, a bright multi-colored bow of color, a brilliant spectral arch, that illuminated our faces with its clarity. By George! *O mi Dios!* It must be a sign from God that we should be here, in the Diocese of Las Cruces, New Mexico, as missionaries of the Sacred Hearts, as a community-in-mission. At least that is how we interpreted it. It appeared over the mountains as we drove down the highway. It appeared in all its beauty, in all its hues of color. It appeared like the one that appeared to Noah and the passengers on the ark in the Old Testament, as a sign from God to show us that we were in the right place at the right time, that God was with us, that a covenant was present. And, we welcomed that rainbow, that covenant, in all its glory, as a confirmation, as an affirmation, of our purpose as religious missionaries of the Sacred Hearts, as a community-in-mission.

It was that rainbow that we followed down the mountain to our new home in Artesia and the Pecos Valley, to serve the people there, to help them to find a greater presence of God in their lives, and more specifically, to find a greater presence of God's love in their lives.

But, what we discovered was that WE ourselves found God in a new, awesome and sometimes frightening way, that God's love existed in what seemed like a desolate place to us. As we tried to be good missionaries to the people, the people became good missionaries to us. We helped each other to find God in, sometimes, a familiar, and, sometimes, an unfamiliar way! And, it all started in the central Pecos River Valley of southeastern New Mexico, between Roswell and Carlsbad, between the "aliens" and the "bats". That is where this book began. That is where a group of religious and the people we journeyed with found God in a way that was to be a prophetic witness to all of us. And, it was where God found us. That, by living together in community, in mission, we discovered God within ourselves, within each other, and within the context of a multicultural milieu of history, time and place that proved so real, so genuine, so from-the-heart, that it surprised and shocked us. It transformed all of us in some way, I truly believe, in our hearts, with a new sense of what it means to have faith, to have hope, and, especially, to have love in God.

Thanks, in part, to that rainbow over the mountains of southern New Mexico, we were given affirmation that our ministry was about to begin with the people of Artesia, Dexter, Hagerman and Lake Arthur, New Mexico, a period of time in which we all were to discover, and rediscover, the God of our pasts, of our presents, and of our futures in the Land of Enchantment, in Satan's Paradise.

But, finding God involves a deep dive into the people, places and events of the past because that is where God's presence speaks, as in Scripture, through the triumphs, tragedies and totems of history.

New Mexico, Southeast New Mexico and the SE NM Pecos River Valley: The Past Regional History

THE PAST REGIONAL HISTORY

INTRODUCTION

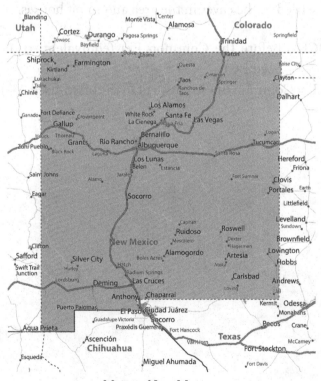

MAP OF NEW MEXICO

Present-day southeastern New Mexico, along the Pecos River, between the cities of Roswell to the north and Carlsbad to the south is a place of flat land, open range, dairies, fields of alfalfa, chiles, cotton, feed corn, oil fields and few people. The Pecos River that runs from north to south just to the east of the four towns of Dexter, Hagerman, Lake Arthur, and Artesia, is, presently, little more than a dry, creek bed. For much of the year, the Pecos River is completely dry. There is no water at all flowing down its course due to upriver irrigation and reservoiring. The water that irrigates the land is found in the aquifer that lies just below the surface of the parched land. This area is located on the southwestern edge of the vast Ogalalla Aquifer that extends all the way from Texas to North Dakota. The area was home to groups and tribes of people, the relatives of the "Sandia Man", around 25,000 BCE*. Nomadic hunters wandered the area, hunting buffalo and other game, over the next several thousand years. In the 1300's CE*, a more sedentary group of people called the "Basket Makers" settled in the caves in the area and in pit houses.

*   BCE = Before the Common Era (equivalent to the often-used BC)

       CE = Common Era (equivalent to the often-used AD)

A little background on the Pecos River, the lifeblood of the region:

The Pecos River flows through New Mexico and Texas, emptying into the Rio Grande. The headwaters of the Pecos River are located north of Pecos, New Mexico, at an elevation of over 12,000 feet on the western slope of the *Sangre de Cristo* mountain range in Mora County. The river flows for 926 miles through the eastern portion of New Mexico and neighboring Texas before it empties into the Rio Grande near Del Rio, Texas. The river's drainage basin is about 44,300 square miles in size.

Multiple dams have been built along the Pecos River. Two dams are located north of Carlsbad, New Mexico, at Avalon Dam and Brantley Dam, to help irrigate about 25,000 acres as part of the Carlsbad reclamation project (established in 1906).

The river was named "Pecos" by the Spanish from the Keresan Indian name of the Pecos Pueblo, *p'oeyok'ona*. The river played a large role in the exploration of Texas by the Spanish. In the latter half of the 19th century, "West of the Pecos" was a reference to the rugged desolation of the Wild West. The Texas storekeeper, bartender and justice of the peace, Roy Bean, a native of Kentucky, was often described as: "The Only Law West of the Pecos", a phrase made popular from the 1956 syndicated television series, *Judge Roy Bean*, with Edgar Buchanan in the starring role. In the series narration, "West of the Pecos" is described as:

"the wildest spot in the United States virtually beyond the reach of the authorities, the railroads, then

> pushing their way west, attracted the
> most vicious characters in the country.
> It was said that all civilization and law
> stopped at the east bank of the Pecos."

New Mexico and Texas disputed water rights to the river until the U.S. Government settled the dispute in 1949 with the Pecos River Compact. The Pecos River Settlement Agreement was signed between New Mexico and Texas in 2003.

Near Carlsbad (it was called Eddy before 1899), the Pecos River Flume is a modern aqueduct carrying irrigation water over the Pecos River. Construction took place from 1889 to 1890 and was part of the Pecos River Reclamation Project. It was originally constructed of wood and spanned 145 feet. It carried water at a depth of eight feet. In 1902, a flood destroyed the flume and it was subsequently rebuilt using concrete. In 1902, it was identified as the largest concrete aqueduct in the world.

The four southeast New Mexican towns of Artesia, Dexter, Hagerman and Lake Arthur can be described as being medium to small in size, with less than 15,000 in population in each (based on the most current US Census), with Artesia being the largest at around 14,000. Dexter and Hagerman each having around 1,200 in population, with Lake Arthur being the smallest at around 500 in population. Each town is its own little enclave of people, separated by miles of dry land and fields. Each town has its own identity, its own sense of being, its own character, its own history, yet its people are connected in many ways by family, by culture, by work, by school, by church and by history.

Southeast New Mexico is a place of significance by the sheer fact that it is an area that was inhabited and continues to be inhabited by Native Americans, settlers with Spanish roots, immigrants from south of the border in Mexico and Anglo settlers. Historically, the role of the divine in such a place was one of master, protector, provider, nourisher, judge, friend, and ultimate controller of destinies, although the independent spirit of the frontier was planted deep within many a hearty soul. The place could be described as flat, wind-whipped, dry, dusty, fertile, productive, or beautiful, depending upon where you were and when you were living there. From the southern end of the region, around the town of Carlsbad, to the town of Artesia, some 25 miles north of Carlsbad, to further north, around the towns of Lake Arthur, Hagerman and Dexter, the region is affectionately called the "Valley", as in Pecos River Valley. The region has always been somewhat remote and, for the most part, sparsely populated.

The history of the area includes such diverse elements as the Chisum family, German WWII prisoner-of-war camps, mineral water, water rights, an underground civil defense bomb shelter school and the face of Jesus on a tortilla!

It is a region that has been sculpted from many "clays", from the Apache and Comanche tribes that traversed the mountains, valleys, deserts and high plains, to the Spanish Conquistadors in search of legendary gold, to the Mexican forces that pushed north from Azteca, to the U.S. Military troops reconnoitering, to the Texas cattle barons and cowpokes of the nineteenth century, to the Anglo settlers from the East in search of land, to those seeking a better way of life for themselves and their families, and, to the farmers, dairy workers and oilfield workers now trying to make a better living, the central Pecos River valley of southeastern New Mexico has been, is, and will continue to be, a place of dreams, dreams fulfilled, dreams dashed, and dreams yet to be. It is a place where God has been found, lost, then found again, where faith, hope and family are treasures that endure from generation to generation, *por los siglos de los siglos.*

To find God in a place like this requires some digging, some uprooting, some sifting and some letting go. This God can be an awesome God, a healing God, a comforting God, a challenging God, an absent God, a war-like God and a fiesta God. This was, is and will continue to be the God of the Pecos River Valley of southeastern New Mexico. It is an ancestral God that has been handed down from great-great grandparents to the present generation. It is a God that was brought there by settlers. Sometimes, this God has been lost in translation from place to place. Sometimes, it has been a God of the desperate, a God of survival, a distant God, but, in the end, a God of hope and enduring love.

Carole Larson, in her book, *Forgotten Frontier*, describes, very well, I believe, the environment in which this search for God has taken, continues to take and will take place in southeastern New Mexico in these words:

"[Southeastern New Mexico] *is not an easily accessible land, not a land immediately assimilated into human emotions. It overwhelms; it is subtle, vast, even savage in its stark forms and endless horizons. Its very largeness can conceal forever the intricate beauties of the small-scale natural phenomena found within it. It presents the individual with a continual choice between watching its larger outlines or pausing to absorb the valley places, canyon places, mesa or desert places within it. It will not be tamed. It will be windswept, self-determining, dynamic under a sun that seems to hold the land as laboratory to test its own powers of intensity. The air itself takes on visible shimmerings under the sun's relentless penetration.*

It is a landscape one either grasps and feels imprinted on one's soul or else finds vaguely unsettling, taunting, even repugnant and antithetical to the civilizing ways of people. There are on the wide stretches of the plateau plain no deep green grass carpets, no lush forests, no shaded tumbling streams, no craggy peaks over misted valleys. There are, in short, no places to hide, to be caressed by nature, no places to believe

6

in abstract beauty; there is no surcease from reality, no real smallness within which to shield oneself from the largeness, no aids from nature encouraging belief in one's uniqueness or protected status. And yet, ultimately, there is something in the landscape that enfolds, uplifts, strengthens, and places people firmly in a tapestry being woven into geological, anthropological [and] cultural history."

PRE-1800

INTRODUCTION

From 1150 CE to 1450 CE, living along the banks of the Pecos River gradually diminished, but the inhabitants retained their hunter-gatherer lifestyle. By 1450, most of the native peoples had migrated to the mountains and foothills west of the Pecos River.

From 1450 to 1800, which includes the Spanish explorations in the late 1500's, hunting-gathering remained the lifestyle among the native peoples, while *rancherias* (small settlements or encampments) appeared with the Spanish explorers as well as with some of the *Indios* (Indians).

Roaming bands of Apaches, Comanches, Kiowas and other Plains tribes kept Euro-American settlement of southeastern New Mexico in abeyance until later.

A number of Spanish explorers passed through the Pecos River area. One, Castäno de Sosa, became lost in the vicinity of present-day Artesia and was guided back to his camp by *luminarias* (lit candles set in bags made of paper or other material). Another of these explorers, Antonio de Espejo, was the only one, however, who praised the Pecos Valley area and suggested colonization. The Spanish eventually left and displayed no interest in colonization of the arid land. When explorers struggled through the area, their major thoughts were on finding water, not gold. Their path approximated "The Trail of Living Waters," a series of widely separated springs by which many a later buffalo hunter or pioneer made his way across the New Mexico area. The Apaches held the white soldier at bay for years by the simple expedient of poisoning water holes.

Catholic Franciscan missionaries accompanying Spanish troops from New Spain to the south (Mexico) began to evangelize by baptizing Pueblo Indians along the New Mexico Rio Grande River, to the west of the Pecos River. Rather than see the Indians revert back to their "pagan" native religion, the Spanish Crown permitted the Franciscans and the colonists to stay. Missions became New Mexico's sole reason for existence in the Spanish empire of New Spain. Church and state were to cooperate in settling the frontier, and the welfare of the church was an important responsibility of the officers of the state. Instructions, which the Spanish Crown's chief political official in New Spain, Viceroy Luis de Velasco, gave to Onate in 1595, upon appointing him to colonize New Mexico, exhibit this cooperation:

> "You should try to bring the natives of these provinces to you and to induce them to hear the word of the holy gospel, that they may receive and accept it, converting them to our holy Catholic faith, causing them to understand, by means of interpreters of their languages, if you are able to get them, so that in the various tongues they may be able to communicate and undertake their conversion, or as it may best suit the present occasion or when the priests find it convenient. You shall hold them in personal respect and reverence like ministers of the gospel so that the Indians may attend and revere them and listen to their sermons and instruction, for experience has shown that this is very important......You shall arrange all things regarding it wisely and harmoniously, always

ordering everything for the glory of God and the increase of our holy faith."

In New Mexico, the Spanish mission, of limited utility elsewhere, served on the frontier to pacify and Hispanicize Indians as well as to save their souls. Garrisons or presidios were established to protect nearby missions from Indians whom the Spaniards termed "barbarous" (*indios barbaros*). The kind of missions that worked reasonably well among California Indians, however, failed among the mounted, highly mobile Plains Indians of Texas and Eastern New Mexico.

DESERT, PLAIN AND VALLEY

GREAT CHIHUAHUAN DESERT

In the southern part of the Pecos River Valley in southeastern New Mexico, just outside the southern limits of present-day Artesia, the very northern edge of the Great Chihuahuan Desert, which extends deep into Mexico to the south, brought early inhabitants of the Pecos River Valley in touch with peoples from further south, from what is now Mexico. These peoples were also hunter-gatherers and brought with them their own customs and beliefs. The lifestyles of these indigenous peoples were quite simple and devoid of excessive material things. In the sixteenth, seventeenth and eighteenth centuries, these *Indios* would have had contact with Spanish explorers, or *Conquistadors*.

CONQUISTADORS

Many religious artifacts and *alajas* (church valuables) attributed to these Spanish Conquistadors as objects of their Christian, and, specifically, Catholic faith, were found in the remains of the Spanish and Indian *rancherias* as well as in the encampments of the *Indios* who raided and stole them from the Spaniards. *Santos* (images and statues of saints), *rosarios* (rosary beads), *medallas* (religious medallions), *campanillas* (small bells), missals (prayer books), stoles (vestments), maniples (vestments), *hostiarios* (wafer-boxes), *casullas* (chasubles-vestments), *oleos* (oils), altar cloths, *sabanas de ruan* (altar linens), and *hechuras de santos* (figurines of saints) were all found among the Spaniards and *Indios*.

FRANCISCAN MISSIONARIES

Franciscan missionaries accompanied the Spanish colonists to New Spain, but these missionaries never achieved the political and economic power or influence over the native Indians that their Jesuit brethren had in other parts of the New World. Nevertheless, many of the Franciscans were zealous missionaries. They established themselves among the Indians, and these people told them about the more populous Indian nations to the north, that is, the tribes of New Mexico. In 1581, one of the friars, Agustin Rodriguez secured the help of Captain Francisco Sanchez Chamuscado, and that year a small party of nine soldiers and three friars embarked on a journey to the north, towards what is now New Mexico.

They were the first to travel the Royal Road up the Rio Grande River to the Pueblo Indian country in northern New Mexico, and although they probably never entered the valley of the Pecos River of southeastern New Mexico, their tales of the Pueblo Indians inspired a more formidable expedition the following year.

Early missionaries reported that the general area was exceedingly impoverished and so dry that it would support only wild and spiny brambles. The Spaniards constantly had difficulty in finding water for themselves and their animals when traveling or campaigning in the area. Some of the *Indios* were living from pools of rainwater or from the moisture from wild plants, roots, and the bark of plants and trees. In most of the area, the Spaniards considered the major portion of the water holes as exhausted the greater part of the year. The peoples of the general region were considered to have had no, or only a slight amount of, agriculture. Without a year-round water source very little agriculture was practiced and there was very little animal life. A few grew corn, but many wandered the entire year over the places where food was most available, hunting what they could obtain with their arrows. These were an "untamed", an "un-Christianized" people, although, an early seventeenth-century writing told of a non-Christian Indian near whose house and *milpa* (field) the Christian doctrine was taught.

Marriage within Indian tribes or bands was uncommon. Inter-band marriage was more the norm. Such matrimonial ties between bands cemented alliances. Some evidence of both maternal and paternal family structure existed. Polygamy existed, alongside monogamy, as well as possibly group marriage. Separation or divorce was common. Women had premarital freedom but liaisons were rather brittle. At each Indian *rancheria*, men who had the greatest reputation for valor among them usually became chiefs for the band. This chieftainship could be inherited, making kinship and age important to the leadership of the band. Leaders, however, were not to be *tatoleros* (talkers) or cowards, though a chief could be killed by members of the band if the chief was considered too strict and ruthless.

There was much discord among some of the bands and some even had the custom of killing and eating each other and of capturing each others' children. Even under missionization, deaths between bands caused enmity. Revenge was an important immediate cause in maintaining hostile relations with neighbors. Besides the revenge motive, killing the enemy for prestige and ceremonial reasons was important. No particular individual was to be blamed for any specific killing committed, but all of the tribe were responsible. The size of raiding parties ranged from small groups of six to twelve men to large forces of well over one hundred warriors for mass attacks. Some raiding parties of *Indios* that stayed out for considerable periods of time were accompanied by women who helped the men keep camp. One band had the women and children along to make arrows for the warriors.

Some of the characteristics of the religious and ceremonial life of the peoples of the Great Chihuahuan Desert were dancing, ceremonial killing and cannibalism, self-sacrifice or bloodletting, and the use of the narcotic peyote (a mescal cactus). This ceremonial behavior was associated with a number of different activities, including warfare, hunting, sickness, and the formalization of inter-band peace and alliance pacts. *Mitotes* (dances) occurred at any time of the year, but particularly in the summer when food was more plentiful.

Some dances were held for war and as celebrations for happiness or sadness. These lasted for up to eight consecutive days and nights. Drunkenness would frequently be a consequence of these *mitotes*. The use of peyote (a small, spineless cactus which contains psychoactive alkaloids, particularly mescaline) was common throughout these dances, accompanied by singing and chanting. The peyote was often ground and mixed with water and sometimes mixed with the powdered bones of a victim. Other aspects of these dances could include snake dances, beliefs about owls and a reverential attitude toward fire. Spaniards looked upon the dances, which sometimes included child sacrifices, as ordered by the devil. At the missions, native dancing was continued, but reoriented toward the divine. The Indians would dance all night on Saturday night, and would be so tired the following day, that they were unable to attend Mass.

Shamans, or medicine men or women, were often involved in armed resistance to the Spaniards. One writing reported an undercurrent of talk concerning a certain old mountain lady who was held in great veneration. She was angry because her people had accepted the Spanish priests. Attempts to pacify her with clothing and other gifts did not mitigate the ire.

"Ceremonialism" often took place at inter-band meetings, especially when a war alliance was being forged. Less complicated customs also occurred when people of different bands met and when inter-band peace pacts were drawn up. Another ceremonial occurred when a *bandera* (banner) was sent by a Spanish governor to a band as part of peace negotiations. Before setting the banner up, word was sent to all of the nations that they meet together to see the banner and to kiss it as the insignia of the King, Our Lord, and that when all had come together it was put up and that the governors and chiefs went first passing underneath the banner kissing it consecutively. After them, all the men and women, young and old, did the same, and they carried out *mitotes* with great pleasure, saying that that *senal* (sign) was true peace and that by means of it they had the assurance of the promise of pardon, and that against this peace, not a single thing was heard. Later, when two Franciscan friars went out to visit them, the Indians lined up in the style of war with their banner which they waved to the priests and then, one by one, they went to kiss the habits and hands of the Franciscans.

Shamans, or curers, usually old men from the band, were reported to attend the sick in the *rancherias*. A fire was usually kept burning. The shamans would see visions of various supernatural figures. The sacrifice of a newborn infant presumably prevented the death of, and would cure, a sick person. One case that occurred soon after the beginning of missionization was that of a woman who had dreamt that her relatives were going to die. When she awoke, she strangled (*ahogo*) a child who had just been born, thus preventing the deaths of the others. Infanticide, for this reason, was said to be common.

Large dances (*mitotes*) were held to turn the tide of plagues. Visions of supernatural beings in the form of fire, deer, serpents, or a figure armed to the teeth (*de punta en blanco*), would threaten the natives with illness because they had become Christians. The way to placate such spirits was to dance, the dances lasting three or four days and nights, the participants performing before an idol without eating until they would fall to the ground. Diseases such as smallpox, measles and *mal de ojos* (the evil eye) were common. Two *ninos* (children) were strangled (*ahogados*) upon birth because the old men (shamans) had dreamt of wars and disturbances and had persuaded themselves that these children were going to grow up and be troublesome and the cause of much harm. The sacrifice of the firstborn was also practiced. The "superstitious" killing of children, it was said, left the Indians less encumbered in their rovings.

INDIAN SHAMAN

During one *Indio* revolt, a medicine man, or shaman, tried to whip the people into a rebellion. Another medicine man had a vision in which he apparently received a message for the people, connected with a revolt against the Spaniards. The vision involved a great lord (*Senor*) who had appeared to him several times in the form of a human being, a deer, or other wild animals (*fieras*). These supernatural manifestations seemingly had told the medicine man that this "lord" was coming from the east to kill all of the Spaniards and laborers (*gente laboria*), thus freeing the *Indios* from them. However, for this, the natives would have to take his message westward in order that all of the nations living in this region (*en esta derecera*) would recognize and obey him. The old medicine man gave his relative a bow (as in bow and arrow), which he claimed belonged to this great lord. All of the *viejos* (old Indians) revered this bow, and they kept it with much veneration in a house, because, they said, he who did not venerate it would die. An Indian from another band learned of this, went to the house, took the bow and stomped on it with his feet, causing a great deal of wonder among the elders when he did not perish immediately.

Some chiefs presumably possessed supernatural power, and some may also have been shamans. One chief, during a *mitote*, performed a ritual in order to communicate with the supernatural. He filled a gourd container (*calavazo*) with water and covered it with a large piece of cloth (*pano*)

Holding this in one hand, he took a cross with the other and announced to the rest that God had just come down from the "most high" and spoken with him. The message was not to surrender to the Spaniards at this time but to flee, as the Spaniards were planning to kill them. On one occasion, when the Indians were being pursued, they invoked the devil, repeating the word *neblina* (fog). Immediately, a bank of fog came up between them and the pursuing Spaniards.

The early missionaries reported many occurrences of visits to the *Indios* by, and visions of, supernatural beings, which they (the *Indios*) considered to be manifestations of the devil. Some of these beings let themselves be seen in daylight. They were said to be "horrible" figures, sometimes, a black man who shot fire from his eyes or expelled blood from his mouth and ears, or other times, a wild beast that caused dread, terror and fright. One figure was in the image of a woman who would talk to people. The commands of these beings were backed up by the threat of sickness or death. One *Indio* was disturbed by the devil in the figure of a black man who, however, was dispelled when the Indian was baptized. Other *Indios* had visions of "wonderful things" which included a figure suspended in the air who taught them to cross themselves and pray. A chief from one tribe took a missionary to a large *pena* (rock) and removed a stone that covered a hole. This he showed to the Franciscan missionary, stating that before he and his people had become Christians, the devil had destroyed many people at this place, disappearing later down this hole. In another supernatural occurrence, there appeared a *nagual*, or guardian spirit.

It concerned a youth whom a *demonio familiar* (supernatural being) constantly accompanied. The being seemingly would appear to the boy (*mozo*) in various forms and would help him in many ways. Possession by a *nagual* was customary among some peoples. An old woman in one tribe kept a *lagarto* (lizard) in a cage (*enjaulado*). She said that it was her God whom she adored and feared a great deal. A priest attempted to demonstrate to her that this was not true by throwing the lizard into the fire where it was consumed by the flames. Another woman from the same tribe was gravely tormented by the "devil", who every day would raise her from the ground over an *estado* (a foot) in height in the air, whirl her around, make froth on her mouth, and also make her face become twisted.

Some instances of death and burial exhibited a certain amount of religious syncretism of native and Christian elements. The dead were usually buried, although some were cremated. Some endocannibalism (eating the flesh of a human being from the same tribe after they have died) and the pulling out and cutting of hair in mourning were practiced. Aside from burial, hair cutting and the destruction of property seem to have been customary features. A mourning wail would also be practiced at burials, usually by the women. One tribe was known for its extraordinary wailing. Friends and relatives of the deceased would get together at the grave, with their faces painted or blackened, and then the men and the women would wail their sorrowful tune. Singing and dancing were part of mourning activities, and women friends and neighbors acted as mourners or *lloraderas* (cryers).

The qualities of the deceased would be sung. One tribe believed that all of those present at the time a death occurred would also die. So, anyone who was considered to be in the last throes of dying would be taken to the *sepultura* (grave) to die there or be buried alive so that the rest would not be present when death occurred. During the mourning and burial of one Indian woman, the old men and women were seen to throw themselves forcefully upon the ground, to beat themselves, to dance and sing together, bewailing and crying over the deceased, and coming to the burial of the deceased with all of the *trastos* (things) and *baratijas* (trifles or trinkets) that she possessed. The old mother of the deceased woman buried herself alive with her dead daughter and was covered up with earth with her deceased daughter, and she remained buried all day until the afternoon, when, coming back, the others found this mother of the deceased alive.

Whirlwinds were also connected with the spirit world. People who saw a whirlwind would throw themselves on the ground, saying to each other, *Cachinipa*, the name which they gave to the devil or to whom they feared, and revered, in that whirlwind, because they did not know how to explain who it might be. The people believed that the devil, named *Cachiripa* (in another place simply *Chiripa*, and another, *Cane*), was inside the whirlwind, and they would prostrate themselves so that they would not die. Spirits were connected with natural phenomena and objects such as rivers, springs and trees around which rites and beliefs were focused. There were also beliefs about heavenly bodies influencing or controlling sickness and health. One priest, after being captured by tribes, was asked by one of the chiefs for some Holy Earth that the missionary had with him. Horses and mules were eaten because they were swift animals and some of this swiftness was believed to be transferred to the eater of their flesh. The *Indios* also ate the flesh of their own people in order to acquire whatever special traits the deceased might have possessed, such as healing powers or hunting skill.

Thus, early, pre-1800 indigenous and explorational inhabitants of the desert areas of the Pecos River Valley of southeastern New Mexico exhibited their spiritual lives in ways very different.

North of the Great Chihuahuan Desert, however, a somewhat different pre-1800 history unfolded in the valleys and plains in and near what is now the towns of Artesia, Lake Arthur, Hagerman and Dexter in the Pecos River Valley of southeastern New Mexico.

The eastern half of present-day Chaves County east of the Pecos River was occupied almost wholly by the *Llano Estacado* (Staked Plains).

THE LLANO ESTACADO

Just as agriculturalists expanded into southeastern New Mexico with the improved environmental conditions of the tenth and eleventh centuries, they withdrew later from the area in response to deteriorating conditions. The bison, too, were affected by the deteriorating environmental conditions, but were not as heavily impacted, however, as the plant resources were that had formed a large part of the area's subsistence.

The agriculturalist groups along the Pecos River withdrew to the northeast. The local hunter-gatherer groups along the Pecos River, on the other hand, responded by becoming highly nomadic bison hunters.

Abandonments began in 1300 CE in the Penasco River Valley, south and west of present-day Artesia, and that by 1400 CE southeastern New Mexico had been abandoned by agriculturalists with the exception of two areas in south central New Mexico. There are two explanations for this pattern of abandonment — environmental deterioration and inter-group conflict. Three sources for these inter-group hostilities were: conflict with pre-Apache, non-sedentary groups that had inhabited portions of southeastern New Mexico; inter-village hostilities among agriculturalists; and conflict with "pre-Apache foot nomads of the Plains, who may have been feeling the pressure from Apaches or other groups pushing down the western Plains.

The path to exploration of the Pecos Valley actually began back in 1527, when Panfilo de Narvaez, a Spanish *adelantado* (a representative of the Spanish Crown), received a vast grant in what is now the southeastern United States from Charles Hapsburg, King Charles I of Spain.

Outfitting an expedition at its own expense, Narvaez and his followers landed on the west coast of Florida that same year (1527). He sent his ships west across the Gulf of Mexico while he and the rest of his party marched north and westward into the interior lands along the Gulf of Mexico. The two groups were supposed to reunite, but the ships never came back. When Narvaez and his men realized they were stranded, they resolved to head west and then south towards the coast of New Spain, north of Vera Cruz, Mexico. So, they fashioned five rude barges and set sail. Three of the barges were lost in rough seas in the Gulf of Mexico. The remaining two boats were swept to Galveston Island, off the east coast of Texas. Eighty men survived the ocean, but as soon as they landed, Indians in the area enslaved them, and starvation and disease began to take their toll. By the early 1530's, only four men remained alive. They became the famous *Naufragios*, the Shipwrecked Ones, and their odyssey across the deserts and plains of the present-day Southwest United States ranks as one of the greatest adventures of the New World.

In 1534, the four of them managed to escape their Indian masters and headed west from Texas. They hoped to reach the outposts of northwestern New Spain (in what is now California), but had no idea that half a continent separated them from their countrymen. During the next two years, they slowly made their way from tribe to tribe across Texas and southern New Mexico. They were the first Europeans to penetrate what is now the southwestern United States and the Pecos Valley region. They never encountered the Pueblo tribes to the north, however. But, their second-hand, untrue tales of great cities tantalized the Spaniards and spurred others to launch expeditions into the lands the *Naufragios* only touched.

The Spaniards reached a village of one hundred lodges somewhere in the vicinity of Big Spring, Texas, along the North Concho River in what is now west Texas. From there they headed toward the Davis Mountains to the west. But the Spaniards were afraid the mountains to the west led to the coast, and all the coastal tribes they had encountered had been hostile. So, they turned north and "proceeded along [a] stream upwards" until they met two women carrying cornmeal who led them to a rancheria of twenty lodges. This "stream" was probably the Pecos River. The women carried water because the Pecos River was notoriously saline, especially in its lower reaches (in west Texas). From the rancheria, one of the *Naufragios*, Alvar Nunez Cabeza de Vaca, wrote:

> We turned inland [away from the river] for more than fifty leagues, [175 miles] following the slopes of the mountains, and at the end of them met forty dwellings.

The wanderers ascended the Pecos River Valley as far north as present-day Carlsbad and then turned westward up the Penasco River drainage until they reached the forty-lodge rancheria somewhere on upper Elk Creek in the mountains west of the Pecos River (Guadalupe and Sacramento Mountains). Leaving that village, they traveled west, descended the Rio Tularosa and crossed the Rio Grande. The forty-lodge rancheria may have been located in the Sacramento Mountains west of the Pecos Valley and was a temporary settlement.

After the *Naufragios* finally reached New Spain (Mexico), Cabeza de Vaca wanted to return to the lands he passed through, but the viceroy, Antonio de Mendoza, chose Francisco Vasquez de Coronado instead to lead a new expedition.

The Spanish *entrada* (entrance) into the Pecos Valley area occurred in the spring of 1541. The Coronado expedition, searching for the gold of *Quivira* and the cities of *Cibola*, encountered on the *Llano Estacado*, bison-hunting nomadic Indians whom they termed the "Teyas". Fray Agustin Rodriguez and a Spanish Captain led a small party of missionaries and soldiers in 1581 whose primary purpose was to assess the need for missions among these Indians.

In the fall of 1582, a party of soldiers, civilians and priests set out from Chihuahua, New Spain (present-day Mexico) for the northern province of New Mexico to rescue Franciscan friars left behind by past expeditions. They probably traveled up the Rio Grande Valley before heading east. This was the Espejo expedition, which returned southward to Mexico in the summer of 1583 by traveling down the Pecos River. They did not encounter any Indians until they reached the *rancherias* of the Jumano Indians near present-day Pecos, Texas, where they encountered three Jumano Indians who led them to their villages near the junction of the Rio Concho and Rio Grande. They did note several great forests of mesquite, perhaps in the same locations where cattlemen would establish their camps centuries later, and also places where mosquitoes were very thick. One of the explorers stated that, "Although the whole region is full of dung and bones, God willed that we should not see any buffalo."

In May of 1590, a band of colonists under the leadership of Gaspar Castano de Sosa set out from New Spain for New Mexico, following the Pecos River route explored by Espejo. They encountered numerous bands of "dog" nomads (named for their use of dogs as beasts of burden) along the Pecos River in Texas, and a cache of shelled corn in "*ollas*" (ceramic jars) near what is now Carlsbad, in New Mexico, but no signs of Indians.

It took Castano and his party twenty-six days to travel from the Rio Grande to the Pecos. Once they finally found the Pecos River, which they appropriately called the *Rio Salado* ("salty river"), they faced a journey northward of five hundred miles into New Mexico.

While ascending the Pecos in Texas, the colonists ran into a group of the nomads near a salt bed. Castano's "Journal" reads "These people had with them many loaded dogs, as is the custom in those regions, and we saw them loaded, a thing new to us, never before seen."

On the 2nd of November of 1590, a handful of Spaniards approached a group of these "dog nomads" standing on the banks of the Pecos River. The colonists attempted to persuade the Indians to join them, but they refused. Finally the Spaniards went back to camp, leaving one member of their party, Juan de Vega, an Indian, behind. Seeing that he was alone, the Querecho warriors threw him into the river and shot him with three arrows. The next day they ran off some of the colonists' cattle, and Castano ordered one of his men, Cristobal de Heredia, in pursuit of the Indians.

There was a battle that occurred between the Spaniards and the Querechos in west Texas. The Querechos probably ranged up and down the Pecos along the western edge of the Plains, hunting buffalo and foraging in the mountains, transporting their belongings by dog. Although they were not very formidable in Castano's time, fifty years later, by 1640, they and other Plains tribes would have the horse, thanks to the Spanish, and the whole pattern of life along the Pecos frontier would change.

Continuing north, Castano's party saw fewer Indians, but they did come across evidence of occupation, and also saw their first buffalo, somewhere along the Pecos River in the vicinity of what was called Horsehead Crossing in west Texas. Within sight of the Guadalupe Mountains to the west, they found a large corral which they thought the Indians used to enclose stock, but since none of the natives in the area had domesticated any animal other than the dog, the corral was probably a game trap. Near present-day Carlsbad, they located a spring with a cone of mineral deposits built up around it, and in a nearby grove, stumbled across an *olla* (ceramic jar) containing ears of recently shelled corn inside, evidence that the people of the area were either cultivating small plots of maize or trading for it among their more settled neighbors to the north and south. A few miles north of Carlsbad, the colonists discovered a large, deserted *rancheria* on the banks of the Pecos River. From there until an advance party reached Pecos Pueblo at the upper reaches of the Pecos River, the narrative fails to mention any more Indians or Indian remains. When Castano did order Cristobal de Heredia to search for natives of the area, the scouts reported that, "They had neither found people nor any trace of them." After that, the Spaniards found only a trail and a burned patch of savanna to indicate that they were not completely alone.

New Mexico was not to be successfully colonized until Onate and his followers arrived in the Pueblo Indian country in what is now central New Mexico in 1598, but, by then, the Rio Grande Valley had been established as the highway between New Spain and New Mexico to the north, and the Pecos River Valley was forgotten.

In the 1600's in New Spain, there was strife between the Franciscan missionaries and the *encomenderos*, who were ranking citizens appointed by the Spanish Governor to provide protection, aid and education to Indians and military support for the government in return for collecting tribute.

When they left Pecos Pueblo and the northern Pecos River, Coronado and his men marched in a southeasterly direction for four days until they came to another stretch of the Pecos River. There they built a bridge to cross the river and traveled east and south across the plains eight to ten days before they encountered their first huge buffalo herd.

The Querechos, as they were called by the Pueblo Indians, lived along the Canadian River near the *Llano Estacado* in northeastern New Mexico. They ". . . were a gentle people, not cruel, faithful in their friendship, and skilled in the use of signs." They were nomadic and subsisted entirely on buffalo, following the great herds with trains of dogs (the "dog nomads").

Captain Arellano, one of Coronado's officers, explored more of the Pecos River. He reached the river some thirty leagues (105 miles) below the bridge the *conquistadors* had constructed, somewhere in the vicinity of modern-day Fort Sumner, New Mexico, and followed the river southward. Inhabitants gave the Spaniards a cool reception. No more Europeans were to visit the middle stretch of the Pecos River in New Mexico for another forty years.

Lack of mineral wealth and the difficulty of maintaining a colony so far from the Hispanic population centers of New Spain to the far distant south virtually destroyed early Spanish settlements in the northern province of New Mexico. During the seventeenth century, New Mexico was run as a royal mission colony whose main purpose was to win over new souls. The history of the New Mexico colony between 1610 and the Pueblo Indian Revolt against the Spaniards in 1680 was one of conflict between the Franciscan friars and the civil governors and of exploitation of the Pueblo Indians (living near the Rio Grande River in central New Mexico) by both sides.

The Apaches took advantage of the political in-fighting between the Catholic Church and the Spanish Government in New Mexico to escalate their raiding. Hostilities increased in the 1630's, when the Spanish governors authorized slave raids against the Apaches, who were now ranging as far south along the Pecos River as the Seven Rivers area just north of present-day Carlsbad. In 1629 and 1632 there were missionizing expeditions to the Jumano Indians, but by the 1650's pressure from the Apaches had moved the Jumanos south to the Rio Grande River in west Texas.

In the 17th century, the Apaches reigned supreme in eastern New Mexico and western Texas. Against the highly mobile and increasingly horse-mounted Apaches, the Spaniards had superior fire-power but were spread too thinly to control the Apache depredations.

In the 1750's, the Mescaleros were first spoken of by that name. They were thus called because of their custom of eating baked mescal (*Agave Americana*, a cactus which provided fiber, food and drink to the Mescaleros). Their territory extended on the east through the mountains west of the Pecos River, on the west to the Rio Grande, south through the region now known as Coahuila and Chihuahua, Mexico, and to the White Mountains of the present State of New Mexico in the north.

Although the Apaches constituted the most serious threat to Spanish security, they were joined in the early 1700's by intruders even more ferocious than they. The newcomers were called "Komantcia" (Comanches) by the Ute Indians, which means "anyone who wants to fight me all the time." Unlike the Apache, they were strictly a Plains tribe, superb horsemen, and possibly the best Indian warriors in the west. In the space of fifty years, they made themselves undisputed masters of the southern Great Plains.

While the Indians raided almost at will, the Spaniards were worried about European intruders as well. Their greatest rivals on the northern frontier were the French, who were active among the Missouri tribes by 1720. The Comanches refused to allow the French to enter Spanish territory, because they did not want their enemies to receive French arms. By 1748, however, the Comanches had broken the backs of the Apaches. They began to barter with the French themselves. French influence in the area was not effectively neutralized until France ceded the vast territory of Louisiana to Spain in 1762.

To protect the northern provinces, the Spaniards had constructed a string of garrisons, called *presidios*, from west Texas, through New Mexico, and down to Sonora, Mexico. Frequently, the Indians carried better weapons than the Spanish soldiers, and were constantly running off presidial herds, leaving the garrisons stranded for months at a time. Throughout the 17th and 18th centuries, the *presidios* were able to wage little more than defensive action against their Indian foes.

This situation began to change in the 1760's when a thorough investigation of each *presidio* was commissioned by the King of Spain. The Rio Grande *presidios* in New Mexico bracketed the Pecos River Valley, to the west, but the Pecos Valley still remained outside Spanish control.

The northern frontier of New Spain was in a deplorable state of affairs between 1771 and 1776 when Indian raiders murdered and plundered the area.

But, the Spaniards were coming into heavy conflict with the Comanches by the mid-1700's. In the 1760's and 1770's, the Pueblo

Indians, in such places as present-day Pecos, New Mexico and the easternmost Spanish settlements were almost constantly at war with the Comanche. In 1779, military campaigns turned the tide of Comanche dominance, and by 1785, the Plains nomads were ready for peace. Unrelenting campaigns waged against them, losses to smallpox in 1780-1781, and a growing alliance between the Spaniards and Indian tribes of east Texas brought about this willingness to live in peace. Nomadic Indian groups during the Spanish colonial period in New Mexico continued to be the Apache, the Comanche, the Kiowa and the Pueblo.

The Apaches, by this time, had developed a very strong dependence on mescal as a staple of their diet. The mescal plant, a small, spineless cactus with rounded stems, and button-like tops was traditionally chewed during religious ceremonies for its hallucinogenic effects. Now, it had become the Apaches' major food source. The mescal abounded in the mountain foothills west of the Pecos River Valley. The Mescaleros were also using pinon, acorns, datil and other plant resources that required considerable processing and storage.

There was a great emphasis on ceremonialism associated with the mescal plant. Mescal was generally collected in the spring and sometimes in the fall by small groups of women. Actual base camps were established by a group of families and collecting took place in a radius around those camps. A roasting pit was prepared to roast the mescal. Among the favored mescal collecting areas included the Guadalupe Mountains of southeastern New Mexico.

By 1800, the major differences between the Mescalero Apaches and the hunters and gatherers of the 11th and 12th centuries had to do with the use of horses and other beasts of burden and the use of firearms obtained from the Spaniards.

Long before Europeans arrived, each of the Native peoples of the Southwest had formed an integral relationship with its homeland, including the Mescalero Apaches. For the Mescaleros, it was the Sacramento and Sierra Blanca Mountains in southeastern New Mexico. The land and the people remained connected through the people's belief in a supernatural power that pervaded the universe. Rooted in origin stories and reinforced in ritual and ceremony, this spiritual link with the land set them apart from the Europeans and lent them a sense of conviction in their unique destiny. After Spanish settlement, beginning in the late 1500's, adaptation had moderated that sense of uniqueness, but still, natives retained a separate identity. They had long known the Spaniards and Mexicans; they did not yet know the Americans, who would pose further challenges to the tenacity of their beliefs many years later. American policy makers believed that Indians should become Christians. Like the Navajos, the Mescalero Apaches had long retained their mobility on the perimeter of the Spanish and Mexican settlements.

The Pecos Valley area had become a gateway to the Southwest as other Indians, Spaniards, Mexicans and an occasional Frenchman, Englishman or American came to inspect the rivers there.

Years before any formal claim was made to this land, travelers and adventurers on their way west stopped to rest. Often gusty winds filled the air and waters with sand and dust because the rain clouds coming across the mountains to the west and north remained so high nearly all moisture dissipated before reaching the earth. Snows were few and light.

The first Europeans (the Spaniards) to enter the Pecos country did so nearly a century before English colonists settled the east coast of North America.

If Mexico had remained a part of the Spanish empire, and if the chaos that followed the establishment of the Republic of Mexico in 1821, had not occurred, perhaps the Pecos Valley would have been settled much earlier.

Spanish control along the frontier began to disintegrate. The Apaches, Comanches and even the Navajos and Utes resumed their raiding. It was not until the U.S. Military began its Indian campaigns in the 1850's, that tenuous peace was re-established.

The religion of the Spanish colonial period, up until 1821, as a result of the efforts of the missionaries, was a peculiar polytheism in which native gods disappeared but their personalities and attributes became attached to Catholic saints. The son or daughter of the Spanish-Mexican immigrant of mixed or indigenous culture developed in an environment of personal attitude based on tradition, convention and supernatural belief.

The person identified with indigenous or mixed culture interpreted their own activities and those outside of themselves by a peculiar criterion all their own, or went to people they considered authorities, but who knew as little of modern scientific interpretations as themselves. Their concepts, like those of such authorities, were generally based on unquestioned convention and on the intervention of the supernatural, an attitude traditional from remote times and little changed by contact with modern civilization. Such an individual treated their sicknesses with herbs or some other folk remedy, accompanied by magic ritual. If their own efforts were not enough to cure them, they went to a medicine man or a witch, and only in a rare and extreme case did they consult a doctor. To settle troubles with their neighbors; to fight drought, fire or flood, loss of crops, and catastrophes of all kinds; or to prosper materially or succeed in love affairs, they turned also to magic, pagan religion and supernatural help. This "folk-lorism" went back to pre-Hispanic times.

During the Spanish colonial period, this folk-lorism was similarly practiced. There was on one side Spanish professionalism and also Spanish superstition and folk lore, and, on the other, Indian professionalism and also popular superstition and folk lore.

The indigenous peoples that lived in Mexico, south of New Mexico, in pre-Hispanic days, professed a great variety of religious conceptions, from the most rudimentary, such as the fetishism and animism of the savage tribes in the mountainous and desert regions, to the most advanced systems, as in the case of the Aztecs and pre-Aztec tribes, who, it appears, came to believe in an impalpable supreme God called *Tloque Nahuaque*.

AZTEC GODS

Material objects, the stars, meteorological phenomena, plants and animals, the protecting spirits, heroes and leaders, gave origin to greater and lesser gods, adverse and favorable, visible or occult. The arrival of the Spaniards, and the Catholic religion, brought about a mixture of a large part of this polytheism with Catholicism to form a "mixed religion" or pagan-Catholic religion. It came about, however, that a large section of the native population was uninfluenced by the religion and customs of the Spaniards. The missionaries, who were usually preceded by the *conquistadors*, brought about during the colonial period, either through skillful artifices or kindness, the slow assimilation of some of these tribes into the Spanish colonies, with the result that the autochthonous (indigenous) and Catholic religions were both found there.

The indigenous tribes that up to the present time preserve their autochthonous religions (such as the Lacandones, Seris, Mayas of Quintana Roo, etc.) offered great resistance to true incorporation into the Catholic Church. Their religion was derived directly from various pre-Hispanic local cultures, but for several reasons it degenerated considerably. One of these reasons was the hostile pressure of civilized neighboring groups, which caused them to conceal and so to repress their religious ceremonies.

The ritual of the Catholic Church, its numerous painted and carved images, the tithes and tributes it imposed, the sacrifice of human beings that it effected through the Inquisition — all these characteristics made it more or less acceptable to the Indian, as the resemblance in rites, images, tributes and sacrifices facilitated amalgamation of the Catholic and indigenous religions. The Spanish priests and laymen on their part did everything possible to accelerate that religious fusion. As examples we might cite the substitution of the cult of the Virgin of Guadalupe in place of the worship before given to the Aztec goddess Tonantzin on the same hill of Tepeyac in Mexico; the dances "Moors and Christians," "Huehuenches," and others, that are a fusion of pagan dances and Spanish-Moorish dances then much in vogue on the Iberian Peninsula and still danced in Spain. In Michoacan, Mexico, the "mass of three priests" developed into a folk dance in which the natives wore the same embroidered ritual robes that the priests used at Mass.

VIRGIN OF GUADALUPE

To appreciate the general character of the mixed religion, it was necessary only to witness some of the Christian-pagan ceremonies held during religious festivities, not only in villages and ranches, but even much further south, in the vicinity of the capital of Mexico.

The Indians of the mixed religion confirmed their children, were married, and died in the bosom of the Catholic Church. At the same time many ceremonies that were of great importance in their lives presented distinct pagan tendencies. Thus, in parts of New Spain, when the cornfields began to germinate and the tender stems were sprouting, the Indians held it indispensable that some old Indian, guardian of mysterious charms, preserved the plantation from harmful animals, particularly from the deer that on silent moonlit nights came down from the hills.

We must also take into account the moral standards of some of the priests that molded the mentality of those "pagan-Catholics". There were Catholic priests who truly comforted and aided with sincere Christian charity. Such priests, generally Indians or *mestizos* (mixed race, Indian and Spanish blood), were worthy of respect and consideration. Unfortunately, their number was small, while there were many more ministers of God, generally foreigners or *mestizos* and "white" Mexicans (those with European blood), that perverted the religion they should have ennobled, exploited the populace, and dishonored the people that formed their churches.

Generally, Mexican Catholicism was essentially the same as Roman Catholicism, but it presented differences in form imposed by historic causes.

Religious dancers, *matachines*, for example, were popular. Saints were important, like *San Isidro*, who directed the clouds and made seeds grow. *San Santiago* was a crafty rascal and enriched himself at the expense of the people, and they were afraid of him. *San Mateo* sent the wind and the frosts.

Spanish Catholics and their Indian converts seem to have been urged by necessity to preserve and pass on the faith themselves.

The Franciscans, deeming themselves missionaries to the Indians primarily, had regarded the Hispanic faithful in a more or less casual manner outside the Sacraments of baptism and marriage. It wasn't any wonder, then, that these isolated Catholics, deprived of regular clerical ministry, would develop a form of parish life in which the Sacraments became secondary to a personal/communal piety that could count on lay leadership. A faith totally integrated with one's daily life was centered in the home, where parents (particularly mothers) saw to it that prayer and religious education were part of the activities of each day.

"The religious and familiar feeling, the concept of duty, the cult of decorum and honor, and the profound piety which Spain left in America owes itself in great part to the women who from the beginning guided and oriented the spirituality of the foundations. When one speaks of the glory of the *conquistadors* and the missionaries who civilized all the world, one ought to associate always in the same memory the women who went with them."

These early Spanish laywomen were entrusted, as were Anglo Protestant women later, with the spiritual and moral qualities of a civilization, while simultaneously relegated to a status within the institutional structures of church and society subordinate to and dependent on patriarchal organizations.

The policy of secularization, which had been adopted by all Spanish colonies in America, was to replace missionary order priests with secular clergy, subject to a bishop, as soon as a frontier area had enough domesticated Indians and Spanish colonists to support a priest and parish. This policy endorsed and implemented the unifying tendency of the Council of Trent by placing more emphasis on bishops who could exercise territorial power, and less emphasis on orders with the varying charisms of their respective founders. The arrangement was to staff each parish with two clergymen, one whose role was pastor, and another whose role was ecclesiastical judge and vicar for the bishop. While one priest was always in residence, the other rode the circuit from one Spanish settlement to another. These diocesan priests faced the same dangers and difficulties as earlier religious missionaries and often died just as dramatically in the execution of their ministry.

In New Mexico, secularization was not successful, however. Many of the secular clergymen sent to New Mexico were discouraged by the poverty and ruggedness of Church life there and returned to

Mexico, aggravating the preexisting problem of insufficient clerical services for Hispanics. Early conflicts between friars and local political leaders became intertwined with conflicts over Franciscan and diocesan jurisdiction, further complicating secularization. In 1747, when Don Antonio de Orendal y Maza arrived in New Mexico as presidial inspector, he joined the faction of Governor Tomas Velaz Cachupen, and, composing an unfavorable report to the Franciscan administration, proposed secularization as a deliberate shift of ecclesiastical and secular power, rather than as a pastoral decision. By 1789, the three New Mexico towns of Santa Fe, Santa Cruz and Albuquerque (as well as El Paso, Texas) were diocesan parishes of Durango, Mexico manned by secular clergymen. Regular celebration of Mass and legitimate administration of the Sacraments by clergymen were then joined to the folk religious practices of the people in those villages, temporarily combining both organizational and expressive forms of Catholic Christianity.

For Indians, as for most primal cultures, religion was not an experience or activity separate from one's economic, social or political life. It was an integral part of one's whole cultural complex. Thus, Christian "conversion" for Indians has most often not meant a total abandonment of past religious traditions, despite American civil and ecclesiastical attempts to effect such a rejection. A sort of spiritual compartmentalization enabled the indigenous cultures to adopt Christian ceremonies, rituals and symbols without changing their native world view.

The Franciscan friars had attempted to replace one religion with another. They had made excessive demands on the Indians' time, energy and loyalties to support the mission system, had even "persecuted their Indian leaders, destroyed sacred paraphernalia and denounced certain ceremonies as works of the devil." But they could not destroy native religious traditions. Nor could their oppression provoke revolting Indians to reject those aspects of Christianity they had made their own.

Syncretistically, Indians accepted part of the Catholicism imposed upon them. Those aspects of the Catholic calendar of celebrations that fit into pre-existing native beliefs and values, especially the saint's day fiesta, had become part of native life. These celebrations frequently were related to the cycle of natural seasons, and so to a particular place at a particular time. Another element of these celebrations that emphasized the importance of place was the procession that served as the transition from the church to the plaza, from the sacred place where the Catholic hierarchy officiated to the sacred place where a native spiritual leader presided *Genisaros* (nomadic Indians who had been taken captive by Spaniards and kept as servants in their households) were often separated from the dominant ethnic group in their religious lives. These Indians were not accepted by either the Spanish or the Pueblo Indians.

The contrast/conflict between two forms of the same faith can be seen in the ancient interplay of two traditions within Church life, one called the "great tradition," the other the "little tradition." A distinction can be made between the formal structures of the official institution, which tend to be abstract, universalistic, and often historically grounded" (the great tradition), and the informal traditions of common people in their everyday lives, which tend to be "more immediate, ahistorical, and particularistic" (the little tradition). Although originally, "Catholicism embraced a dialectical interchange between its great and little traditions," the Council of Trent inaugurated a period of "centralization, rationalization, and literacy" in the Church which emphasized the primacy of the great tradition over the little tradition. Spanish Catholicism, however, despite the Council of Trent in 1545 and the promulgation of the Roman Ritual in 1614, continued to be influenced by the national character of the older Rite of Toledo. And it was this form of Catholicism, a type of little tradition, that came to America with the friars and *conquistadors*. Somewhat later, a form of Catholicism more representative of the one universal great tradition developed in the Eastern and Midwestern portions of the United States. It was this "minority group along the Atlantic coastline from which the mainstream of American Catholic life took its rise that set the pattern for future Catholic development." And (with the exception of some religious order missionaries), it was this emphasis on the great tradition that so often characterized the approach of an American secular clergy to the establishment of the Church in the Southwest region of what is now the United States. Among Hispanic Catholics isolated in Southwestern villages the meeting of these two traditions made for fierce ethnic and religious conflict. The great tradition frequently manifested itself in a concern with Church authority, organization, doctrine, official establishment of jurisdiction, and adherence to the streamlined, universal, official way of administering the Sacraments, subordinating (if not condemning) the little tradition.

For example, *La Conquistadora*, Our Lady of the Conquest, has long been associated with Hispanic history and cultural conflict in the Southwest. Originally brought to New Mexico in 1625 by Fray Alonzo Benavides, Franciscan Superior of the Missions of the Kingdom of New Mexico, this little statue of Mary immediately attracted the veneration of colonists and Indians who visited Santa Fe, New Mexico. A Marian Society was formed, which quickly grew into a confraternity, or lay association. These devotees honored her as the Queen of Heaven, our Lady of the Rosary, and the Queen of their new Kingdom of New Mexico and their Villa de Santa Fe.

LA CONQUISTADORA

At the time of the Pueblo Indian Revolt in 1680, the fleeing Spaniards took the statue with them to El Paso, and when they returned twelve years later, reconquered the land in her name.

Another way of showing veneration to Our Lady was by using pious salutations that included the name of Mary.

> "The way to introduce oneself in a house was to say, on opening the door: "*Deogratis*" (Thanks be to God) or "*Ave Maria Purisima*" (Hail Mary Immaculate) and the answer received was: "*Para Siempre bendito sea Dios la Siempre Virgen Maria: pasa adelante*" (forever blessed be God and the Holy Virgin Mary: come in). . Another kind of pious and interesting salutation was used by persons at a distance from each other. The one who could first address the other by the words "Ave Maria" had the right to be answered by the recitation of the whole Hail Mary for [their] intention."

This brief history of the land and its peoples and of religious beliefs and the spiritual prior to 1800 in the deserts, valleys, mountains and plains of the Pecos River Valley reflects a path that was full of struggles and solaces. It engendered a spirit of fierce independence and wanderings, of conflicts and peace, of the holy and not so holy. The God of the peoples of the Pecos Valley region, prior to 1800, was a God that fulfilled the mystical world beyond human explanation, the God that was the familiar God of ritual and devotion, and the God who meant survival in a hostile land.

POST –1800

INTRODUCTION

The modern (post-1800) history of the Pecos River Valley of southeastern New Mexico can be divided into four distinct periods, coinciding with the four modern historical periods of New Mexico. These periods were: The Late Spanish Colonial Period (1800-1821), the Mexican Period (1821-1846), the U.S. Territorial Period (1846-1912) and the U.S. Statehood Period (1912-present). The Late Spanish Colonial Period was the time when the Spanish and missionaries continued their spiritual work in the New Mexico of New Spain. The Mexican Period followed, as Mexico gained its independence from Spain and lasted up to the United States war with Mexico. As a product of the US victory over Mexico in the Mexican-American War, New Mexico was made a territory of the US and ushered in its Territorial Period. This was followed by the Statehood Period, when New Mexico was finally, after many attempts, made a state of the United States, which it continues to enjoy to this day.

LATE SPANISH PERIOD (1800-1821)

By the early nineteenth century, there was a sparsely populated concentration of Mexicans (those born in Mexico) in what was later to become part of the United States, the territory, then the state, of New Mexico. It was relatively isolated with much of the land under Indian control. Northern Mexico was tied more closely to New Mexico than to Mexico. Major economic activities for both Mexicans and Anglos were subsistence agriculture and cattle ranching.

The orderly way in which the Spaniards from New Spain settled and governed their northern frontier stands in contrast to the haphazard way in which Anglo Americans would move into the Far West in another 25 to 30 years. In New Spain, the Catholic Church worked closely with the State to introduce civilization. There was very little separation between Church and State.

After more than two hundred years of Spanish occupation, New Mexico remained an isolated, sparsely populated frontier province whose trade was strangled by merchants in Chihuahua, Mexico and by Spanish commercial regulations. New Mexico's secular and religious problems were largely ignored by Spain. Even the Church, whose influence had helped to maintain New Mexico as a Spanish colony, could not serve the New Mexicans well. In 1812, when Pedro Bautista Pino traveled to Spain to represent New Mexico in the newly formed *cortes*, or parliament, he wrote a graphic description of New Mexico's problems. This is what he said.

> "The twenty-six Indian pueblos and the 102 settlements of Spaniards, which constitute the population of the province of New Mexico, are under the spiritual supervision of the diocese of Durango [Mexico]. These pueblos and settlements are served by twenty-two missionaries of the order of Saint Francis from the province of Mexico. In only one pueblo of the district

of El Paso and in the capital [Santa Fe] are the parish priests secular clergymen. All of the missionaries and the priests receive an income from the treasury, excepting those of the villas of Albuquerque, Santa Cruz de la Canada, and the capital [Santa Fe], who have no income other than the offerings at the altar.

It is noteworthy that the distance from the [Indian] pueblos, in which the missionaries reside, to the Spanish settlements range[s] from eight to ten leagues [28-35 miles]. In view of such long distances, therefore, not all the parishioners can go to one town to hear mass, nor can the parish priests say mass in two towns on the same day; it is also impossible to have vicariates, because the income or allotment assigned the missionaries for the spiritual administration of those towns is itself insufficient. The present allotments were made at an early date without considering the 102 settlements which have been established since the year 1780 for the preservation of the province.

For more than fifty years, no one has known that there was a bishop; nor has a bishop been seen in the province during this time. Consequently, the sovereign provisions and the instructions of ecclesiastical discipline have not been fulfilled.

The misfortunes suffered by those settlers are infinite because of the lack of a primate (bishop). Persons who have been born during these fifty years have not been confirmed. The poor people who wish, by means of a dispensation, to get married cannot do so because of the great cost of traveling a distance of more than 400 leagues [1400 miles] to Durango [Mexico]. Consequently, many people, love, live and rear families in adultery. The zeal of the ministers of the church is unable to prevent this and many other abuses which are suffered because of the aforesaid lack of ministers. It is truly grievous that in spite of the fact that from 9,000 to 10,000 *duros* [a *duro* is a Spanish or Spanish-American *peso* or silver dollar, approximately $750 to $833 US dollars in present-day *duros*] are paid by that province in tithes. For fifty years, the people have not had an opportunity to see the face of their bishop.

Agriculture, industry and commerce are the three bases of all prosperity. The province of New Mexico has none of these because of its location, because of the neglect with which the government has looked upon it up to the present time, and because of the annual withdrawal of the small income that it is able to derive from its products and manufactures. This income is so small, as we have previously stated, that until recently the majority of its inhabitants had never seen money. Who would believe that such conditions exist in North America?

The province of New Mexico does not have among its public institutions any of those found in other provinces of Spain. So backward is it in this matter that the names of such institutions are not even known. The benefit of primary letters is given only to the children of those who are able to contribute to the salary of the school teacher. There are no physicians, no surgeons, and no pharmacies."

By 1821, when Spain lost its hold on Mexico, a distinctive culture had developed on the far northern frontier of New Spain, in what would become the territory and state of New Mexico. Originally Spanish, but modified by exposure to Mexican and Southwestern Indians and tempered by geography and isolation, this frontier society had become truly Mexican. New Mexico, where sixteenth-century customs and language were transmitted most directly from Spain, remained the most "Spanish" of the frontier provinces, but there too, modification of Spanish customs and institutions occurred, and considerable mixture with Indian blood took place.

A social institution, for which there was little evidence during the early colonial period, seemed to have developed in the late colonial period along with and perhaps in consequence of the rise of the livestock industry. It was the *patron* system, which was typical of Spanish social structure in many areas of the New World, and there are even those who feel that subservient attitudes toward and extreme dependence upon those in authority are part of the personality configuration of those of Spanish descent. There is little to indicate that the early farming villages described were anything but egalitarian.

As the Spanish Period ended in New Mexico and the Mexican Period began, things were changing.

MEXICAN PERIOD (1821-1846)

At the time of the Mexican Revolution against Spain in 1821, the Hispanic colonists in New Mexico, with the indigenous Pueblo Indian population along the Rio Grande River, formed an "island" of sedentary agriculturalists in a "sea" of often hostile nomadic Indians. Beginning at approximately this time, a small number of Hispanic settlers and seasonal herders began moving out of the Rio Grande corridor and into the edges of what is now the Pecos River Valley region near Roswell.

In 1821, Mexico declared its independence from Spain and, in 1827, issued a decree exiling all Spanish-born residents of the United States of Mexico. This left missions and Hispanic parishes in New Mexico vulnerable to physical and spiritual neglect on the part of Spanish-born clerical leadership.

Again, lay leadership emerged. This time, in the form of a *cofradia* (confraternity) called *La Fraternidad Piadosa de Nuestro Padre Jesus Nazareno* — the Penitentes. Their importance was undeniable in continuing communal parish functions, such as funerals and Holy Week services, just as *santeros* (persons who make religious images) continued to create devotional images and women continued to encourage personal devotions, religious education, and the use of such sacramentals as blessings, pious sayings and blessed objects. One woman recalled how her aunt awakened the family early in the morning with her hymn at dawn, greeted people in the name of God, knelt at a home altar for prayer, and blessed the family children at the end of the day as they kissed her hand in respect. These memories of an expressive faith are more vivid for her than those of official Church functions directed by clergy.

PENITENTES

There is ample evidence to indicate that throughout the Mexican Period there was a great deal of trade between New Mexico and Mexico. The annual trading caravan called *la conducta*, or *el cordon*, occurred regularly. Many features of social organization, as well as other specific culture traits, were shared by New Mexico with Mexico. Folklore and song, baptism, wedding and funeral customs, the *compadrazgo* (extended family kinship, co-parenthood), the *cofradia* organization (Catholic laymen responsible for the care of religious images, pilgrimages and ceremonies), Passion plays, secular dances, courtship customs, protection and seclusion of unmarried women, inheritance rules, beliefs concerning health and disease, witchcraft, extended families living in multi-family dwellings, male authoritarianism and many other items were either identical or very similarly patterned in both areas, New Mexico and Mexico. The lowest social class in both areas was composed of Indian slaves and servants (*Genizaros*), poor mestizos and rural peasants, regardless of race.

As the United States expanded westward along cattle and stagecoach trails and began to build railroads in the Southwest, and, as a consequence of the US-Mexican War, American expansionists inhabited the new U.S. Territory of New Mexico.

U.S. TERRITORIAL PERIOD (1846-1912)

Even before Mexicans and Americans came into contact with one another in the borderlands between the two cultures, they had formed negative impressions of each other inherited from their respective mother countries, Spain and England. Seventeenth-century New Englanders such as Samuel Sewall and Cotton Mather, for example, who had little direct contact with Spain or Latin America, took a view of Catholic Latin America that was based largely on what they had read in literature from England. Sewall believed that Latin American Catholic culture was doomed to fall before a triumphant Protestantism. Mather took the trouble to learn Spanish in order to write a missionary tract for Spaniards in the New World which was designed "to open their eyes and be converted . . . away from Satan to God."

Anti-Spanish views inherited from England were far more complex than simple anti-Catholicism, however. The English colonists also believed that Spanish government was authoritarian, corrupt, and decadent, and that Spaniards were bigoted, cruel, greedy, tyrannical, fanatical, treacherous and lazy. In responding to these charges, Spanish historians have found it convenient to give them a pejorative label: the "Black Legend". In defending themselves from the blackening effect of this "legend," Spaniards have often gone to the other extreme of whitewashing Spain of all faults, giving rise to what Spain's detractors called a "White Legend".

As more Anglos inhabited New Mexico, there existed, what one writer has termed "the fantasy heritage" a dichotomy between things *Spanish* and things *Mexican*," which both Anglo-Americans and Mexican-Americans in the Southwest seem to have come to accept. Anglos who glorified the region's Spanish heritage while they discriminated against Mexicans suffered from this "fantasy". By the 1850's, Mexican-Americans who preferred to be called Spanish, Hispano or Latin American, in order to disassociate themselves from more recent arrivals from Mexico, were also deluded by this "fantasy" that their ancestors and heritage were Spanish.

The "fantasy heritage" manifested itself in the myth that Spain's rule over the Southwest was a bucolic, romantic period when pastoral life was simple, beautiful and virtuous. Paradoxically, accompanying this romanticization of the period of Spanish control of the Southwest was the notion that Spain's failure to build strong, prosperous provinces in the Southwest resulted from despotism, Catholicism and the mixture of the races — the notion that Spain, an inept colonizing power, had populated the Southwest with inferior peoples of mixed blood and had equipped them with inferior institutions.

Yet, predisposed to view the Catholic Church and Spanish government as regressive, Hispanic peoples as lazy, and mixed bloods as inferior,

Anglos failed to realize that conditions on the Mexican frontier closely resembled those on the American frontier.

Some Anglo Americans, combining their inherited belief in the "Black Legend" with racism and their exposure to frontier Mexican culture, came to the conclusion that Mexican people were inferior. They were contemptuous of Mexican government and of Catholicism, and they viewed Mexicans, especially Mexican men, as indolent, ignorant, bigoted, cheating, dirty, bloodthirsty, cowardly half-breeds. Mexican women were referred to as "Spanish" while Mexican men were "Mexican".

The Mexicans, in turn, did not fail to notice and comment on some Anglo Americans' feelings of superiority. Especially evident to Mexicans was some American's attitudes toward people of color — Indians and Negroes. The "fanatical intolerance" of some Americans was evident in many ways.

Some Americans viewed Mexico's "primitive inhabitants" as no better than American Indians and that Mexico deserved to be conquered because it was less industrious and efficient than the United States.

And, in small ways, there seemed to be some disrespect toward Americans by Spanish-Americans. For example, Miguel Sena, a member of the Santa Fe town council, or *ayuntamiento*, complained that the Americans mocked the system of justice and acted shamefully in the courtroom: "As soon as they enter, they stretch themselves or recline on the seats, and if they are not ordered to stand, they give their answers in that position, and with their hats on their heads." The following year, the *ayuntamiento* of Santa Fe found it necessary to require that Americans close their shops on Sundays "to avoid public scandal, and to keep the Day of the Lord with due respect."

The more common view held by Mexicans seems to have been that the "gringos", as Anglo Americans were called, were arrogant, aggressive, unscrupulous racists who endangered the very existence of Mexico as a nation. So intense had anti-Americanism become that many Mexicans were willing to fight a war to protect their homes, religions, language and customs from the odious "Anglo-Saxon race" which seemed to threaten to enslave all Mexicans.

Yet, at mid-19th century, American General Kearny addressed the mostly Hispanic inhabitants of Las Vegas, New Mexico from an adobe rooftop with the following words:

> "My government will protect you in your religion. I know you are all great Catholics. My government respects your religion as much as the Protestant religion, and allows each man to worship his Creator as his heart tells him is best. Its laws protect the Catholic as well as the Protestant. I am not a Catholic myself — I was not brought up in that faith; but, at least one-third of my army are Catholics, and I respect a good Catholic as much as a good Protestant."

AMERICAN GENERAL STEPHEN W. KEARNY

In the Treaty of Guadalupe-Hidalgo of 1848 whereby the United States, after defeating Mexico in the Mexican-American War, took over government of the land previously owned by Mexico in the Southwest including New Mexico, the words of Article IX (prior to amendment by the US Senate) read:

> "[A] guaranty shall be enjoyed by all ecclesiastics and religious corporations or communities, as well as in the discharge of the offices of their ministry, as in the enjoyment of their property of every kind, whether individual or corporate. This guaranty shall embrace all temples, houses and edifices dedicated to the Roman Catholic worship; as well as all property destined to its support, or to that of schools, hospitals and other foundations for charitable or beneficent purposes. No property of this nature shall be considered as having become the property of the American Government, or as subject to be, by it, disposed of or diverted to other uses."

John C. Cremony, an interpreter to the U.S. Boundary Commission, serving the New Mexico Territory from 1849-1851, commented in 1850 on the religion of the Apaches:

> "When you talk to [an Apache] of a Creator, he replies that he admits that fact; and when you endeavor to explain the attributes of the Most High, he tells you of the necessity to propitiate the devil. Any attempt to make him comprehend the Trinity is laughed to scorn, and he hesitates not to tell you that lie, simply because it is beyond his comprehension..He is as dogmatically convinced of his superiority as you are of yours...... Experience has shown the futility of all attempts to... christianize the North American savage.
>
> Most Indian tribes believe in the existence of two gods, who divide the universe between them. One

of the divinities is the author of all good, the other the father of all evil. The good god is deemed a quiet and inactive spirit, who takes no decisive part in the affairs of mankind, but relies more upon their desire to escape the evils brought upon them by the bad spirit than upon any direct efforts of his own. He contents himself with the knowledge that after mankind has been sufficiently tormented by his great adversary, they will seek him as a source of refuge. On the other hand, they invest the evil spirit with powers of unequaled and inconceivable activity. He is everywhere at once, and takes the lead in all schemes and pursuits, with the view of converting them to his ultimate use. The first duty of the Indian, exposed as he is to the influences of these two spirits, is to propitiate the most active of the two, and the one which will control his everyday avocations. His next object is to approach the good spirit and ask his pardon for having made terms with his one great enemy.

The Apaches believe in the immortality of the soul, but they also place credence in two divinities, the one of Good and the other of Evil, between whom power is so evenly balanced that it is beyond the faculty of man to determine which is the greater, although the ultimate superiority is credited, without hesitation, to the Good Spirit, but they modify this superiority in so far as we are concerned, by curtailing the activity and interest which the Good Spirit takes in our behalf; while the Spirit of Evil is represented as being infinitely watchful and interested in the affairs of the Apache people. The Spirit of Good is in the distant future; but the Spirit of Evil takes part in our daily and hourly affairs. The result is that while they look up to the God of Good with extreme reverence and ultimate trust, their orisons, or usual petitions, are made to the divinity which they suppose to shape their earthly ends. This may be called the excess of barbarism and heathenish mythology; but, permit me to ask, is there any difference between the untutored and savage Apache and the apparently christianized, civilized and refined man of the world? Does not the latter put off his worship of Jehovah and take to that of Mammon quite as fully and steadfastly as the Apache endeavors to conciliate the spirit which he believes will yield the most immediate and material response to his prayers?

The Apaches have no tradition whatever of the [F]lood [of Noah]. They are quite ignorant of their origin, and unhesitatingly state that they have always lived in the same country, and been the same unmixed people. They pride themselves on the purity of their blood."

And, concerning the religious ceremonies and lack of veneration of the Apaches, Cremony wrote,

"Of religious ceremonies, the Apaches have very few, and these are limited to the immediate concerns of life. The occasional scalp dance and its accompanying purification of weapons, the feasts made at marriages, and when the girls attain the age of puberty, and the ceremonials observed at the sepulture [burial] of noted warriors, comprise the whole among a people not overburdened with reverential ideas, or prone to self-humiliation. Their prayers for success, if any such are ever made, are addressed to the Evil Spirit, who is supposed to rule entirely over the apportionment of fortuitous or prejudicial results to the people of this world. It is greatly to be doubted whether the bump of reverence was ever discoverable in an Apache skull. It would be, as it has always proved, a sheer waste of time and labor to make any effort at inculcating sentiments which have been abjured by them from the earliest periods, and to which they have become wedded. The teachings of christianity are so diametrically opposed to all their received opinions and crystallized ideas, that they regard them with abhorrence. To tell an Apache warrior that when he is smitten on one cheek it is his duty to receive a slap on the other, is to proclaim the teacher a fool and an unworthy person, in his opinion. To instruct him that it is criminal to deprive other people of their property, is to inform him that it is his duty to starve in order that his enemy may prosper. An endeavor to explain to him that he should forgive his enemies and harbor no feelings of vengeance for their assaults, would at once convict his instructor of such unmitigated nonsense as to forever debar him from all future consideration. The most that can be effected is to enforce his submission to superior power, which being accomplished, it should be our aim to exhibit that leniency to which he is a stranger, and make a start from that point."

Bishop Lamy, a French Catholic priest-missionary-bishop, arrived in 1850 and attempted to institute reforms in the local folk religion prevalent at the time. However, the *Penitente* organization, which had helped keep the folk traditions alive during the so-called secular period, that is, after 1800, when the Franciscans began to dwindle in numbers, remained viable and only slightly altered by the new circumstances of Lamy's arrival.

During the Civil War, in the 1860's, minor skirmishes took place in New Mexico, which remained loyal to the Union. Many of the soldiers who fought in the west stayed on, married daughters of Hispanos and founded many of today's prominent families of Anglo surname but Spanish heritage.

Just as civil boundaries in the region remained unsettled into the second half of the 19th century, so too did Catholic Church ecclesiastical boundaries.

In 1850, New Mexico, the only Vicariate Apostolic (a Vicariate Apostolic was a form of territorial jurisdiction of the Roman Catholic Church established in missionary regions and countries where a diocese had not yet been established. It was essentially provisional, though it may have lasted for a century or more) in the region, included the territory conceded to the United States by the 1848 Treaty of Guadalupe Hidalgo, except for the towns of Dona Ana and Las Cruces whose names were somehow omitted from the document, and which remained under the jurisdiction of the bishop of Durango in Mexico, until their annexation to the Vicariate of New Mexico in 1858. The New Mexico Vicariate Apostolic also included most of Arizona.

In 1853, changes in jurisdiction included raising the New Mexico Vicariate Apostolic to become the Diocese of Santa Fe. In 1859, those southern portions of Arizona and New Mexico ceded to the United States from Mexico by the Gadsden Purchase of 1854 were annexed to the Diocese of Santa Fe.

There were, however, still difficulties between American civil authorities and Durango diocesan Catholic priests from Mexico continuing to work in New Mexico.

It is possible that this pattern of shifting ecclesiastical jurisdiction imparted to Catholics a sense of marginality until the Church was officially established among them.

In 1868, Arizona and the southern counties of New Mexico became a Vicariate Apostolic.

During a seventeen-year period in the late 1800's, six new dioceses joined the Santa Fe Diocese, which became an Archdiocese. Until 1884, Santa Fe was the only diocese located in the American Southwest.

At mid-19th century, most Catholics maintained a subsistence economy based on agricultural and pastoral (non-religious) pursuits.

Most of the early Catholic agricultural or pastoral settlements in the New Mexico region were founded by Hispanic peoples who had received land grants from Spain or Mexico.

In the Southwest, along the Rio Grande watershed of New Mexico, Hispanics and Pueblo Indians were served by Spanish and Mexican priests prior to the arrival of U.S. Military forces in 1846.

The modernizing tendencies of the civil government of the United States were also reflected in the Americanizing policies of the U.S. Catholic Church.

The establishment of Catholic parishes for Anglo whites coincided with the renewal of home missionary concern among American Protestants in the post-Civil War years. A century earlier, the First Great Awakening (1740-1776) had produced a Protestant vision of Christianizing a continent through evangelical zeal. This interdenominational movement, based on a belief in the necessity of a conversion experience and a consequent need to bear witness to it, was supplemented by a general sense of Manifest Destiny. By the time of the Second Great Awakening (1780-1830), a growing fear of barbarism on the rapidly developing Western frontier, as well as this desire to create a righteous empire, spurred Eastern churchmen to establish churches and provide a ministry to these new settlements.

The great fear was that people of the West, being far removed from the civilizing and Christianizing influence of the settled communities of the East would revert to "barbarism" and subvert the moral order of society.

This belief in the superiority of American Protestantism over Catholicism, and even of one form of Catholicism over another, characterized much of the religious conflict at mid-19th century in the Southwest. Hispanic Catholics, both priests and people, had become accustomed to a sort of religious autonomy during three centuries of isolation and neglect. Bishop Lamy's formal arrival in Santa Fe in 1851 aroused the suspicion of both laity and clergy.

"Since the Americans had come to New Mexico, people and priests had noticed that among the newcomers were many Protestants, Jews and *quien sabe que* (who knows what else), so that when they heard that a new bishop had come, without having been previously announced, their first impression was that he might very well be anything but a Catholic dignitary."

In New Mexico especially, this fear of strangers, especially of Anglos and their foreign religions, soon gave way to a sort of ethnic resignation to the inevitable, but 300 years of isolation from the centers of Catholic orthodoxy, followed by the aggressive reorganizing effort of an imported American hierarchy, left enough discontent among the people to make them potential converts to Protestantism. With American occupation of New Mexico came Baptists, Methodists, Presbyterians, Congregationalists and other Protestants. At first, concerned with Anglo settlers, they eventually designed a plan to deliver Hispanics from the "ignorance and superstition" of their Catholic faith. Primarily through the dispersal of Spanish Bibles, these evangelists encouraged Hispanics to question Catholic tradition. A follow-up program of tracts to supplement Bible reading confirmed a growing conviction for many that Roman Catholicism was truly in error. A Protestant history of its ministry among New Mexico

Hispanics presents the following example of the necessary price for rejecting "superstition:

> "In the 1870's, near Las Vegas, New Mexico, Jose Inez
> Perea, previously awakened by contact with the Bible,
> protested to his mother that the wooden image of the
> Virgin Mary which hung in a prominent place in the
> house should be removed. During a quarrel which
> ensued, Perea, in dramatic display of iconoclastic zeal,
> put a bullet through the statue. For this deed he was
> banished from his home and cut off from his family."

Clearly, one's conversion from Catholicism to Protestantism was not easy. But, in New Mexico, some think that the way had been paved by the public conflict between Bishop Lamy and the popular, secular clergyman from Durango, Mexico, Padre Antonio Jose Martinez. Some Protestants even considered him as the "forerunner and foundation layer of Protestant missions in New Mexico."

To further capitalize on their gains, and, in response to the dramatic neglect of education in the Southwest, Protestants set up more than sixty schools in New Mexico between 1879 and 1891. The Catholic response was more negative:

> "Many of them [Protestant schools] were frankly
> educational institutions for the betterment of the
> people. But others, those called "Spanish Mission
> Schools," went all out under the guise of education
> to take away the faith of the poor and ignorant by
> offering them an education which the Catholic
> Church at the time could not afford. Their procedure
> was to blacken Catholicism in the eyes of simple folk.
> What these sects did effect too well was to confuse
> souls; they took away the faith of many and left them
> not Protestants, but infidels and scoffers."

In addition to their disdain for Protestant schools, many Catholics also feared public schools. This attitude was common among 19th century American Catholics and was related, in part, to the mandate of the Catholic Third Plenary Council of Baltimore for more Catholic parochial schools.

Three hundred years of Catholic presence before the arrival of American modernization and Protestant evangelicalism made for poor inter-faith relations in the area during the 19th century. Brigham Young and the Mormons insisted on an efficient agricultural system of separateness. By the very nature of its teachings, such as polygamy, Mormonism awakened antagonism. National disapproval came to Utah not only in the form of U.S. Military force, but also in the form of moral outrage and militant Protestant evangelization. Although Catholics were numerically the largest of the Gentile religious groups, they, like the Episcopalians in the territory, took little part in the conflict. The main concern of these two sacramentally focused churches was to provide for the spiritual welfare of their own members, not to proselytize.

Even after the Catholic Church in the United States was removed from the jurisdiction of the Congregation of the Faith in Rome in 1908, terminating the mission status of the American Church, Catholic parish life in this region continued to be dealt with in a missionary approach to widely dispersed populations.

In the region, despite the arrival of the railroad at the turn of the 20th century, much of the area remained isolated. In 1900, in the Archdiocese of Santa Fe, there were nearly nine times as many parishes without priests as there were parishes with priests. Even the achievement of statehood in 1912 failed to generate an increase in industry or population for New Mexico.

In taking a close look at local Catholic church life in the region at the time, one was aware of two distinct modes of religious conduct: an expressive style and an organizational style. While some differences between the two can be explained in terms of historical and geographic conditions, the most basic difference is ethnicity. In New Mexico, Catholic parish life was from the beginning an expression of Hispanic politics and culture in an isolated and undeveloped desert frontier. These Hispanic and Indian Catholics came under the jurisdiction of an American Catholic Church in 1850, however.

In the mid-1850's, Anglo ranchers began moving into the Pecos Valley, and Comanche demands for food and gifts that had been tolerated by the Hispanics became grounds for Anglo demands for military protection against the Comanche.

The first American military exploring expedition to pass through the middle Pecos River Valley region of southeastern New Mexico was that led by Captain Randolph B. Marcy in 1849.

Fort Stanton was established in the mountains west of the Pecos Valley.

Once the Confederates had been defeated and driven out of New Mexico during the American Civil War, the Union army reoccupied the forts in the southern part of the state.

Illiteracy was widespread in New Mexico by the time American rule was established. The problem was compounded by the fact that English was not the mother tongue of the majority of New Mexicans. In 1860, in New Mexico, an estimated 46,000 of a non-Indian population of 82,000 were illiterate. That was over half of the non-Indian population. Practically all of these non-Indians were Hispanic.

During the post-Civil War, post-Indian resettlement period, the Mescalero Apache tribe came increasingly into conflict with Anglos who were settling the river valleys and mountain flanks of the Sierra Blanca mountain region west of the Pecos River.

In the late 1870's, a violent power struggle took place between two prominent Anglo political and economic factions in southeastern New Mexico. It was called the infamous "Lincoln County War".

The history of the Pecos Valley of southeastern New Mexico during the American Territorial Period was distinct from that of the rest of the Southwest and especially from that of the rest of New Mexico. The southeast New Mexico Pecos River Valley was shared by Texas ranchers and Mid-Western agriculturalists. There were no Indians to be worried about after 1881 and very few Hispanos, and it was a more homogeneous white, Anglo-Saxon Protestant population than to be found anywhere else in the Southwest. Roswell was typical of ranch supply centers in West Texas, while Eddy (Carlsbad), south of present-day Artesia, on the Pecos River, was like a bit of Kansas transplanted. The fact that, eventually, by the 1890's, the rail lines led south from Eddy to the Texas & Pacific Railway hub at Pecos, Texas and northeast from Roswell to Amarillo, Texas, and had no direct connection whatsoever with the rest of New Mexico, strongly sustained the Texas-Midwest character of this part of the Pecos Valley.

The era of military exploration and protection finally ended in 1881, by which time the Comanches and Mescalero Apaches had been permanently confined to Reservations.

The era of the cattle empires covered the period from 1866, when the first herd of Texas longhorns was driven into the Pecos Valley, until 1889, when massive droughts brought an end to the great livestock boom. The era of land and water speculation, railroads and homesteads covered the period from 1885 to the first decades of the twentieth century.

Anglo infiltration into the Pecos River Valley of southeastern New Mexico actually began when, in 1866, two Texas ranchers named Charles Goodnight and Oliver Loving decided that the best way to tap into the cattle market generated by the mining boom in Colorado was to drive their cattle west to the Pecos River in west Texas and then follow the river to the north into New Mexico.

In 1867, several other groups of Texans began moving cattle north and west on the Goodnight-Loving Trail, despite trouble with the Comanches in Texas and with the Guadalupe Mountains bands of Mescalero Apaches once they reached the Pecos.

Regarding Hispanic settlement near the Pecos River Valley of southeastern New Mexico, several small Hispanic villages were founded west of Roswell along the Rio Hondo, in the 1850's and 1860's. La Placita (later renamed Lincoln) on the Rio Bonito was settled by immigrants from the Manzano or Socorro areas of north central New Mexico and occupied until Fort Stanton was abandoned during the American Civil War and the Mescalero Apaches regained control of the area. In 1866, a group of 30-40 Hispanic families from the Estancia Valley near Albuquerque settled on the Rio Hondo west of Roswell. Many of the men had been employed as freighters on the Santa Fe Trail, and they named their village Plaza de San Jose or La Plaza de Missouri in honor of St. Joseph, Missouri, the beginning point of the Santa Fe Trail. Missouri Plaza, as the village came to be called, was occupied until the 1870's when many of the downstream communities on the Rio Hondo were abandoned because large upstream irrigation projects led to reduced water flow.

Fort Stanton, constructed in response to the hostility of the surrounding Mescalero Apaches, probably fostered the establishment of several small Spanish-speaking communities such as Missouri Plaza, *San Patricio*, *La Hunta*, *La Boquia*, *El Repente* and *Las Tablas*. By 1870, 43 of 50 households in this highland region west of Roswell were Hispanic.

The influx of Anglo population into eastern New Mexico — gradual at first, but in ever-increasing numbers, included cattlemen from Texas and then ranchers, farmers and homesteaders from throughout the United States and from many foreign countries who arrived in the Pecos River Valley and moved into the Sierra Blanca uplands, west of the Pecos Valley. The small villages of Hispanic subsistence farmers and herders were overwhelmed by the big ranches and new towns. Lacking the tight cultural integration and land-based economic and political power of the Hispanics of northern New Mexico, the Hispanics of southeastern New Mexico were reduced to the status of second-class citizens, and soon many were living in segregated communities within the larger Anglo towns.

In other parts of New Mexico, outside of the southeast part, conflicts between Hispanics and Anglos during the Territorial Period occurred, many times, because of boundary disputes. The Treaty of Guadalupe-Hidalgo, which ceded New Mexico to the United States, contained specific provisions designed to protect the property rights of Mexican citizens. The authorities of the Treaty, however, were working within a framework of British and American legal precedent, while the holders of the New Mexican land grants viewed property from the Hispanic perspective of usufructory rights (the right to use and enjoy the property of another) to traditional use areas and ties of kinship and patronage. There were long drawn-out legal battles over land rights. But not in southeast New Mexico, since it was mainly Anglo and had no land grants.

On the American frontier, by the 1870's, frontier churches played a minor role in the initial phase of exploration and settlement. A church was proverbially constructed in a town only after several saloons had been built. By June of 1875, the last of the Comanches surrendered. The buffalo had been nearly hunted to extinction by Anglo hunters, thousands of the Indians' best horses had been confiscated, many of their leaders were in prison in Florida, and the people were confined on Reservations in Oklahoma. The Comanche were gone from eastern New Mexico, and except for a few nostalgic visits by New Mexicans to the Oklahoma Reservations, their century-old trade relationship with the Pueblo Indian and Hispanic populations of New Mexico was at an end.

At first, those who were driving the great cattle herds up the Pecos River Valley into New Mexico were simply passing through. One of those trail drivers saw the potential of the Pecos River Valley for cattle ranching, however, and came to stay, building one of the largest cattle empires of the American West. His name was John Chisum. Chisum first drove cattle up the Goodnight-Loving trail in 1867.

Many of the new settlers in the Pecos Valley were from Texas, and some of these had an implacable hatred of "Mexicans", owing both to the bitter events of the Texas War for Independence and to the *comanchero* complicity in Comanche atrocities in Texas. One of the worst episodes of racial violence took place in the winter of 1873-1874. The five Harrell brothers and their associates had left Texas after being involved in a bitter blood feud and had settled their families at a ranch on the Rio Ruidoso west of Roswell. In December of 1873, a Hispanic deputy sheriff in Lincoln attempted to arrest one of the Harrell's and two other Anglos on drunk and disorderly charges. The deputy and one of the men killed each other in a gunfight. An angry Hispanic mob killed the other two Anglos. The Harrell's took their revenge by killing four Hispanic men and wounding a woman at a dance in Lincoln. Attempts to arrest them failed, and they went on to kill four Hispanic freighters and a young Anglo settler who had a Hispanic wife. Finally, the whole Harrell gang left for Texas, but not before an Anglo posse from Roswell tracked them down and killed at least two of them for stealing livestock.

Cattle rustling reached epidemic proportions in southeastern New Mexico. Many small ranchers attempted to establish themselves in the Pecos Valley of southeastern New Mexico in the 1870's. Most of these ranches belonged to honest, hardworking men, but some were simply a front for the multiple gangs of outlaws who had migrated to southeastern New Mexico to escape the pressure being put on them in Texas by the Texas Rangers and other law enforcement personnel. Several of these unsavory individuals settled along the Pecos River in the Seven Rivers area south of present-day Artesia, and, in 1876, John Chisum's brother, Pitzer, and his foreman, Jim Highsaw, found clear proof that the Seven Rivers outlaws were rustling Chisum Jinglebob Ranch cattle. Over the winter of 1876-1877, several confrontations ensued, some ending in bloodshed. In 1877, rustling by outfits based at Seven Rivers reached major proportions, and finally Chisum and his cowboys laid siege to the Beckwith Ranch near Seven Rivers where many of the rustlers worked. Corruption and violence were endemic in Lincoln County, which included the Pecos Valley, in those years. The Lincoln County War in the 1870's was a range war, a struggle for commercial and political power.

Just prior to the intensive agricultural development in the 1890's in southeast New Mexico, surface and underground water sources in the region were especially productive. Artesian wells, which tapped the underground water, quickly multiplied by the end of the nineteenth century.

In the half-century following the Civil War, westward mass movement of Americans and eastward drifting of small groups of New Mexico Hispanics led to settlement of the Pecos River Valley region. Cattle-ranching was the first economic activity to start up, but by 1890, drought had all but closed it out. The very southern end of the region, south of Artesia, near a village called Seven Rivers, and just north of present-day Carlsbad, became a haven for outlaws escaping justice in Texas from 1885 to the end of the 19th century The turn towards law and order was completed, however, when artesian water was discovered at Roswell in 1891, and its development throughout the valley promoted widespread irrigation and a rapid influx of people. The railroad reached Eddy (Carlsbad), south of Artesia, in 1891, and

Roswell, north of Artesia, in 1894, irretrievably setting the course for urbanization of the Pecos River Valley of southeastern New Mexico.

Most of the Anglo settlers of southeastern New Mexico were Southerners. The first actual wagon trains of settlers came to the Pecos Valley near Roswell in 1878 or 1879, bringing eight families. Farmers began moving into the region near Roswell in the late 1870's and 1880's to take advantage of the fertile Pecos Valley and the then abundant water. The discovery of artesian water near Roswell in the early 1890's fueled intense land speculation and resulted in the opening of thousands more acres to farming. The economic picture of the region became fully developed when the railroad arrived in the mid-1890's, providing access to national markets for sale of products and the easy acquisition of goods from other regions. The agrarian base of ranching and farming provided a solid economic base for the Pecos Valley of southeastern New Mexico.

The years 1909-1910 were years of extremely low precipitation and were considered drought years. The years of 1896, 1899 and 1903 were lower than the mean by more than 2 inches, and in an already moisture-deficient area, also qualified as years of drought. Two of these extremely dry periods, 1903 and 1909-1910 (with probable resulting crop failure) occurred during the major occupation of the region. Some quotes from the Roswell newspaper about one of the drought years:

> "Old-timers do not remember a longer dry spell than this has been." (1904)
> "Several hundred hides from cows that died on the plains from drought were brought to the city and sold." (1904)
> "No rain in June yet" (1904)
> "No good rain for a year. Plains are grassless. Cattle dying by the thousands. Lambs are being

killed to save dams. One rancher killed 10,000
lambs." (1904)

Farmers often survived the precariousness associated with dry
farming [no irrigation] by engaging in other economic pursuits such
as freighting (the hauling of cargo) or manual labor and by raising
large families to assist in management of the land. Irrigation farming
was an alternative agricultural strategy that required intensive
labor, available capital, and usually crop specialization. The average
homesteader of low economic status could hardly afford to irrigate.
The Federal government finally authorized the construction of large
reservoirs to provide irrigation water through the Reclamation Act
of 1902, but even this did not help the small landowner. Farmers
frequently found that it was more economically secure to commit a
portion of their lands to ranching or the raising of livestock in order
to supplement their livelihood. After the severe drought of 1885-1887
in the West, along with overgrazing and poor land management, the
cattle industry collapsed and the outcome was smaller cattle holdings
combined with the adoption of grain agriculture. Homesteaders
seeking to earn a living from an inhospitable land frequently filed
land claims on open lands with water sources which were being
used by cattlemen. Conflict between homesteaders and ranchers
developed as homesteaders forced the cattlemen to move to more arid
areas by fencing off the land, culminating in recurring outbursts of
open hostility between the two.

At the end of the Mexican-American War in 1848, there were 75,000
Spanish-speaking peoples residing in the Southwest with 60,000 in
New Mexico. By 1900, there were 6,649 new immigrants of Mexican
birth in New Mexico. Massive Mexican immigration did not occur,
however, until approximately 1908, and a large migration after 1910
was thought to have been the result of the Mexican Revolution of
1910-1920. The primary condition encouraging immigration from
Mexico was the large differential in real per-capita income between
Mexico and New Mexico. Poverty in Mexico certainly served as

a push. Thus, most Mexicans who immigrated were economically motivated.

As Anglos became the major landowners, they used Mexicans as cheap laborers on the large ranches. Mexicans were generally confined to the poorer lands in outlying settlements. When cotton production became significant, its requirement for extensive hand labor created a demand for cheap Mexican labor. Another major source of employment for Mexicans was the railroads, which needed a plentiful supply of cheap labor for the construction and maintenance of the railways. Most of the Mexicans coming into the Pecos Country after 1900 may have worked on the railroads at one time or another.

The status of the Mexican in the economic system of the nineteenth century was summarized in these words: "the Mexican is in his own country an outcast, a poor relation. Lacking capital, he is shut out from all participation in development, except as a laborer." Socially, the Mexican of the nineteenth century Southwest frontier was also forced into a subordinate position. The frontier was not an inevitable leveler of rank and station, but rather divisions became evident as communities began to develop. Nowhere was this social segregation more evident than in the development of bi-cultural frontier settlements. Frontier towns were usually dual communities composed of distinct Anglo and Mexican societies sharing a common perimeter. These social segregations were, and still are, most evident in the border states of the Southwest, such as New Mexico, as evidenced in Roswell, where Mexicans lived in their own communities, spoke their native tongue, and maintained their own culture. A typical comment from the period stated that the New Mexico population was not "American," but "Greaser" — persons ignorant of our laws, manners, customs, language and institutions.

By 1900, the many Texans moving to southeastern New Mexico gave it the nickname of "Little Texas". There were large land and stock holdings in the area by outside interests. In 1880, the only towns of significance were Seven Rivers, Lincoln and White Oaks (a gold mining community in the mountains west of Roswell). Roswell was only a cattle trail trading post. In fact, by 1880, the population of Roswell was only 279.

In 1904, the construction of the New Mexico Military school in Roswell began and the opening of a Mexican school in Roswell occurred. In 1911, the first Spanish newspaper was printed in Roswell: *El Registro de Roswell*. Roswell's growth was historically, and inextricably, tied to the development of the cattle industry in southeastern New Mexico, then, to the coming of the railroad.

Sheep raising had been traditionally associated with the Spanish-speaking peoples of New Mexico. There was a hierarchical ordering of those engaged in the sheep business, however. The owners of sheep ranches were granted the highest esteem and in southeastern New Mexico were frequently Anglo. Next came the sheep shearers who, although migratory, considered themselves an exclusive group and were never a part of the lowest group, the herders. Both of these groups tended to be Hispanic. Sheep shearers were often seasonal workers. With the help of the railroad, the sheep business surpassed the cattle industry in importance in southeast New Mexico.

Attempts to draw settlers to the Pecos Valley for the express purpose of homesteading or pursuing agricultural endeavors lagged far behind the onrush of cattlemen and sheep ranchers, however, until promotion picked up after the turn of the twentieth century.

The lack of water still played the major role in the unsuitability of the land for agriculture. Farmers and ranchers continued to struggle over water even though artesian water was discovered in 1890.

With the discovery of artesian water, however, the Pecos Valley was advertised in 1905 as apple country better than Oregon, with soil richer than the Nile Delta in Egypt.

Freighting (transporting cargo overland by wagon) was an important component of the early southeastern New Mexico transportation system.

Prior to 1885, Roswell had only one store. By 1899, there were more saloons than grocery stores in the town.

By 1902, the sheep business had supplanted the cattle business in importance in the Pecos Valley.

In the early 1900's, there lived six Hispanic and eight Anglo families some miles west of Roswell, whose artifacts were discovered by archaeologists. One of the Hispanic families, the Ontiveros', had their infant children baptized at San Juan Bautista Catholic Church in Roswell starting in 1903 while they still lived at their homestead west of Roswell. One of the older Ontiveros' had lived in or near Roswell since 1902. Neither Mr. or Mrs. Ontiveros could read, write or speak English. Within a few years, the Ontiveros family moved from their homestead back into Roswell into the Hispanic *barrio* (neighborhood). The Hispanic and Anglo families living in the homestead settlement west of Roswell probably moved away by 1913. From 1897 to 1913, there were 7 Hispanic and 7 Anglo families living at the homestead. Most of the Hispanic men were laborers while most of the Anglos were farmers or retired soldiers. Cooperation between Hispanic and Anglo homesteaders was evident in that they used each other nondiscriminantly as witnesses when filing homestead claims.

During the first decade of the twentieth century, Roswell had a viable, but segregated, Hispanic community to which outlying Hispanic settlements were tied, socially and economically. Back in 1878, a colony of "well-to-do" Mexican sheepmen settled at the head of the North Spring River near present-day Roswell. They began to dig a large irrigation ditch but eventually abandoned the area and moved to the vicinity of the Rio Grande River to the west. Some, however, joined an existing Mexican settlement on the Berrendo River on the northeast outskirts of present-day Roswell. The Berrendo settlement was later attacked by a band of outlaws who forced the residents to leave the area. In 1885, another small group of Hispanic settlers located southeast of Roswell near what was called Lea Lake.

Within the present city limits of Roswell, was a Hispanic community, called "*Chihuahuita*" which is still viable today.

The 1900 census listed 254 Spanish surnamed people in Roswell while the population count for that year was 2,049, indicating Hispanics composed at least 12.4% of the population of the town.

An important social force drawing Hispanics to *Chihuahuita* would have been the presence of a Roman Catholic Church. The first Catholic Church in Roswell was organized in 1902 as *San Juan Bautista* Roman Catholic Church, referred to as St. John's, and was located in *Chihuahuita*. By 1904, the church had 130 Spanish families on the rolls. Another church, established as a mission by the Salvation Army, was organized in 1900 and was also located in *Chihuahuita*. It was called the Mexican Baptist Church. In addition to a mission church for Hispanics, the Salvation Army also ran a school on the outskirts of *Chihuahuita* for Hispanic children. The school had 41 pupils, aged 5 to 18, and classes were taught in English. St. John's also conducted a school for Spanish children by 1904. The local independent school district did not operate a school for Hispanic children until 1915. The failure of school systems to educate Hispanic children was not recognized as a shortcoming in the first few decades of the twentieth century. At that time, educators viewed Hispanics as outside American society and if schools were operated for Hispanics, they were separate facilities far from comparable to their Anglo counterparts. Frequently, the justification for maintaining separate schools in the Southwest was that Hispanics had a language problem and could not keep up in schools where classes were taught in English. The development of *Chihuahuita* followed that of communities in southern Texas where Anglo and Hispanic populations lived side by side. It was a bi-cultural system, where the populations interacted economically but were spatially and socially segregated. Prior to 1910, there was little effort in the Southwest to "make them [Mexicans] a part of the country to which they had come." Hispanics aggregated in separate communities like *Chihuahuita* where they continued to speak their native language and follow their own culture. Mexican enclaves always seemed to be "on the other side" of something. The separateness of such communities was usually fostered or developed by the contemporary Anglo population due to attitudes of social and/or racial superiority. This attitude was prevalent in early twentieth century Roswell as it was in virtually every town with a bi-cultural population. Roswell, however, was no worse than any other community of its kind. Anti-Mexican attitudes were characterized like this in the Roswell newspaper:

> "Outlaws drove out a community of Mexican sheepmen on the North Spring River in 1878."

> "In 1883, a group of men from Texas went on a rampage in surrounding Lincoln County, killing Hispanic residents. It was called the Harrell War."

> "In 1885, twenty cowboys drove a Mexican sheepman's 4,000 sheep to a point northeast of Roswell and left him to retrieve them as best he could."

> "Roswell was composed of bearded men from the mountains, blue-shirted cow-men from the plains, and swarthy Mexicans from nowhere in particular." (1900)

> "A letter written in 1903 describes Roswell as nearly all Caucasians with Indians and his half-brother, the Mexican, being only noticed because so few." (1903)

"A bunch of Mexicans were around town and then left. They more resembled Indians than Mexicans." (1904)

"An Anglo's life was saved by his Mexican cook. The name of the Anglo is mentioned, but not the Mexican cook." (1904)

"Forty Mexicans were sent out on a train for lambing and shearing. Most were of the 'greaser' type." (1904)

"Two Mexican shepherds got in a fight and one was severely hurt. Had he been other than a Mexican the injured man would have expired instantly... it seems impossible to kill a Mexican by cutting him... it has been said that the only way one could kill a Mexican by cutting him would be to cut his head off or his heart out." (1904)

"I never saw a Mexican until I came to Roswell a few weeks ago, and I do not hear many kind utterances in regard to the race. Some people here do not appear to regard them as any better than negroes, and I understand that there was a certain amusement house that banned Negroes and Mexicans." (1904)

"The development of 'Little Texas' in southeastern New Mexico was due to the 'magic wand of Anglo-Saxons' as opposed to the culture of the greaser [who] is too lazy to keep up; and [who] smells too badly to be endured." (1906)

The community of *Chihuahuita*, however, would have nurtured the Hispanic population of Roswell and surrounding areas through its accepting social environment, religious offerings and school programs geared specifically to Spanish-speaking citizens.

Contemporary Roswell newspapers in the early 1900's were full of names of Anglos coming in by the trainloads, mainly from the Midwestern areas, to regain their health or to retire.

> "There is no field, or belt, or stratum of artesian waters in the world which is more constant in its flow or more accessible than that in the Pecos valley, within the limits of Chaves County. Water wells have been in constant operation and have furnished an unvarying supply of clear, cold, pure water for the past ten years. What was once considered the Great American Desert, of which Chaves County is a part, is being made to "blossom as the rose". The great volume of the artesian flow is used for irrigation. One well will irrigate 160 acres of land under very heavy croppage, and much more when the land is devoted to fruit trees and crops adapted more or less to growth in an arid country. The soil of the valley is rich in those minerals which nourish vegetation; the air is dry and pure and discouraging to all forms of parasitical life which create such havoc to the fruits and grains of other sections of the country."

In 1850, there were more than twenty-five million buffalo on the western plains! By 1900, there were less than one thousand!! In 1850, not a single town or road existed in southeastern New Mexico. By 1900, the area had five county governments, several sizeable towns, growing commerce and agriculture, and a population of over 25,000. The total population of New Mexico in 1900 was 196,310. Thirteen percent of the entire New Mexico population in 1900 resided in southeastern New Mexico.

The discovery of artesian water supplied the one thing needed to make the Pecos Valley a garden of the world. The proven artesian water field in Chaves County was about seventy-five miles long and twenty miles wide.

The town of Roswell was incorporated in 1891 and remained a village until 1903, when it became a city. By 1907, Roswell had over 120 artesian wells in its environs. In 1906, a hospital was built by Catholic sisters in Roswell.

The Pecos Valley Immigration Company was organized in 1905 and brought more immigrants to the valley than any other organization. It had about 400 agents located over the United States from New York to California and played a major role in the development of the Pecos Valley.

Hispanics and Native Americans have tended to be invisible in histories of this region or, even worse, to have appeared only in "bad guy" walk-on roles in the dramatic accounts of cattle barons, range wars, railroads and homesteaders.

The gradual contiguous spread of Hispanic colonists during the nineteenth century was a little-known event of major importance. Overshadowed in the public mind and regional history by Indian wars, cattle kingdoms, and mining rushes, this spontaneous unspectacular folk movement impressed an indelible cultural stamp upon the life and landscape of a broad portion of this part of the Southwest. It began in a small way in late Spanish Period times, gathered general momentum during the Mexican period, and continued for another generation, interrupted but never really stemmed until it ran head on into other settler movements seeking the same grass, water and soil.

In the lower Pecos Valley of New Mexico, the boom in homesteading arose in response to water development projects.

At its peak, the Pecos Valley Irrigation and Improvement Company was the largest privately financed irrigation project in the world. The company built a railroad spur linking the lower Pecos Valley of New Mexico with Pecos, Texas and commenced six major water development projects.

At the same time that the Pecos Valley Irrigation and Improvement Company was building massive dams and huge canal systems to bring the salt-filled water of the Pecos River to farm fields, artesian wells were being drilled throughout the Pecos Valley to bring fresh water to the land.

By the turn of the century, and on into the first decade of the 20th century, the major factor in settlement and development within the Pecos Valley was the railroad.

Between 1850 and 1900, New Mexico changed from Spanish settler region to western frontier society to modernizing territory on the verge of statehood.

A very considerable proportion of the population of New Mexico was Spanish-American, the descendants of those who pushed across the Rio Grande and settled in the midst of the hostile Indian country long before this territory was detached from Mexico.

A social problem of racial adjustment existed as well as a missionary problem. There was a definite racial question between Spanish-Americans and Anglo-Americans. Spanish-Americans were confused in popular thinking with the Mexicans. There was a more deeply seated prejudice between the Spanish-Americans and the Mexico Mexicans than there was between the Anglo- and the Spanish-American. Mexican immigrants did not identify themselves with the Spanish-Americans. In very many areas where there was a large Spanish-American population there were no Mexican immigrants. Mexicans had begun to come for railroad work and to industrial centers, and were, as elsewhere, largely migrants. The Spanish-Americans, on the other hand, were generally farmers owning their own land. The misunderstanding and jealousies between the Spanish-Americans and Anglos were largely the result of political rivalry and intrigue. It was partisan politics. The situation had many points of similarity with that in the U.S. Territory of Hawaii between the native Hawaiians and the American elements in the population.

Nearly a hundred years of Anglo-American aggressiveness, influenced by this assumption of the Spanish-American, tended to produce a certain amount of chronic distrust and bitterness.

In striking contrast with the Mexican immigrant, the Spanish-American natives of New Mexico were thoroughly loyal to the United States. Many thought the Spanish-Americans had been slow to appreciate the public school and some of the other institutions of American life, and explained this by the adverse influence of the Catholic Church.

There was considerable difference of opinion as to the relations in which there were most evidence of racial feeling between Spanish-Americans and Anglos. Very many thought it came out most definitely in political relations, though one discriminating writer pointed out that this feeling in political relations had a background in the differences of religion. Only a very few thought there was much evidence of race feeling in the economic field, however.

While some thought it would require one or many generations to bridge completely the differences between the Spanish-Americans and the Anglo-Americans, only a very few felt that there were permanent racial characteristics which would keep them apart. The strongly-opposed types of religious allegiance would long separate them, and some felt that the Anglo-Saxon superiority complex was a very stubborn disease.

The instances of personal prejudice against Spanish-Americans even in churches existed. Whatever was said as to the desirability of separate Spanish/American churches to give opportunity for spiritual expression and development, one ought to have been able to expect in the churches a welcome to those who had chosen the church's invitation to its mission school.

The Spanish-Americans in New Mexico built houses, maintained irrigation ditches, grazed their livestock, cared for their sick, buried their dead and celebrated the holy days of the Catholic religion. Neglected by both church and state, they developed a relatively autonomous system for maintaining law and order, socializing the children and perpetuating the faith and their culture in general.

The *cofradia* organization of the Catholic church was very early transplanted to New Mexico, as well as to other parts of the New World, and it is likely that the so-called Penitente Brotherhood, a somewhat later development than the *cofradia*, was an outgrowth of these earlier religious and beneficent societies. Even without the sacraments of the church, which often had to be foregone in the absence of a priest, the rituals of life continued. In addition to the patriarchal extended family, the *compadrazgo*, or system of godparent-hood, continued to be an important institution, serving to strengthen rights and obligations among kinfolk.

Recreation consisted largely of the celebration of the various life crises and of the holy days of the Catholic calendar, including the day of the village's patron saint. In addition to religious observances, conducted by officers of the *cofradia* or by a priest — if one was available — there was feasting and the inevitable dancing (except in the event of a funeral, which was, however, a kind of social occasion also).

Anglo settlers had been filtering into the New Mexico Territory up until 1900 when the trickle became a wave, resulting in an Anglo majority sometime after 1920.

Southeastern New Mexico, encompassing fifty thousand square miles, was one of the least known areas of the Territory of New Mexico despite its stunning and varied landscape and its rich and exciting history. The region was long known as 'the empty quarter'. It was different in tone, feel of land, culture, accent and historical tradition from the rest of New Mexico. It was the 'Old West' where there were ranchers and farmers, politicians and judges, teachers, old-timers, young people, business people and leaders of the Hispanic community.

Southeastern New Mexico, a compelling blend of pure frontier West and the dynamic cultural eclecticism characteristic of the Territory as a whole, was the region settled latest and yet the one whose name became synonymous with the dangers and opportunities to be found 'west of the Pecos'.

Southeastern New Mexico was, in fact, one of the driest regions in the entire United States, where rainfall averaged less than twelve inches a year, and the Pecos River was the only perennial source of surface water in an area of sixty thousand square miles stretching from the Sacramento Mountains in the west to Lubbock, Texas, in the east.

Just as it integrated space and claimed wholeness, so too did this land demand recognition that time was eternal and circular, not to be conceived in the short gulps of human breath in the marked-off centuries.

The people of southeastern New Mexico were, in fact, bound together as much by their history as by the feel of the land they occupied. For what the entire *Llano Estacado* and the trans-Pecos region had in common was that it was their destiny to be among the last frontiers of the American West to be tamed and permanently settled.

It was generally held that a belief in Christianity was a civilizing tool used in the Manifest Destiny policy of the United States. It was assumed that the Indians could be persuaded to change their way of life from semi-nomadic to agricultural, sedentary, and Christian, writing in one report that only the first generation would remember the old ways, while the children would grow up as members of a new generation with new ideals of virtue and duty, becoming "tamed" and "civilized".

Having begun as a trickle during the 1850's and 1860's, emigration to the southeastern New Mexico Pecos River frontier swelled during the 1880's and 1890's and on well into the 20th century like water rushing through a break in a sea wall. An unmistakably American brand of rugged individualism flourished. In addition, the very suddenness of the region's surge in historical momentum tended to attract individuals who were either especially ambitious, or outcasts, wanderers, or outlaws, or simply in need of new beginnings.

Southeastern New Mexico became a crossroads where incoming groups from a number of distinctive origins converged. Out of this confluence of settler groups there emerged a new society with its own social order based on cultural, economic and religious differentiations.

The Hispanic people of New Mexico continued to speak Spanish and to perpetuate the customs of their Spanish and Mexican heritage, a right guaranteed them under terms of the Treaty of Guadalupe-Hidalgo, which made them citizens of the United States. Throughout the Territorial Period, and on into the Statehood Period, all official documents and voter ballots in New Mexico were printed both in Spanish and in English, in recognition of the dual language reality.

Even by the turn of the 20th century and the decade that led to statehood in 1912, a difference between the Hispanic settlements in the mountains and the one at Roswell ("*Chihuahuita*") was apparent.

Chihuahuita, in Roswell, became a multigenerational community with an eclectic Hispanic culture merging the folkways of Mexico, the

Mexican traditions of Texas, and the more purely Spanish traditions brought from north-central New Mexico.

Ethnic intermarriage between Anglos and Hispanics was one of the means by which some Hispanic customs were introduced to Anglo settlers. But, separatism marked the tenor of social relations between Anglos and Hispanos, generally. The Southern influence (from the American South) predominated in the Anglo community.

In the early decades of the 20th century in the Pecos Valley, there was a trend toward the growth of local government, growth of sizable communities with all their attendant institutions such as schools, churches, banks, commercial establishments, and newspapers, and growth of a non-agrarian, usually Anglo, middle class, composed of professionals of various sorts and business people.

Southeastern New Mexico did work as a safety valve for America's demographic and social tensions, even as it demonstrated as convincingly as other frontiers that inequity was not abolished, only recreated in new shapes, in frontier society. Nowhere else was there quite the same mix of interacting forces in quite the same proportions. Nowhere else did the same cast of characters influence the interplay of existing forces. Southeastern New Mexico continued for some time to experience such aspects of frontier life as isolation, dependence upon emigration, and the lack of many amenities taken for granted elsewhere.

For the sky-swept vastness of southeastern New Mexico, the changes that time brought could even now seem compressed under the weight of two ever-present realities. One was the land itself, which remained an open, wild, sweepingly free and somehow remote interior portion of the continent. And the other was a human community that evolved out of, and still reflected in startlingly direct ways, the legacy of a frontier past that saw ethnic groups, determined individuals, and disparate economic interests engaged in a struggle for their place in the Western sun. Southeastern New Mexico blazed with activity from the late 1860's on into the 20th century as its daunting, varied lands were sought for cattle and sheep range, gold and coal mining, cropland and townsites. The lingering effects of the social divisions that accompanied the boisterously optimistic American settlement, however, are visible even today.

The frontier legacy was one of an eclectic, layered, evolving society, as well as one still learning to live with the inherent limits of a dry land in which water was a precious commodity affecting the region's economic and population-growth potential.

The events that were pounded into the soil and the voices that resounded in the harmonies and disharmonies of human discourse could seem eerily alive in the very silence of the plains, river valleys and mountains.

Here, the past was part of the present, because this was a place still in the process of being discovered, and because the land itself insistently fused past and present. It may be the destiny of southeastern New Mexico to be forever frontier.

The history of church life in the Pecos Valley was a story of struggle. It was the drama of a diverse people searching for authentic ways to acknowledge God's Presence in a sparsely settled land. It was the tale of individual and communal wrestling with the resistant forces of nature, with a dependent economy, with the multiple traditions of an indigenous non-Christian culture, with radicalism and militantism, and with contrasting forces within the church itself. Such a history considered concrete evidence of the geographic struggle (physical, political and economic). It described the ethnic struggle of Native American and Hispanic minorities with the dominant Anglo society and with each other, as well as the multicultural conflicts of nationalistic European immigrants. There was an interplay of complementary but often conflicting principles within, especially, the Catholic Church: hierarchical order and the prophetic principle, organizational style and an expressive one, the "great tradition" and the "little tradition," and the communal impulse and personal needs.

A sense of geography (physical, political and economic) was basic to an understanding of the area and its people. The very immensity of the region, a variety of imposing landforms, and pervasive dryness created awesome obstacles to the civilizing tendencies of humankind. The late establishment of both civil and ecclesiastical jurisdiction caused considerable confusion and delayed the development of organized church life. As settlements were formed around agricultural enterprises or railroad activities, frontier faithful sought visible religious communities where they could fulfill their religious duties and celebrate the important events in their lives. Evangelizing efforts and a militant presence often contributed to inter-religious tensions. The lack of early industrialization in the region, along with the boom-and-bust phenomena related to the shifting populations of relocated railroad junctions, delayed stabilization of the population and its movement from rural to urban settings. These geographic and demographic conditions contributed to a sort of economic colonialism from which the region has only recently emerged. Church life generally retained a rural missionary character. The region's low population density was characterized by the predominance of rural communities and isolation created by the great distance between urban centers. The majority of churches would have been considered more rural than urban. There were good examples of a spirituality that remained one with its surroundings. One group in a desert environment that invested spiritual energy in obtaining the necessary blessing of rain was the Hispanic Catholic ranching community of eastern New Mexico. When Fabiola Cabeza de Baca Gilbert recalled her childhood on the *Llano Estacado*, she says:

> Money in our lives was not important. Rain was important. We never counted our money; we counted the weeks and months between rains. From childhood

we were brought up to watch for signs of rain. . . . As
a child, prayer was the only solution to the magic of
rain. . . . On reaching middle age, I am still praying
for rain.

Could the prayerful and prudent traditions of Indian farmers and
Hispanic ranchers, combined with a realistic awareness of the limited
benefits of federal reclamation projects, and the church's own rich
tradition of water imagery be a source of regional spiritual energy
contributing to the solution of one of the fundamental problems of
life in this region?

The relatively late determination of civil boundaries contributed
to the rural character of church life in this region. Negotiating
acquisitions and creating subsequent subdivisions into territories of
the United States forestalled settlement in the area and, thus, delayed
the development of formal parish life.

In the rural, mobile settlements of white immigrants, cut off from
their European roots and from Eastern ethnic ghettos, it was likely
that the expression of one's faith was not as intimately bound to
one's entire cultural complex as it was for isolated communities of
Hispanics with hundreds of years of a lay tradition. It may be also
true that immigrant Europeans had become aware in America of how
the centrality of an elaborate sacramental system, especially in the
Catholic Church, in their religion made for greater dependence on
clerical leadership than they observed in other American churches.
Thus, these early white settlers came west for individual reasons,
confident that their clergy would follow to minister to what they
saw as their basic spiritual needs. For example, even before Catholic
railroad workers began to come into the region, Catholic military
men stationed at forts were visited by passing clergy or Indian
missionaries eager to extend the grace of the Sacraments to whites
on a somewhat lawless frontier. Perhaps European immigrants, more

easily Americanized than Native Americans or Hispanics, were seen as "civilizing" agents by the American institutional Catholic Church.

In the region, where missionary work among Catholics had not accustomed many of these foreign-born clergy to the great distances and difficulties of frontier life, diocesan priests were the first to bring their ministry to Catholic settlers. For order and secular clergy alike, the few priests assigned to a diocese or vicariate regularly covered large areas as circuit riders. The same was true in the Protestant churches.

Back in 1895, Pope Leo XIII addressed an encyclical to the American Catholic Church. In *Longingua Oceani*, there were praises for "the young and vigorous American nation, in which we plainly discern latent forces for the advancement alike of civilization and Christianity." Lauding "the prosperous condition of Catholicity," the Pope gave credit "to the virtue, the ability, and the prudence of the bishops and clergy" with the "main factor, no doubt" being "the ordinances and decrees of your synods." Clearly, the institutional aspects of the American Catholic Church were his primary concern. His expressed belief that the Catholic Church had greater opportunity for prosperity in a country where it was supported by the state rather than "as in America, dissevered and divorced", was not well-received by Catholic Americans. There is no doubt that ecclesiastical organization contributed greatly to the stability of clerical leadership, but it was not the only force at work in the development, preservation, and celebration of the faith.

Building programs for parishes, like clerical and lay leadership traditions, suggested some differences between early regional and other approaches. In the American Southwest, in places such as New Mexico, the Catholic Church had been built not by Indians under the direction of friars with royal subsidies as in Spanish colonial times, but "at the expense of its Spanish citizens."

The phrase "at their own expense" became a common way of describing local lay initiative for the building of churches in Hispanic areas.

Despite national economic depressions, such as the one in 1893, Catholics and other religions continued their pioneering struggle to provide what they considered the essentials for proper church life. After gathering for months or years in schools, homes, hotels, halls, saloons, stores, log cabins, or courthouses for the celebration of Mass and the Sacraments, and church services in general, these immigrants were eager to worship in what they considered a more sacred space.

Churches for Anglos were built only after subscription lists of pledged financial supports were collected.

Once arrangements had been made by circuit-riding clergy to provide church services on a regular basis and to build churches, then, was consideration given to religious education.

Home religious education was of such value to Catholic missionaries that even after parochial schools had been established, "these schools [could] accomplish very little in inculcating religion in the hearts of the young if the work [had] not been commenced at home."

A complementary socializing activity in some Hispanic homes was the Christian education of Indian servants, an important obligation that the Spanish family took very seriously. These Indian servants, or *criados*, both children and adults, were prepared for baptism and sponsored by the families with whom they lived.

Institutionalized programs of religious education in the New Mexico Territory could best be understood in a national context that included both civil and ecclesiastical attitudes toward education and the role of women in it. One of the beliefs growing out of American Puritan society was that without education (both secular and religious) a person would retain a greater tendency toward evil than toward good and, thus, for the sake of social order, instruction in Godly living was essential. This attitude was deepened by the experience of the American Revolution and the fear of freedom generated by an irrevocable break with traditional authority. How would this newly liberated people create and maintain social order in a new governmental form? "[American Revolutionary] ideology stressed that liberty depended upon popular virtue; the American people must be pious, disinterested, and unworldly if the Republic were to survive." And it was women who were entrusted with the responsibility of passing this piety on to their sons and daughters and, thus, preserving the republic. For Protestant women, this role was fulfilled not only through motherhood, but also by their conspicuous participation in revivals and prayer meetings and by individual evangelizing efforts. The principle that evangelical activity proved the authority of one's conversion experience applied to Protestant women as well as to men.

But how did Catholic women whose religious experience did not include emphasis on personal conversion share in this national belief? Hispanic women in the region seemed to have possessed a similar sense of responsibility as culture bearers for an ancient code of honor that blended religion with personal refinement. Among Anglo Catholic women in America, religious women (usually representing European congregations) carried the visible social responsibility for bringing civilization, refinement, and a sense of American culture to Native Americans and Anglos alike, via formal institutions for learning. This was an extension of the ancient role of women as prayer leaders, or, in the Hispanic culture, *rezadoras*.

The rationale for Catholic parochial schools had to do with the conflicts between European and American ways of life and between Catholic and Protestant social goals. A transitional period in America's religious history occurred when two great waves of European immigration created serious social, political and economic problems in this country. Catholic fears over the loss of the faith outside Catholic schools conflicted with Protestant resolve to create a public school system designed to pass on the faith of America's Protestant "beginnings." By the time the mandate was carried to the Western frontier, it bore the marks of the old Protestant fear of barbarism.

In the New Mexico Territory, schools run by Anglo missionaries, both Catholic and Protestant, were instruments not only of civilization, but of acculturation in a very particular American mode. Hispanic boys often attended Protestant schools "out of sheer necessity of learning English, for in these parts it was necessary for trade with Americans of the United States that the Spanish people made great and protracted sacrifices to send their boys to schools where English was taught."

As the New Mexico Territorial government slowly established public school systems, members of Catholic religious orders were often asked to conduct these schools. Despite the willingness of Catholics to cooperate with the bishops by building and supporting parochial schools, the services of religious and lay teachers in academies and public schools seemed to have been more common.

Although religious education programs had always been a valuable element in parish life, either where a parochial school was unfeasible or where many Catholic students did not attend the parochial school, they grew in number and improved in quality dramatically as Catholic parochial schools struggled to survive and sometimes failed. Early parishes in newly developed towns often could not afford a building or could not obtain teachers for a parochial school, and so, organized Sunday schools for the first ten or twenty years of their existence. Some also provided Mass and Catechism every Sunday for the students. Religious education programs extended themselves to students through these Masses and Catechisms. These 19th century beginnings of religious education programs in the New

Mexico Territory may have seemed second best to parochial schools at the time, but they set precedent for what became a nationwide 20th century priority.

Perhaps the most common, but unavoidable, concern of most Catholics, and, of all faiths, was fund-raising. Most often, funds were raised for the construction of buildings and other organizational expenses. From the 1850's onward, after Bishop Lamy in New Mexico energetically reinstituted the earlier tradition of tithing, in a circular letter of 1854, he stated in Spanish:

> "The faithful of this territory, having no pretext for complaining of the parish taxes, nor of the collection of tithes; [they] will know that we have withdrawn from Pastors the facility of administering the Sacraments [nor may they] give ecclesiastical burial to the heads of families who refuse to pay their share of the tithes."

This early tithing system was more diocesan than parochial; however, in later years when pastors could not collect the amount of contribution they felt was suitable, they appealed to the bishop to use his influence in forcing payment of tithes. At one parish.

> "[i]n addition to the tithes, which they split with parish and bishop, and the first fruits, which they retained, the priests could also keep income from fiestas, Holy Week sermons, and other such special ceremonies, and the stipend offerings for Masses .. A large portion of their income was spent in building and rebuilding."

At another parish, parishioners paid either the *diezmo* or the *primicias*. The former was a 10% tithe paid in different commodities or with manual labor; the latter was a commitment by parishioners to designate some portion of their hay or grain-producing land, and the harvest from it, to the church, their "first fruits".

Finances for rebuilding and other parish projects came from a variety of sources. Often, the religious order serving in the area built the first churches for Anglos. At other times, a local secular clergy or even a visiting bishop bought the land and paid for the first simple structure. In the period of early settlement, railroad companies, power companies, or wealthy civic leaders frequently donated land or money for the construction of a parish church.

Despite help from secular and ecclesiastical sources, the laity of most parishes in the region assumed the major responsibility for the building and continued maintenance of its churches. As evidence of their commitment to the congregation and its building program, parishioners often signed subscription lists professing their intention to financially support the project. Frequently, it was the women who devoted their time and talents to collecting funds for the building. While the women were busy collecting funds, the men were occupied in volunteering hours of labor to build the churches themselves.

In many parishes, pew rental was a regular means of raising funds. When names of parishioners accompanied by a statement of amounts given for this purpose and for special collections were published in church announcements or bulletins, negligent or poor parishioners must have been shamed into further efforts to contribute.

Happier ways of raising funds involved special projects that had a social as well as an economic goal. Some parishes accrued heavy debt, however.

Special fund-raisers frequently involved the domestic talents of women. But, public relations skills were also important when religious women went begging for funds to build schools. Both clergy and laypeople needed to use ingenuity in gaining financial support for frontier parish needs.

In addition to monetary contributions, personal contributions of time and talent were vital to the establishment of most parishes. The two most common societies in most parishes (because they fulfilled necessary functions on the parish level) were the Altar Society for women and Holy Name Society for men. Sometimes called Altar and Rosary Society, the women's group was committed to the upkeep of the sanctuary, altar decorations, vestments and altar linens. The Holy Name Society often served simply as the Men's Club, focusing on building and overall maintenance efforts.

A sort of predecessor of these voluntary groups existed and continues to exist in parishes without priests among Hispanic Catholics in New Mexico. The *mayordomos* were one couple or more who committed themselves for a year to care for the church. "It was always considered a high honor to be entrusted with the keys to the church." So dependable were the parishioners who served these ongoing material needs of the congregation that they often were in complete charge of a church that found itself without a resident pastor.

Often, parish societies served ethnic, national or material needs, but some confraternities (or *cofradias* as they were known among Hispanic Catholics) served primarily spiritual needs. In addition to the well-known *Hermanos de Nuestro Padre Jesus* (the *Penitentes*), whose own prayers and penances were supplemented by spiritual and corporal works of mercy, *La Cofradia de Nuestra Senora del Carmel* also served parishioners.

As an advancing U.S. immigration through Indian lands in the late 19th and early 20th centuries soon became a full-scale invasion of Anglos moving westward with military, economic and political might to support their advances, the indigenous peoples were clearly the losers. In the end, the Christian churches, too, would act as agents of U.S. domination in the Americanization and Christianization of Native Americans, especially.

As far back as 1870, tired by ineffective treaties and drained by the economic cost of numerous military campaigns intended to subdue the American Indians, U.S. President Ulysses S. Grant created a Peace Policy that enlisted the aid of religious institutions in acculturating indigenous peoples. Christianization became the means of Americanization and the Reservation boarding school its method. Not only were the many U.S. Christian Churches asked to participate in this cultural domination, but they were arbitrarily assigned particular tribes as their charges, regardless of the religious faith or preference of the Indians themselves. Consequently, Indians who had learned to accept one form of Christianity were suddenly expected to adopt another. This caused not only interdenominational conflict, but a loss of continuity in developing a religious stance that could include both native tradition and an imposed culture.

Catholic bishops throughout the country protested this aspect of Grant's policy, when, in 1873, they organized the Bureau of Catholic Indian Missions to deal more effectively with the injustices they perceived. There were many disappointments to add to the trail of broken promises.

Early indigenous Indian education was part of the Franciscan mission system. As the decrease in Franciscan clergy became greater than the increase in secular clergy from Durango, Mexico, Indian education suffered. During the episcopacy of Bishop Lamy, during the latter half of the nineteenth century, attempts were made to transfer Indian schools from administration by the U.S. War Department, which insisted on conducting classes in English, to the Catholic Diocese of Santa Fe, which would instruct in the more familiar Spanish; but it was not until 1886, during the episcopacy of Archbishop Salpointe, that a contract was made with the U.S. Government for seven day schools and one boarding school. Proposed day schools were set up, but they lasted only a few years. One boarding school for boys received the last of its federal aid in 1894.

Hispanic Catholicism was also modified by the imposition of a different mode of religious conduct, different from what Hispanics were used to, the Americanized and Americanizing institutional Church. The "little tradition" had flourished for Hispanics during the geographic and cultural isolation of both the Spanish Colonial and the Mexican periods and continued on into the Territorial Period. When Bishop John Baptist Lamy and his party of U.S.-sponsored clergy arrived in 1851, Lamy came into conflict not only with the few Hispanic clergy serving his new vicariate, but also with the folk religious customs these Catholics had developed during nearly 300 years of separation from institutional influence.

Lamy spoke of the Mexican clergy:

> "[I hoped] to keep them under fear. Perhaps that will change them, but I doubt it I must be patient and catch them doing wrong. I suspended one of the senior clerics, perhaps that will serve as an example for the others."

Although Lamy later sought to encourage the ordination of native clergy, his initial approach to the New Mexican priests as wayward subordinates, and his repeated importing of European clergy to take over their duties, had sufficiently offended the local Catholic Hispanics to prevent their filling the clerical ranks of the institutional Church in New Mexico.

Lamy judged as inferior not only the New Mexican clergy, but also the religious expression of the people. He perceived, repeatedly, that, "the people were well disposed and showed a strong attachment to their religion on the surface. The people went to Mass, observed the feast days, kept their religious sodalities active enough, but for the most part failed to adhere to the Sacraments, upon which all else depended."

A series of diocesan regulations pertaining to proper administration of the Sacraments stressed instruction for the recipients, clearly a function of the "great tradition's" emphasis on intellectual knowledge and literacy.

One boost to ethnic identity and cultural expression was granted his Spanish faithful by Bishop Lamy, however, his insistence on foreign-born clergy learning and using the Spanish language. Lamy wrote most of his own pastoral letters in Spanish and even used that language in official documents when Latin was not required. The majority of parishes in his jurisdiction continued to use Spanish in all parts of their services, as many throughout New Mexico continue to do today. Most rural Hispanic parishes in New Mexico expressed their ethnicity as an unbroken tradition without national recognition. Lamy had always to deal with the problems of a Hispanic Catholic majority population vis-a-vis an Anglo (and mostly Protestant) power structure.

Left for so long to their "little tradition", then criticized by representatives of the "great tradition", Hispanic Catholics in New Mexico depended on the family, on the community, and on lay *cofradias* (those brotherhoods that simultaneously sought to fulfill the people's religious needs and to help them maintain a sense of cultural identity). In New Mexico, the Hispanic people participated in public rituals under the leadership of the *Penitentes*, expressed privately and publicly their devotion to particular saints, and communally celebrated feasts of the liturgical year and major rites of passage with elaborate local custom.

During the time when Hispanic villages in New Mexico were most isolated from the regular care of clergy, the *Penitente* Brotherhood conducted funerals and Holy Week services for local Catholics who would otherwise have gone without the consolation of religious support and an appropriate expression of their faith. In ministering to the dying, villagers under the leadership of the Penitentes would pray with the dying person, prepare the body and the grave, keep vigil (*velorio*) with the family, lead the singing of *alabados* (hymns of praise) composed for the occasion, conduct the funeral procession, and even conduct the interment. The Requiem Mass and the blessing of the plot could wait for the next visit of the priest, but the deference shown the departed, the consolation afforded his or her family, and the public expression of communal religious values could not.

The words of the *alabados* were very beautiful in the Spanish originals. Essentially mystic in spirit, they had a direct simplicity, an "earthy" concreteness of expression similar to that of seventeenth-century metaphysical poets. One of the *alabados* was a funeral hymn sung as the body was being carried to the *Campo Santo* (graveyard or cemetery, Spanish for holy ground). In it, it is the dead man who speaks and says good-bye to the world he is leaving. The song is typically Spanish in its stoic acceptance of life and death, and in its mixture of the homely and the Divine. Other *alabados* are long narratives of the whole story of Christ's life and death; shorter ones in praise of the Virgin; and many, of course, apply directly to the discipline of penance as a means of salvation or purification of the heart.

GOOD-BY TO THIS WORLD

Good-by, all this company,
Who have been here at my wake,
The hour and time have come
When you must take me out.

Good-by, my loving parents,
Who conserved my life,
The hour and time have come
For me to take my parting.

Good-by, my dear children,
And my wife, much beloved,
Good-by, all this company,
Now I go to the other life.
Good-by, all my kindred,
Good-by, my sweet morada,
Good-by, all my companions,
Now I go on the Journey.
Good-by, all this company,
My last hour has arrived;
Accompany me to my interment,
Which is my true house.

What a wearisome journey,
And such a hard road!
Now I am going to another life,
As my God has determined.

My strength has all left me,
And my mind has left me;
Now I leave all the
pleasures of this world so
confusing.

Accompany me to the sepulcher;
From me my soul has
separated and is going to
confess its sins, surrounded
by angels.

Good-by, all this company,
I am going to the Campo Santo,
and with me all my kindred,
who weep bitter tears.

Now I separate from all,
And from the world in general,
Until we meet in glory
In the universal justice.

It is possible the God of my soul
May look in on me
Inside the sepulcher
Where my bed will be.

The sepulcher is my bed,
The earth my proper seat;
And souls are frightened
When they consider themselves inside.

Now I am going to the church
Preceded by prayer,
And by all my kindred
Whose hearts are broken.

What one cannot see,
When he stops to consider,
That this bitter step,
All have got to take!
This life is a riddle,
And it keeps us in a dream,
And we invent amusements
In order to support the pain.

From the earth I was made,
And the earth shall eat me,

The earth has sustained me,
And at last earth I shall be also.
God made me by the power

Of His Divine Spirit;
And I trust in His Goodness
He will guide me by a good road.
Good-by, all this company,
All has been completed;
Put me in the sepulcher.
In the earth of forgetfulness.

Of nothing I was formed,
By the hands of the Creator,
And in the universal justice
He will be my defender.
To God I kneel humbly,

Of my faults repented;
He will forgive me
For the wrong way I have served Him.
In God I await to repose,
In God I await consolation,
Trusting in His tremendous justice
He will open Heaven's gate.

I am of my Jesus the brother,
I belong to Jesus and always will,
because I yield gladly,
And to Jesus I surrender.
Good-by for the last time,
Those who see me on this earth,
Place me in the sepulcher
Which is truly my house.
Good-by, all those present,
All who accompany me, Pray a *sudario*
[a burial shroud]
In order to overtake me.

Good-by, all my neighbors,
All, all in general
Commend my soul to God,
And do not forget me.

THE END-AMEN

During Holy Week, *Los Hermanos de Nuestro Padre Jesus* (*Penitentes*) often participated with the townspeople in public and non-penitential dramatizations based on the Stations of the Cross, but they also held their own private penitential "re-enactment of Christ's crucifixion on Good Friday, when one of the Brothers was tied on a full-size cross he had carried to the *Calvario*, raised up on it, and left for some time, frequently until he fainted." In the parish dramatization, Christ was portrayed by a great "*bulto*", a life-size image with movable limbs, often referred to as the *Santo Entierro*.

The primary purpose of the passion plays was never dramatic excellence; instead it was always the involvement of the people, both performers and congregation, in a gripping religious ceremony. By cutting spoken lines to a minimum and drawing the congregation away from aesthetic contemplation and into reciting prayers of the Stations of the Cross and singing the *alabados* characterized by narrative structures and portions of the dialogue of the sacred personages themselves, the New Mexico passion play erased as nearly as it could the distinction between actors and audience. It joined them all into a performance, which, while it did not fail to be a play, displayed the features of a religious ceremony.

During the U.S. Territorial Period in New Mexico, one woman remembered her visit to a *Penitente morada* (combined chapel and meeting place) with a mixture of pride and fear.

> "Moved by curiosity to see the inside of the *morada*,
> I once asked a *penitente's* wife, who was going to pay

a votive debt to the *santos* at the *morada*, if I might accompany her We climbed the hill on which the *morada* stood in the upper town and were admitted to the chapel. On the wall of the hall dividing the chapel from the secret room hung a row of whips. The woman crawled on her knees from one statue to another, placing lighted candles before each. I was left kneeling before the statue of the Crucifixion. Paralyzed with fear, I could not move, for there before me on the mud altar stood the statue of *La Muerte*, Death."

Both Bishop Lamy and his successor, Jean Baptist Salpointe, denounced the *Cofradia de los Hermanos* for the severity of their penitential practices. Salpointe, towards the end of the 19th century, was a determined enemy of the *Penitentes*, and it could be that during his regime anything that smacked of New Mexico folk religion was put aside in favor of official services and French and Italian devotional practices." Many believe, however, that without the constancy of this *cofradia*, Catholic parish life among Hispanics in New Mexico might well have been lost to neglect.

In Catholic circles, the problem of neglect was aggravated by the ecclesiastical condemnation of Hispanic folk religious practices, so that disillusionment with the official Church led many either to ally themselves with what some historians call Padre Martinez's schismatic church, or to convert to some form of Protestantism. One administrative response to these defections was to conduct what became in the second half of the 19th century and early part of the twentieth century, "a commonplace experience in the Catholic community," the parish mission. Subsequent missions served as counter-evangelizing efforts in the traditionally Catholic areas of New Mexico. By this means, American Catholic Anglo clergy "shaped the piety of the people and strengthened the institutional Church. The "great tradition" exerted its domination over the "little tradition". Eventually, the *Penitentes* fell into disfavor, but not all elements of

Hispanic folk religion were condemned. Since devotion to particular saints and to Mary, Queen of Saints, had popular appeal among many ethnic groups and had some doctrinal foundation, Catholic Church officials permitted related customs.

It was a nearly universal custom that Catholics would build shrines to particular saints who might intercede for them in obtaining favors. In the isolation of New Mexico Hispanic villages, these shrines contained not plaster statues imported from Europe but wooden *santos* or *retablos* crafted by a local artisan. Since the goal of making a *santo* was to create an instrument of holiness and power rather than an artifact for detached contemplation, the connection between the saint in the picture and the saint of reality was a matter of great importance. . . .[T]he artifact is intrinsically holy not merely because of what may be done with it (prayer) but because it was made by a holy *santero* working within this multiple holy tradition.

RETABLO   *SANTO*

One woman recalled, as she claimed solidarity with both the people and the ruling hierarchy, the treatment of *santos* in her family *hacienda* and chapel. A shoemaker came to her village to make "lovely tin frames for

Grandma's collection of *santos*, donated to her by the [then-Mexican] bishop and priests who stopped at the house during the year. There wasn't space left for another frame of the sanctuary wall of the *capilla*, so thickly was it covered with frames of all sizes. And when the Bishop came to administer confirmation, he told one parish priest that there were too many *santos*."

CAPILLA

In addition to private devotions to saints, public celebrations in honor of a local patron saint were common among Hispanics in New Mexico. In one place, there was a celebration of the feast of *San Geronimo* as both an Indian and a Spanish *fiesta*.

In the Hispanic villages or communities not attached to Indian pueblos, *la funcion*, the parish *fiesta* in honor of their patron saint's feast, was, and perhaps still is, the most significant expression of popular piety These were usually extended celebrations consisting of Vespers with a procession around the plaza on the opening evening, and a High Mass followed by an even larger procession on the next morning. In some parishes, the *cofradias* carried the *estandanes* (banners) and chanted the traditional *alabados*. Then the day was given over to visiting, eating, games and, sometimes, the special *Matachines* dance. *La Funcion* would usually close with a large dance. Not only members of that parish, but villagers for miles around traveled to neighboring parishes to share in this celebration. The *funciones,*

> "were the complete and valid self-expression of a traditional group not so formal as the Latin rituals of the Roman Catholic Church, of course, but taken nearly as seriously. And with good reason, for this public or semi-public ritual activity flowed from the people's true sense of its place among the other inhabitants of the cosmos, and each ceremony in its turn served as a proclamation of the village's selfhood, which taught and reinforced its common being."

In addition to the ability of a particular saint to give a particular village or community a sense of identity, sometimes a saint associated with one's ethnicity or one's cultural history evoked expressions of popular piety. *Santiago*, the patron saint of horsemen, and, in colonial New Mexico, the protector from wild Indians, was still honored on his feast in many Hispanic villages and communities. In addition to Mass and processions in his honor, an abbreviated version of the medieval drama, *La Danza de los Moros y Cristianos*, was revived as part of the *fiesta.*

LA DANZA DE LOS MOROS Y CRISTIANOS

Ethnic and historic ties to a particular saint projected personal devotion beyond the private realm to the public sphere, and, yet, the celebration remained part of the "little tradition". It was also true that personal rites of passage transformed by Catholic Sacraments could gather a variety of communal folk customs, illustrating the interplay of the "little tradition" and the "great tradition" in a single celebration. This was particularly evident in those circumstances where lack of clerical leadership breeded an independent attitude toward celebration, and where a traditional emphasis on ceremony and ritual was not curtailed by staunch representatives of the "great tradition's" streamlining, modernizing trend. Both weddings and funerals in Hispanic villages and communities were examples of elaborate expressions of popular piety surrounding a clearly regulated Roman ritual.

Hispanic weddings, both within the central ceremony and in the preparatory and concluding celebrations, contained several blessings of persons and objects. At the *prendorio* (engagement party), in the days before engagement rings were included in the gifts given to the bride, a jeweled rosary was placed over the heads of the couple by the bride's oldest uncle or godfather. This gesture combined the use of a sacramental with a personal blessing given by a significant family member.

The wedding itself was divided into two separate ceremonies, the first for the proposal and vows, the second for the nuptial blessing. Sometimes, between these two ceremonies, a set of coins and rings was blessed by the priest for the couple in the church vestibule before they approached the altar for the nuptial blessing.

Between the wedding ceremony and the reception, formal processions often formed to mark the transition from the church to the home or hall. This custom might have been seen as one way in which popular piety recognized the difference between the places in which one most often conformed to the "great tradition" or felt free to express the "little tradition". Another expression of popular piety surrounding Hispanic weddings took place in the home or reception hall. There was the *entriega*, "the delivery of the wedded couple to their parents by the *padrinos* (sponsors) for a final blessing before departure," a "long string of impromptu verses that the guitarist was addressing to the newlyweds, their parents, and *padrinos*, verses of advice, of parting, and blessings." Whether celebrating weddings or funerals, Holy Week or the feasts of the saints, Hispanic Catholics in New Mexico employed a "little tradition" that linked their religion to their culture. Faced with the imposition of a "great tradition" by an ecclesiastical institution that was unwilling to be mutually influenced, many surrendered the institutional Church in order to preserve an expressive one.

Less enduring or influential in New Mexico than either Native Americans or Hispanics, separate communities of Catholic European immigrants contributed to the history of ethnicity and religion in a variety of ways. Irish and German Catholics were representatives of the earlier waves of immigration that added millions to the population of the country and thousands to the Southwest region. Initially attracted by industrial enterprises, many turned to agriculture and business. Italian Catholics seem to have come in two separate groups, those from the northern provinces first, followed by those from the southern provinces. It was the second great wave of European immigration that added not only larger numbers of Catholics to the U.S. population, but also new ethnic groups from east European countries. Before assimilation obscured their distinctive features, most of these ethnic groups experienced cultural conflict even within parishes. Representatives of both waves of European immigration were found in parishes scattered throughout the Southwest.

Because maintaining an ethnic identity in a largely white, Anglo-Saxon, Protestant society was essential to these 19th century and early 20th century Catholic immigrants, "[t]he parish (as well as the station and mission) was the center of their lives, and they sacrificed a great deal of their surplus resources to build chapels and rectories in their neighborhoods. The local church was the center of the community, surrounded by homes, taverns, stores and shops." A highly charged debate was waged towards the end of the 19th century between Catholic Americanists and anti-Americanists, which was not officially solved until the turn of the 20th century when, in 1899, Pope Leo Xlll condemned Americanism which said that there was a separation between church and state and that individual initiative was more important than obedience to authority.

During the first decade of the 20th century, new parishes in New Mexico served new combinations of Indian, Hispanic and Anglo Catholics. The ethnic variety as well as distances and numbers made for a demanding ministry.

It was during this period that many Indian missionaries began to attack Indian culture as an obstacle to Americanization and Christianization. Missionary attempts to transform once nomadic Indians into farmers met with failure. Extreme poverty and ill-health were common.

As New Mexico transitioned from a U.S. Territory to Statehood by the second decade of the 20th century, the Pecos Valley was poised to embrace its future and its God in new, yet familiar ways.

U.S. STATEHOOD PERIOD (1912-PRESENT)

Several men with ambition and capital undertook an ambitious, privately-funded, commercial irrigation project in the Pecos Valley that eventually failed shortly after the turn of the twentieth century.

By 1921, "Most of the homesteaders in the region had, in spite of proving up [doing required improvements to keep their land], moved away."

Oil was discovered east of the Pecos River in the 1920's, and vast oil and gas fields were developed throughout southeastern New Mexico during the century's first half.

Mexicans, though they might have been American citizens of the second or third generations, nevertheless remained or were kept apart socially, and were almost always called "Mexicans."

The change from the indigenous and mixed cultures to the highly modern civilization of the United States was exceedingly abrupt.

Although, in religion, the Mexican immigrant underwent a great change in the United States, this was not the case in so far as their folk-lorism went. Materially, they became identified with modern American civilization — housing, clothing, domestic utensils, use of machinery, etc. — all these they made their own. But, their folk-lorism was not only retained, it continued developing and spread to Americans of Mexican origin and even to Native Americans.

In most of the life stories collected from Mexicans in America, the folk factor plainly appeared. Some of the ballads, poems, stories and songs were composed in Mexico and retained in the United States, usually with slight change, while others were made in the United States by Mexicans or Americans of Mexican origin. In these latter was found the reflection of the new environment upon the Mexican spirit.

Birthdays, or rather, "saint's days" were celebrated with music and dancing, as were baptisms and weddings. During the 1930's, there was usually a small hired orchestra, or perhaps a piano was rented or hauled to the scene of the *fiesta*. Suppers of Mexican food, *enchiladas* and *tamales*, were served. The music was a combination of American fox-trot alternating with the singing of Mexican ballads to the accompaniment of guitars. Many of the immigrants owned phonographs.

A funeral was an extremely important occasion, and every effort was made to make it as elaborate as possible. Mass was said and there was always a wake, at which there was less drinking than on such occasions in Mexico. On such occasions, the church received financial tribute; funeral masses cost ten dollars, a baptism five, a marriage twenty, and burial privileges in Catholic cemeteries came at a high cost, but they were always paid for.

There were witch women and herb doctors who cured the evil eye and other ills, by means of their own preparations and magical spells. Typically Mexican were the "chills of fear," counteracted with a specially prepared and blessed brew which was accompanied with a ceremony in which Catholicism, European magic, and Indian magic combined curiously. This brew was called "water of fright." Herbs were widely sold and used, though sometimes "the business was spoiled," as one herb-vendor explained, by doctors paid and kept by the companies that employed the immigrants.

Superstitions peculiar to the American-Mexican population in the Unites States and, in New Mexico, particularly, were also numerous. Sweethearts could not give each other handkerchiefs, for this meant forgetfulness and desertion; the guests at a wedding could not dance in the room where the bride sat, as this was a bad omen; girls "wish"ed upon a star or on the moon, with their arms out and body forming a cross; and a wish made at 9:15 at night invariably came true. Meeting a group of nuns in the street meant bad luck, and also, two yellow taxis seen together were a bad omen, to counteract the effects of which the person seeing them pats or strikes his or her companion twice on the back. These few examples suffice to give an idea of how the folk mind of the Mexican immigrant found food everywhere, as well in old tradition as in new.

With regard to Mexican culture, there were four specific areas of concentration: first, *corridos* (ballads), *canciones* (songs) and music;

second, herbal medicine; third, the names of Mexican stores and other places of business; and, fourth, superstitions and magical beliefs.

The *"corrido"* and *"cancion"* were the most numerous types of Hispanic music, and appropriately, they dealt largely with two themes: the *"corrido"* with death and the *"cancion"* with love. An *"alabado"* was a folk poem of exhortation, usually relating to the Passion of Christ. An *"alabanza"* was a song of praise to the Virgin Mary and the saints. A *"despedimento"* was a song of farewell.

Many of the songs composed by the Mexican immigrants expressed their experiences in the new country and their reactions to the new experiences with a fidelity and a naivete which made them a valuable source of information on their likes and dislikes, their hopes and their disappointments. They constituted, taken together, a sort of collective autobiography.

Some of these songs recounted the misfortunes of the immigrant, their disappointment and disillusionment. Many dealt with the unpleasant results of labor contracts entered into through the too unscrupulous labor agent. Here are two such songs:

LOS INMIGRANTES	THE IMMIGRANTS
(Los Enganchados)	("The Hooked Ones")
El 28 de Febrero	On the 28th day of February
Aquel dia tan senalado	That important day
Cuando salimos de El Paso	When we left El Paso
Nos sacron reenganchados	They took us out as contract labor
Cuando salimos de El Paso	When we left El Paso
A las dos de la mañana	At two in the morning
Le pregunto al reenganchista	I asked the boss contractor
Si vamos para Louisiana	If we were going to Louisiana

Llegamos a la Laguna	We arrived at Laguna
Sin Esperanza ninguna	Without any hope
Le pregunte al reenganchista	I asked the boss
Si vamos para "Oclahuma"	If we were going to Oklahoma
Por esas lineas del Kiri	Along the line of the Katy
Pasa un tren muy volador	There goes a very fast train
Corre cien millas por hora	It runs a hundred miles an hour
Y no le dan todo el vapor	And then they don't give it all the steam
Y el que no lo quiera creer	And he who doesn't want to believe it
No mas que venga a montar	Just let him get on board
No mas que monte de noche	Just let him get on board at night
Lo vera donde va a dar	He will see where he gets to
Llegamos el dia primero	We arrived on the first day
Y al segundo a trabajar	And on the second began to work
Con los picos en las manos	With our picks in our hands
Nos pusimos a trampar	We set out tramping
Unos descargaban rieles	Some unloaded rails
Otros descargaban "tallas"	And others unloaded ties
Y otros de los companeros	And others of my companions
Echaban de mil malallas	Threw out thousands of curses
Los que sabian el trabajo	Those who knew the work
Iban recorriendo el "llaqui"	Went repairing the jack
Con martilleros y paleros	With sledge hammers & shovels
Echandole tierra al traque	Throwing earth up the track
Ocho "varas" alineadas	Eight crowbars lined up
Nos seguiamos disgustados	We followed disgusted

A los gritos y las senas	To shouts and signs
Nos quedábamos paraos	We remained indifferent
Decia D. Jose Maria	Said Don Jose Maria
Con su boquita de infierno	With his Hades's mouth
"Mas valiera esta en Kansas	"It would be better to be in Kansas
Que nos mantenga el gobierno"	Where the government would maintain us"
Decia Jesus "El Coyote"	Said Jesus, "El Coyote"
Como queriendo llorar	As if he wanted to weep
"Valla mas estar en Juarez	"It would be better to be in Juarez
Aunque sea sin trabajar"	Even if we were without work"
Estos versos son compuestos	These verses were composed
Por un pobre mexicano	By a poor Mexican
Para difundir la Palabra	To spread the Word about
Del Sistema americano	The American system

VIDA, PROCESO Y MUERTE DE AURELIO POMPA

LIFE, TRIAL AND DEATH OF AURELIO POMPA

Voy a contarles la triste historia	I am going to tell you the sad story
De un mexicano que allá emigro	Of a Mexican who emigrated out here
Aurelio Pompa, asi se llamaba	Aurelio Pompa, so he was called
El compatriota que allí murió	Our compatriot who died there
Alla en Caborca, que es de Sonora	Out there in Caborca, which is in Sonora
El pueblo humilde donde nacio	The humble village where he was born
"Vamanos, madre," le dijo un dia	"Come on, mother," he said one day
Que allá no existe revolución	Over there there are no revolutions
Adios, amigos, adios, Maria	Goodbye, friends, goodbye, Maria
Dijo a la novia con gran dolor	He said to his betrothed very sadly
"Yo te prometo que pronto vuelvo	"I promise you that I will return soon
para casarnos, mediante Dios"	So we can get married, God willing"
"Adios, Aurelio," dijo la novia	"Goodbye, Aurelio," said the girl
Que soolozando se fue a rezar	And she went sobbing to pray
Cuidalo mucho, Virgen Maria	Look after him, Virgin Mary

Que yo presiento no volvera	I have a foreboding he will not come back
El senor cura y sus amigos	The priest and his friends
Junto a la novia fueron a hablar	Along with his sweetheart went to talk
A suplicarele al pobre Aurelio	And to beg poor Aurelio
Que no dejara el pueblo natal	Not to leave his native village
Fueron inútiles tantos consejos	Such advice was useless
Tambien los ruegos de su mama	And so we were the entreaties of his mother
"Vamonos, madre, que allá esta el dolor	"Let's go mother, over there is the dollar
Y mucho, juro, que he de ganar"	And I swear I am going to earn a lot of them"
El mes de mayo de hace cuatro anos	Four years ago in the month of May
A California fueron los dos	The two of them went to California
Y por desgracia en la misma fecha	And through misfortune on the very same date
En una cárcel allá murió	Died there in prison
Un carpintero que era muy fuerte	A carpenter who was very strong
Al pobre joven muy cruel golpeo	Struck the poor young fellow cruelly
y Aurelio Pompa juro vengarse	And Aurelio Pompa swore to be revenged
de aquellos golpes que recibió	For those blows he had received
Lleno de rabia conto a su madre	Filled with rage he told his Mother about it
Y la pobre anciana le aconsejo	and the poor old woman advised Him
"Por Dios olvida hijo querido"	"*Por Dios*, forget it, dear son"
Y el buen Aurelio le perdono	And Good Aurelio forgave him
Pero una tarde, que trabajaba	But one afternoon when he was working
Con tres amigos en la estación de tren	With three friends at the railroad Station
El carpintero paso burlando	The carpenter came by mocking at him
y al pobre Pompa le provoco	And aroused poor Pompa
Los tres amigos le aconsejaban	The three Friends advised him
Que lo dejara y fuera con Dios	To leave him alone and go his way
y el carpintero con un martillo	And then the carpenter with a hammer
muy injurioso lo amenazo	Very offensively threatened him

Entonces, Pompa, viendo el peligro	Pompa, seeing the danger
En su defensa le disparo	Fired in self-defense
Con un revolver y cara a cara	With a revolver and face to face
Como los hombres el lo mato	As a man he killed him
Vino la causa, llego el jurado	The case came to court, the jury arrived
y el pueblo Yanqui lo sentencio	And the Yankee people sentenced him
"Pena de muerte" pidieron todos	"The death penalty" they all demanded
y el abogado no protesto	And the lawyer did not object
Veinte mil firmas de compatriotas	Twenty thousand signatures of compatriots
Pidieron perdon al gobernador	Asked for his pardon from the Governor
Toda la prensa tambien pedia	All the newspapers ask for it too
Y hasta un mensaje mando Obregon	And even Obregon (Mexican President) sent message
Todo fue inútil, las sociedades,	All was useless, the societies,
Todas unidas pedían perdón	All united, asked his pardon
La pobre madre, ya casi muerta	His poor mother, half dead already
También fue a ver al gobernador	Also went to see the Governor
"Adios, amigos, adios, mi pueblo,	"Farewell my friends, farewell my village
Querida madre, no llores mas,	Dear mother, cry no more
Dice a mi raza que ya no venga	Tell my race not to come here
Que aquí se sufre que no hay piedad"	For here they will suffer, there is no pity here"
El carcelero le preguntaba:	The jailor asked him:
"Español eres?" y el contesto	"Were you Spanish?" and he answered
"Soy Mexicano y orgullo serlo	"I am Mexican and proud of it
Aunque me nieguen a mi el pardon"	although they deny me a pardon"
Esta es la historia de un compatriota	This is the story of a compatriot
Que hace quatro anos allí llego	Who four years ago came there
Y por desgracia en la misma fecha	And though misfortune on the same date
en una cárcel muy mal murió.	Died in a dreadful way in prison.

In New Mexico, where there was a large population of Mexican-Americans long established, there was a greater tendency to remain faithful to the tenets and obligations of the Catholic Church. The following paragraph is in the words of a New Mexican Catholic priest.

> "Altho[ugh] there is intense competition between religious sects, the majority of the inhabitants, especially in the small towns, are Catholic and keep up the religious customs of Old Mexico such as paying the priest a peso for every mass which they ask to be said, and bringing him offerings of eggs, bread, fruit and candies. In some parts of the country Mexican-Americans, Mexicans and American Indians act in harmony and with complete propriety in their attendance at church services, and at some *fiestas* they have picturesque processions in the plazas of the towns."

It was clear, however, that a large part of the Mexican immigrants abandoned Catholicism. This fact might have been attributed to the hostility of the American Catholic clergy toward the Mexican immigration.

It could be said that there was hardly a Mexican immigrant home in the United States where the Mexican flag was not found in a place of honor, as well as pictures of national Mexican heroes. Love of country sometimes went so far that very often altars were made for saints and flag or hero, or both, giving Mexican patriotism thus an almost religious quality.

In Spanish-American homes, there was always a saint or religious image on the wall with a small altar (*altarcito*) arranged with flowers, candles, and other decorations on a table in one corner against a wall.

One writer wrote of the differences between Anglo and Spanish Americans:

> "The Anglo works too hard, loves money too much and plays too little. The other goes to the other extreme, perhaps, but can teach us something about enjoying simple, inexpensive pleasures. He meditates and reflects more than the Anglo, is more artistic, has a greater inherent love of beauty. These qualities if developed properly are very valuable. In education the Spanish-American should not be run through the ideals of government, of office-holding, freedom of opinion and speech, of religious life, etc. In that respect he must conform to Anglo notions. In other respects the best education for him is one which will show him how to grow as far as he can according to his abilities. His racial heritage after all makes him somewhat different from the Anglo-Saxon."

There was an apparent assumption of these outsiders (Anglos) that material prosperity meant superiority. While most of New Mexico had been captured completely by the outsiders, not so with the southern and southeastern mountains, where probably the division between these diverse viewpoints had progressed farther. If it were not for a particularly intolerant religious control of the Spanish-American group and a rather exceptional amount of superstition, the prospect of assimilation would have been much more encouraging. By the 1930's, however, there seemed to be little real co-operation between Anglos and Hispanics, and a great deal of political and religious competition existed.

A Spanish-American very wisely suggested teaching of Spanish to Anglo-Americans, lectures in the schools and the churches on friendship between the races, and a public opinion which would condemn the mutual criticism between the groups in public meetings, especially by politicians who kept the prejudice alive for their selfish gains. Although the constitution of New Mexico forbade discrimination against Spanish-Americans, few Spanish-American students went through the high schools and the university. There is little doubt that religious intolerance used racial attitudes as a means of maintaining its dominance. While Spanish was used in the public schools of certain sections of New Mexico and priests taught the catechism in the public schools during school hours, there was sure to be racial friction. In a few places, there was mingling of a small proportion of Anglo-American children with the Spanish-American children in the elementary grades.

One missionary admitted that the priests who dominated the life of the Spanish-American communities did not help them to higher standards.

Many of the Hispanics spent all their savings on the *fiestas* of the saints. By taking part in a *fiesta*, health and happiness were assured, thus it was better to give up money than to miss one of the *fiestas*.

In many Hispanic houses was found the image of a patron saint, placed in the best room, which was given up to it, the people of the house sleeping in the kitchen in order not to disturb it. Only strangers could occupy the same room as the image of the patron saint. At noon the wife and her husband placed before the saint's image a small dish of *copal* (incense) which served the saint as food. Visitors, as soon as they came into the house, went to see the saint's image.

In some Spanish-American communities, if it hailed hailstones, the people took out their patron saint from the church early in the morning and punished it by dunking it in cold water; but, if the harvests were good, they carried it in a procession and made a great *fiesta* for it which they celebrated with liberal drinking of *mescal* and eating of quantities of *tamales*. Every year an old man was selected to represent the patron saint. On the Day of the Dead, the people fastened flowers, especially yellow ones, to the doors of their houses to invite the souls of their friends to enter, and they paid with some offering for every *paternoster* (Our Father) which was said for the dead.

Ordinarily, Hispanic families would spend nothing for doctors or medicine, but would spend large sums on funerals. They would kill a head of cattle, grind as much as four bushels of corn, and provide a barrel of *aguardiente* ("firewater"). The celebration lasted about three days, during which the Indians in attendance danced all night and part of the day beside the corpse stretched out between four candles. Violins and guitars were played and songs sung in honor of the dead person. The family continued to live in the same room as the corpse, and all got drunk. Until the last morsel was gone the fiesta did not come to an end.

As late as 1940, over half the population of New Mexico was of Spanish descent, but again, not so much in the Pecos Valley of southeastern New Mexico because of its larger Anglo population.

Epithets for the new State of New Mexico such as "The Land of *Poco Tiempo*," the "Land of Enchantment" and "Satan's Paradise" — to name only a few of the better known — were commonplace. These referred not only to the physical topography of New Mexico but also to the type of culture found there.

In 1931, New Mexico was referred to as "a country within a country".

Although on the one hand, New Mexico was firmly and strongly integrated with the nation as a whole, it yet presented some, often startling, differences from other areas of the United States. New Mexico was, in many respects, an extension of Latin America into United States territory.

New Mexico was the only state in the union which may be said to have been effectively bilingual. This had repercussions in the school system, advertising media, court system, entertainment world, and religion.

New Mexico was also a different country in that it was relatively unknown and little understood in the eastern states.

It was suggested that one of the important factors in explaining the persistence of Spanish (as well as Indian) culture traits and complexes in New Mexico for so long after its territorialization and statehood by an alien society was the partial commitment of Anglos themselves to the values characteristic of these cultural patterns.

The inter-cultural marriage pattern in New Mexico was still predominantly that of Spanish females marrying Anglo males. The offspring of most of these modern inter-cultural marriages were brought up as Anglos rather than as members of the Hispanic group.

Both Indians and Hispanos adhered largely to the Catholic faith while at the same time engaged in religious practices not considered to be strictly orthodox by the Catholic Church. Both, in spite of inevitable gradual change, resisted acculturation and assimilation into the larger, dominant, Anglo world within which they lived as social and cultural enclaves.

Nearly the whole eastern plains area of New Mexico, including southeastern New Mexico, however, was heavily dominated by Anglos, and the term "Little Texas" was applied to it in recognition of the origin of the majority of the settlers and of their cultural patterns.

The importance and solidarity of the family group among Spanish-Americans was very strong. Most Hispanos included other relatives besides parents and siblings as members of their *familia*. Grandparents, parents' siblings and the latters' children, termed *primos hermanos*, were all considered "close" relatives. Although an eldest brother would ordinarily have been held in the greatest amount of respect by a sibling group, he could lose this position by behaving in a fashion deemed immoral, through laziness, or through failure to fulfill his kinship obligations. However, he would continue to be considered kin regardless of his behavior.

In both rural and urban areas of New Mexico, most social intercourse occurred among relatives and the extended family was the most important social unit.

Divorce, desertion and broken families had been increasing steadily among Spanish-Americans as the 20th century progressed. A number of children were leaving their families and were moving elsewhere, thus destroying the old family solidarity which had existed for years.

Orphans, unmarried children and older people without income were taken care of by attachment to functioning households. All emigrating family members were kept track of forever. Family solidarity continued even though some members spent all or part of their time in large towns. Families did take care of a large circle of poor relatives. The idea of reciprocity among family members still persisted. Those on relief were frequently aided by children and other relatives — especially in the matter of housing.

Regarding the Hispano way of life, the extended family unit remained important in ways unparalleled in the Anglo world. Persons who could not be fitted into some kinship category, however, may have been treated with suspicion, withdrawal and perhaps even shown overt hostility. Spanish-American society was kin-based society and the most lasting, deepest ties were those between kin-related members. Kinfolk continued to call upon each other for economic assistance, when necessary, for advice, moral support and simple companionship.

Even the *compadrazgo*, commonly used in Latin-American countries to extend in a ritual manner the network of kinship relations, had the effect of reinforcing or intensifying family relations. Most of the sponsors for baptism were chosen from within the family circle itself. Visiting and mutual-aid patterns showed the highest amount of interaction among those persons related through both a biological and a ritual kinship tie.

The second primary social unit to which Hispanos became attached was the community. This had in the past usually been the village, but, as the years went on, the city neighborhood, or *barrio*, in many ways replaced the village as the most important territorial identification. The rural community might also have been considered a kinship unit, since its members were frequently interrelated by complex ties of consanguinity and affinity. Few families could not claim at least a third cousin relationship to every other family. In former days, it was not at all unusual for cousins — even first cousins — to marry.

There developed in time, all over Spanish-American areas, a pattern of highly integrated, extended or consanguine family groups. These larger kinship groups almost deserved to be called "clans". A similar concept was called *La Sangrelidad*, or, "the blood relatives."

In the Hispano social system, the individual identified strongly with their village or community of birth and retained a sense of loyalty to it throughout life, even though they may have resided elsewhere temporarily or permanently. One way in which this strong community solidarity was expressed and reinforced was through inter-village or inter-community or even inter-*barrio* rivalry.

The third dimension of social solidarity was that commonly known throughout the Southwest as *la raza*. There was a kind of mystical bond that was beyond the kinship and community ties. This *la raza* was translated "the people", meaning "my people".

From the U.S. Territorial Period onward into the Statehood Period, a two-class system within the Hispanic community appeared to have been in effect with a lower class and a middle class.

Psychological stress in the New Mexican Hispanic community often developed through a confusion of roles and identities. Some of the values of their former way of life remained with them, yet they found them incompatible with their new goals. Many did leave for Anglo neighborhoods, but they returned on Sundays to the old *barrios* to worship in a Spanish-language church, have dinner with their parents and grandparents, etc. When possible, they would dissociate themselves, not only as individuals but as a group, from the lower classes, claiming that the latter were not in fact Hispanos at all, but "Mexicans".

As the years went on, the Spanish-speaking population in New Mexico turned more and more to the large, non-kinship kinds of institutions for mutual aid and community action, which could be grouped under the term "voluntary associations".

Many were the *cofradias* or *confraternidades* (lay brotherhoods) sponsored by the Catholic church. There were confraternities such as those of Our Lady of Light, the Poor Souls, the Blessed Sacrament, the Rosary, the Third Order of Saint Francis and the Guadalupanos.

The primary purposes of these organizations were to maintain the church and the statues of saints, to conduct religious activities in the absence of priests, and to provide mutual aid during times of crisis for the members. The famous *Penitentes* probably derived from this type of organization, as was indicated in part by their full and proper name, *La Confraternidad de Nuestro Padre Jesus Nazareno*, by which the members themselves referred to their society. This society apparently combined the features of an already existing confraternity organization with scourging and blood-letting taken from the Spanish penitential tradition. Certain villages in which the

Penitente movement was strongest were also greatly populated by *Genizaros* [Spanish and non-Pueblo Indian mixtures]. Many other church-associated societies still operate today as before to maintain the Catholic religion and to provide assistance to the members upon death of a relative, illness, etc. Such groups also functioned as social clubs.

In the southern counties of New Mexico, where the major Hispanic population component was from Mexico, voluntary associations seemed less important, but the secular supra-community mutual-aid societies there have had a long history.

The combination of threats to the old village life brought thousands of refugees to the suburban villages surrounding the growing urban centers of New Mexico and southeastern New Mexico.

During the 1940's when the emigration of Hispanos out of New Mexico was occurring, New Mexico began to experience another massive wave of Anglo immigration, many of whom came in connection with the development of defense activities during the Second World War. Between 1940 and 1950, the population of New Mexico was increased by 50,780 Anglos and decreased by 31,680 Hispanos — 27,960 of native New Mexican parentage, 3,720 of foreign — presumably Mexican — ancestry. Most of the Anglos went to the cities. This trend continued during the 1950's.

Besides divorce, there also seems to have been an increase in the number of illegitimate births and subsequent desertion of the woman by the father of her children in the Hispanic community.

Most newly urban Hispanic residents were still carrying a rural, folk culture with them, creating important problems of adjustment in their new environment. By 1966, the institution of *compadrazgo* was still highly viable and important in the structuring of interpersonal relations among city Hispanos.

Institutions like *Esperanza* tried to combat juvenile delinquency.

In the town of Artesia and the Little Texas eastern belt, there seemed to have been a lower percentage of Spanish-American inhabitants than in other parts of New Mexico and prejudice and discrimination against Hispanics seemed to have been so strong that more-educated Hispanos declined to live there.

There was a clear trend toward increasing inter-marriage over the fifty years from 1915 to 1965.

Joining Protestantism was another common reaction of those Hispanics who attempted to adopt the Anglo value system.

By 1967, the percentage of Roman Catholics among New Mexican Spanish-Americans was probably close to 75% of their total number, down from previous centuries, however.

The greatest change in Spanish-American marriage customs was not in the religious denomination, however, but in the great increase in civil ceremonies.

Hispano couples where both partners were Hispanic would choose Catholic marriage ceremonies significantly more often than did those in which only one partner was Hispano.

New Mexico, with all its faults, with all its poverty, nevertheless came closer to the pluralistic dream of American society than did any other area in the nation.

It was becoming recognized that Americans of Spanish descent formed one of the largest and most neglected minority groups in the country. Even though the total number of Mexican-Americans or Spanish-Americans was exceeded elsewhere, no state had such a high percentage of its total population claiming Hispanic ancestry as New Mexico.

It was clear that in New Mexico there was much poverty, juvenile delinquency, crime, illiteracy, poor health and dependence upon public assistance, all of which tended to be largely concentrated among Spanish-Americans, who formed the bulk of the lower class. The relations between Spanish-Americans and Anglos continued to include distrust, even hostility, prejudice and discrimination, which, however, operated in both directions.

By the mid-1930's ethnic intolerance had become rife, even though it was never openly admitted.

The change in status of the Spanish-speaking population of New Mexico, brought about by the changed composition of the state's population as a whole, seems to have led to the origin of the myth, now become a legend, of cultural differences between New Mexico and Mexico. This myth functioned in a fairly clear-cut manner as an attempted means of preserving the dignity, the worth and the prestige of the New Mexican Spanish cultural patterns, while at the same time countering discriminatory behavior based upon perceived differences between Anglo and Mexican culture patterns. In effect, New Mexicans, perceiving themselves in danger of being pushed down or swallowed up completely, fought back by making scapegoats of their Mexican cousins.

In the southeastern part of New Mexico, even in the 1930's, there were still some barbershops and restaurants where the Spanish-American was not welcome. Schools were sometimes segregated along ethnic lines with the excuse that the linguistic inadequacy of the Spanish-speaking child would hold back the Anglo child. Segregation of children was sometimes made on the basis of the fear that Anglo children would "catch diseases" from Mexican children who came from unhygienic homes.

At Christmas time, *luminarias* flickered on the rooftops and pathways of commercial buildings, hospitals, Protestant and Catholic churches, and the homes of any and all who wished them. Carved statues and *retablos* of Catholic saints were the property or exclusive symbols of no particular ethnic group.

In the religious arena, during the first half of the 20th century, the slow transition from missionary priests to secular clergy necessitated requests for more religious order priests to serve the region's Catholic parishes. Parish leadership was often assumed by laypersons. Early churches were rebuilt while many parishes constructed their first churches. Parochial school development experienced an ebb and flow as other religious education programs grew in popularity. The founding of national benevolent societies gave vital support to Catholic efforts in a region where vast distances and insufficient clergy strained existing financial resources. During this period, parish societies and parish-sponsored activities for youth became more popular as a growing need for better social bonds between parishioners became evident.

The 20th century found this region still much in need of priests, especially to serve the previously converted Indians and the traditionally Catholic Hispanics, especially Spanish-speaking priests. Supplementing early missionaries and diocesan clergy in parish life were Catholic religious orders such as the Salvatorians, the Benedictines, the Marists, the Norbertines, the Redemptorists and the Capuchin Franciscans, among others. The number of priests increased significantly during the first decades of the 20th century. But, still, there were examples of lay leadership in areas where priests no longer or irregularly served.

Old Hispanic parishes in locales where economic developments began to draw new citizens joined in the general building movement.

In addition to economic challenges, two issues relating to Hispanic religious tradition created factions within the parishes in New Mexico. The people's fondness for their church building and for many of its old furnishings caused resentment when the building was abandoned and the furnishings were placed either in the school basement or in storage. When construction plans for the new church called for a full basement that would function as a community center, and parishioners opposed the plan because of the complete excavation of the *camposanto* (graveyard) that it required, the next pastor tactfully decided to compromise and excavate only for the heating system and access to it. Here, again, we have evidence on the parish level of the conflict between a Roman/American Catholic organizing tendency to modernize and expand ecclesiastical establishments and the ancient Hispanic Catholic expressive tendency to preserve sacred objects in particular environments.

In 1947, however, the socioeconomic climate that had encouraged and allowed religious men and women to conduct the first public schools in New Mexico came to an abrupt halt.

Summer vacation school for Catholic religious education grew in popularity during the first decades of the 20th century. The program sometimes included merely an hour of Catechism instruction three mornings a week with occasional Catechism tests in lieu of the Sunday sermon. On looking back on these tests that were taken before the entire assembly, one student in the program recalled:

> "The older people probably welcomed this, but for us culprits in the front pews it was sheer agony — sort of like a catechetical spelling bee. If we missed twice we were out — humiliated and dreading the admonition from our parents when we got home. This spectacle, thank God, was a short-lived affair."

Dramatic catechetical expansion was encouraged in Catholic New Mexico by the foundation of religious communities dedicated specifically to catechetical work. In 1922, one such community, the Missionary Catechists of Our Lady of Victory were founded to teach Catechism and to train lay catechists.

On some college campuses in New Mexico, Catholics had the fourth largest representation among students, behind Methodists, Presbyterians and Mormons.

Regularly scheduled social events for youth served to include them in parish life.

The 19th century reality of church women (both Protestant and Catholic) being the financial backbone of local congregations seems to have carried over into the 20th century as well, particularly in the rural parishes. This appears to have been true in Hispanic parishes as well. Reliance on locally donated labor and outside financial support was typical of the economic struggle, in general, to outgrow a dependent economy.

From the first decade of the 20th century onward, the benevolent Catholic Church Extension Society of the United States of America supported, in part or entirely, the building of many Catholic churches in New Mexico. The Extension Society "launched the home-mission movement in this country" for Catholics, pledging to serve "those areas of the United States where the work of the Church was seriously handicapped by a lack of personnel, organization, finances, etc." At a time in this country's history when Protestant denominations were experiencing great evangelizing success on the American frontier (due in great measure to the support of their own home mission societies), Catholic parish life might not have been as firmly established in New Mexico had it not been for the aid of the Extension Society.

Another development in Catholic parish life in New Mexico during the first half of the 20th century, which gave evidence of a growing need for social bonds between parishioners, was the proliferation of societies. The establishment of ethnic societies and local chapters of national societies marked this period. Organizations such as the Knights of Columbus, the National Council of Catholic Women, and the St. Mary and St. Joseph Societies for Indians helped.

Building projects and other internal affairs were not the only concerns of New Mexico parishes during the first half of the 20th century. During the years of WWI and WWII, many New Mexico parishes noted with pride the names of parishioners and priests serving in the armed forces, and most scheduled daily prayers for peace.

Although it may be true, in general, that American Catholics during the first half of the twentieth century moved up the economic ladder and joined the ranks of non-Catholics, who were gaining personal prosperity by means of the capitalist system, this movement seems to have been limited to those urban areas where the success of businesses and the development of complex social systems permitted such progress. In the many undeveloped sections of still predominantly rural New Mexico, struggles with physical and economic geography still characterized the individual and communal lives of Catholic parishioners.

The national, post-World War Il, enthusiasm for religion that characterized the decade of the 1950's in America was paralleled in the Southwest by an unprecedented period of industrial and population growth. This growth made possible within the Catholic Church a great amount of energy and economic support for the expansion of existing plants and the rebuilding of outdated facilities, as well as the construction of entirely new churches.

In some areas, any industrial growth was not always permanent. In that case, parishioners were challenged to discover new ways of financing or to continue their dependence on gifts and fundraisers.

Because of such fluctuating economic and demographic conditions, and because of the continuing rural need for social activities, fund-raising for Catholic parishes in New Mexico continued.

Frequently, these fund-raisers were meals, which in rural areas fulfilled a need for social activity as well. The most well-attended activities in a rural parish were usually the meals sponsored for fund-raising.

This corporate sense of church as community and the role of the laity in it, which had always been present in the Hispanic Catholic Church, became more commonly manifest in all New Mexico rural parishes during the first half of the 20th century in the form of these parish fundraising events. But, it was given theological expression and more conscious attention after promulgation of the papal encyclicals *Mystici and Corporis* in 1943 and *Mediator Dei* in 1947. The impact of these two documents was not felt on a pastoral level in most places until the 1950's, when concern for the lay apostolate and liturgical interest became visible in the formation of local social action groups and the celebration of dialogue Masses. These changes encouraged wider use of the vernacular in the liturgy and greater flexibility in church architecture.

Evidence of this international encouragement to broaden one's notion of church as hierarchical institution with a new understanding of the corporate nature of ecclesia seems to have been limited, however, to church architecture, especially in the new buildings required for burgeoning suburban parishes such as in Albuquerque. In the many rural sections of the region, more dramatic change was delayed until the startling revelations and revolutions of the 1960's, like Vatican Council Il.

Although it is generally held that the parochial school system experienced its most rapid expansion after World War Il, it is hard to prove that this was so. Despite the difficulties of insufficient clergy, isolation and persistent financial concerns, local parishes in the Southwest, New Mexico and the Pecos Valley documented some growth from 1850 to 1960. From initial goals of simply supplying Catholics with access to the Sacraments, to the building and maintenance of physical plants and the development of religious education programs, these predominantly rural parishioners, along with their priests, organized societies and sponsored frequent fund-raisers to sustain what the economic growth of the 1940's and the continued charity of national benevolent societies could not do alone. These frontier conditions, dramatized in some sections of the region by the interplay of expressive and organizational styles of clerical and lay leadership, allowed the missionary spirit that launched the Catholic Church in the region to endure and to serve as a historical basis for the evolution of parish life.

The struggle of the people to express and establish a meaningful religious life is nowhere more dramatic than in the ongoing encounter of one ethnic tradition with another. In this region's Catholic history, it surfaced in an emphasis on the "official establishment" of churches by an Eastern-based hierarchy and a frequent disregard for culturally integrated religious traditions. The imposition of organizational efficiency often offended those for whom expressive celebration was a greater value. Yet, encouragement from a few order missionaries and secular clergy in the region enabled some Native Americans to resist the exclusion of tribal traditions from Catholic life, and Hispanics, to resist the loss of folk religious practices from their cultural tradition. Conversely, the national religious customs of European immigrants succumbed, by and large, to Americanization. Even back during the days before World War l, when American Catholicism defined itself primarily as an immigrant Church, Catholics of recent European extraction were widely dispersed in this region.

But Indians and Hispanics, particularly, made themselves known as "the melting pot that wouldn't." Objects of alternating Anglo disdain and pride, these two ethnic groups had the distinction of being the first and most consistently expressive Catholics.

With the passage of the Indian Reorganization Act in 1934, Native Americans could now exercise more control over their own secular affairs and religious practices. But this federal legislation did not have an immediate impact on Catholic missionary ventures in the Southwest, however.

In those tribes where Christianity failed to present a meaningful faith and where ancient religious traditions were being lost, a "vacuum [was] created by the cultural disintegration that was the result of the impingement of aggressively modernizing Western cultures on the traditional societies of North America." One of the movements that arose to fill this vacuum among Native Americans was the Peyote Cult. Based on practices used by Mexican Indians for many centuries, the cult spread to certain Plains Indians groups and was given its accomodationist form by the Comanche or Kiowa back in the 1880's. Peyotism appealed to those people suffering oppression and deprivation who could neither return completely to the old ways nor totally accept Anglo culture. The pan-Indian nature of the Peyote movement led in 1906 to the formation of a loose organization covering several Western states. As opposition to the cult increased, the federation grew and came to be known as the Native American Church. In 1945 and 1946, chapters of the Native American Church were incorporated in New Mexico.

Peyotists regarded the institutional forms of Catholicism and Protestantism as a white person's faith, appropriate for whites but not meant for Indians. Instead, they conceived of themselves as relating to the same god through a different mediator. The Peyote Spirit encountered in the ritual was sometimes identified with Jesus or the Holy Spirit and served the same mediating functions as did the Christian figures. It was the spiritual means through which divine power came into contact with and could be assimilated by human beings.

NATIVE AMERICAN PEYOTISM

Like early New Mexican Hispanic Catholics, 20ᵗʰ century Hispanic migrants from Mexico were without sufficient clerical leadership. Unlike the European immigrants of the 19ᵗʰ century, the Hispanic migrants of the 20ᵗʰ century did not bring with them priests of the same ethnic group to share their struggles. Instead, foreign-born clergy encouraged the same kind of assimilation their countrymen and women ultimately chose, while the "little tradition" among Hispanics prevailed.

> "Non-institutional religion was the response of a religious people not adequately served by the institutional Church. But the people did not forget to practice their beliefs simply because priests were not around. [They] continued to practice their *religion casera* [home or do-it-yourself religion]. More accurately, it was a community religiosity of mutual help organizations and devotional groups growing out of the home-nurtured faith of the people."

It was not until the 1940's that the Catholic Councils for the Spanish-speaking began to do organized work with Hispanic migrants in New Mexico.

During these decades of Hispanic migrations into New Mexico, Protestant evangelizing efforts were quick to include the Spanish-speaking in their plan to convert the world to Christianity. But, in addition to the appeal of the mainline Protestant denominations, Pentacostalism and other sects began to attract large numbers of disaffected Hispanics, especially in the post-World War I years. This 20th century outgrowth of the Holiness Movement most often appealed to those people who found themselves in the interstices of society, neither in the mainstream nor outlawed. Like the disoriented Native Americans who turned to the Peyote cult, black immigrants to urban areas, poor rural whites, and Puerto Rican immigrants to New York City, all found themselves among the socially dispossessed who hungered for an unmediated religious experience expressed in a spontaneous, unstructured way. Except for those involved in the Charismatic Movement, the American Catholic Church failed to come to terms with this growing socio-religious movement into the Pentecostal churches.

World War Il, it seemed, brought an end to Hispanic isolation in the United States. This spirit became evident on a national level in the organizing of such groups as the G.l. Forum and in strengthening such pre-existing groups as the League of United Latin American Citizens (LULAC) and *Sociedades Mexicanas*. The war also led Hispanics to question their status within the Catholic Church. This new militance was seen by some as the roots of the *Chicano* movement of the 1960's.

As the 20th century progressed, "the more overtly [European] aspects of parish life became less visible" within the New Mexico Catholic Church.

The Apaches of southeast New Mexico, a notorious threat to all from the 16th through the 19th centuries, gave up their nomadic marauding in the 20th century, but had no Catholic parish of their own in the area until the Apache Mission of St. Joseph's was established on the Mescalero Reservation by Franciscans.

ST. JOSEPH MESCALERO APACHE MISSION

During the 1950's and on into the '60's, the migration of new Spanish-speaking parishioners into areas where earlier Hispanics had settled seemed to give new impetus to old customs in some sections of the region.

While European immigrants had some ethnic influence on the quality of New Mexico Catholic parish life, that influence was often temporary and always limited. Native Americans and Hispanics, however, had not only been among the earliest Catholics in the region, but had also allowed the cultural expressions of their faith to become obvious elements of the region's multicultural self-understanding. The interplay of ethnicity and religion was a dynamic in American Catholic life that revealed an official preference for a hierarchical approach and, thus, an Eastern attitude of superiority over the "uncivilized" West. But, it also suggested the possibility of reclaiming a prophetic appreciation of diversity and the inclusion of regional distinctions that could enrich the American Catholic experience in the Southwest.

During the more than five decades since Vatican Council Il in the 1960's, several economic, social, and political changes have taken place that affected the quality of Catholic life in the Southwest and in southeastern New Mexico, and, in some cases, the ways in which the directives of the Council were implemented on a local level. In the face of an environmental dilemma created by the country's growing energy needs, this historically dependent region of the Southwest was determined to have a voice in deciding its own future. Native American self-determination and a revival of Hispanic culture were prophetically influencing the region's social, political and religious life. On the parochial level, these conditions led some to question the limits of traditional parish structures in meeting the individual and communal needs of members, and to ponder the place of the "little tradition" in the renewal of Catholic life.

As it did in the region's early history, geography continued to play a central role in New Mexico's economic, political and ecclesiastical development. "Once distance, space, and remoteness were our curse. Now they are our blessing." Open spaces, unique landscapes and land forms, and an abundance of untapped mineral wealth encouraged governmental defense and science industries, manufacturing (especially of agricultural products), development of wilderness and recreation areas and the exploration of energy resources.

In New Mexico, federal laboratories employing scientists and technicians, as well as Bureau of Indian Affairs contracts and U.S. highway projects, made the U.S. Government the largest contributor to the state's economy. With the lowest per capita income in the Southwest, however, New Mexico continued to reflect the undeveloped condition that had characterized it for so long.

If there was one underlying theme of the people in this region, it was that those who lived and worked here were determined to play a strong role in shaping their future.

Such "voluntary regionalism," concerned with economic and cultural progress and quality of life, was bound to affect the quality of life in the region as well. Parish structure changed as staffs expanded in many instances to include lay or religious members (including permanent deacons) and parish councils added a new dimension to collegial authority.

At one time in the recent decades, New Mexico had the highest percentage (27.3) of parishes in the United States whose staffs consisted of clergy and laity or religious. However, there was no clear data to indicate whether this trend was in any way connected to the Hispanic tradition of lay leadership, to a declining number of priests or to a greater number of religious women included on parish staffs.

A shift in emphasis from parochial schools to sophisticated religious education programs had been evident in the region as well as in the entire American Catholic Church. The rationale for such a shift was the rediscovered value of family-centered religious education, but a practical basis for the change had been an economic one.

Perhaps the most dramatic change in parish structure and style during recent years was the growth of lay ministry. Three of the most highly developed ministries were those to youth, to the sick, and to those who were grieving.

One architectural feature that symbolized the expanded program of ministries and activities in many contemporary parishes in the area was the family center or parish center. There was not the same pride, however, in the structure and its impact on the local environment that characterized so many building projects of earlier decades.

It was difficult to classify Catholic Indian communities in New Mexico as either mission or parish. In a sense, most were both. In some Catholic Indian communities, it was difficult to determine just how many of those who claimed to be Catholic were so and by what standard.

For some Native Americans, Catholicism was the bridge or buffer between two different cultures, tribal life and American society. "Each religion was relegated in a compartmentalized manner to its own distinct times, places and ceremonies. There was little attempt to reconcile Christian monotheistic belief with Indian pantheistic and polytheistic belief." Catholicism was the meaningful system that eased the transition from one culture to the other. In New Mexico, individual priests and religious did what time and circumstance allowed to make worship meaningful.

While Hispanic Catholicism had been an important element in the multi-cultural history of the region for over 300 years, and in certain urban centers for more than eighty-five years, it was only within the past fifty years that an unprecedented infiltration of Spanish-speaking people and the impetus of the Chicano movement made the Hispanic community of greater concern to the entire American Church.

Parishes that maintained the "little tradition" continued to reconstruct village history, revive ancient folk customs, restore old folk art objects and church buildings, and express their faith through celebration. There was a growing concern for saving neighborhoods rich in ethnic and religious history.

Throughout the New Mexico region, restored folk customs included dramatizing *Los Pastores* (a Nativity play) and *Las Posadas* (a re-enactment of Mary & Joseph's search for lodging) and dancing *Las Matachines* (a *matachine* dance was a ritual dance about a struggle for survival). At Christmastime, many churches and homes lighted *luminarias* or *farolitos* to commemorate "the shepherd campfires long ago outside the town of Bethlehem." In some old Hispanic parishes, adaptation and renewal of the liturgy meant restoring old religious artifacts. Hispanic communal custom also included an oral tradition of *cuentos* (stories) and *dichos* (sayings), which transmitted Catholic values in folk religious form to the next generation.

Indian and Hispanic churches contained precious murals, altar screens, *santos, retablos* and basic architectural features, all conceived and executed to enhance worship. *Santeros* (*santo* makers) continued to be prevalent throughout New Mexico.

By the late 20th century, many Hispanics had become comfortable with their middle-class status and were not as aware of the needs of their own people as they might have been. It was a long, slow process to establish *comunidades de base* (basic Christian communities), to initiate religious instruction in Spanish (and from a Hispanic perspective), to address the economic needs of Spanish-speaking immigrants, and to welcome them warmly into parish life, even in this area of the country. Why so?

Some claim a history of Hispanic invisibility in the American Church had been the rule.

> "A dynamic and aggressive Anglo culture had come between the Hispano and their past and was uprooting them from the soil, cutting them off from their ancestors, separating them from their culture. Very little was being done to facilitate their transition from the culture of their ancestors, whose voice was silent, to the culture of the majority, whose voice made their laws and determined their destiny."

What has been preserved of Hispanic Catholic culture in New Mexico has been due more to the resistance and persistence of an isolated people true to their "little tradition" than to any leadership on the part of the "great tradition". Hispanic Catholic observers saw this invisibility in three areas: in ecclesiastical leadership, in parish leadership and in church attendance.

While the Catholic Church in New Mexico struggled to face and to deal with these challenges, evangelists of other faiths were working hard to win Hispanic souls. Early Protestant evangelizing efforts by Presbyterians, Methodists and Baptists succeeded in creating an indigenous leadership among Hispanic converts. Although still subordinate to Anglo leadership in most large Protestant denominations, many educated Hispanics clung to these American Protestant mainstream churches, aware that these were the agents of their education and consequent higher status. Others were influenced by the new wave of conservatism in American religious life and found themselves attracted to fundamentalist, Pentecostal, millennialist and other Protestant sects. Appealing generally to the socially disinherited, these sects frequently offered a religious affiliation that was simple, direct, personal and emotional, oftentimes, in independent neighborhood churches, which had no elaborate ecclesiastical structure or even a national organization to impose customs from the dominant culture.

A Catholic Diocesan Vicar had said:

> "There is a lot of defection from the church locally. For many Hispanics, leaving the church is a defection from society and culture. We have not taken Hispanic culture seriously in the church. We have often Americanized them, not given them the freedom to be Hispanic. This is more of a cultural problem than simply a religious problem."

An elder with a Jehovah's Witnesses Church, pointed to the disillusionment of Hispanics with Catholicism as one motive for their conversion to that sect:

> "I think their main frustration comes from being told that the priest has all the answers and they do not need to know themselves. —When they start asking questions in the church, they find they can't get them. When they find out that the Bible has the answers, they like it."

A National Catholic Hispanic Pastoral *Encuentro*, held in the early 1970's, said.

> "Generally, Spanish-speaking Catholics in the United States feel isolated from the official structures and institutions of the Church and recognize a long history of lack of knowledge about and sensitivity toward Spanish-speaking traditions on the part of the American Church."

By the 1970's, the Catholic Church in America had become a less parochial and more global Church.

In 1978, the Gallup Organization, in its report on the Unchurched American, concluded:

> "Perhaps the most telling of all is the finding that 86% of the unchurched — and 76% of the churched — agree that "an individual should arrive at his or her own religious beliefs independent of any church or synagogue."

This confidence that the prophetic principle as well as the institutional Church could lead one to deeply held religious values was evident in interfaith encounters that may or may not have been formally labeled ecumenical.

Some reports of charismatic groups among Native Americans indicated that they were more divisive than supportive to parish life since native religious traditions seemed not to be consistent with the Catholic Charismatic Movement.

All of this historical perspective gives us a good idea of some of the conditions in which the towns along the Pecos River in southeastern New Mexico were surrounded by and developed in. Now, for the past local history of the southeast New Mexico Pecos River Valley and the individual stories of these towns and cities along the New Mexico Pecos frontier.

Southeast New Mexico Pecos River Valley: The Past Local History

In the Pecos River Valley of southeastern New Mexico, around the town of Artesia, the spirit of the past still breathes along the Pecos where some live much as their ancestors did centuries ago, alongside those whose roots are in the present and who dream of the future.

There were cultural differences of this area from surrounding areas and historical conditions which led to diversity.

Before the turn of the 20th century, the Artesia area was being settled by pioneer ranchmen. There were few towns and transportation was poor. The ranches established were large enterprises and the families who settled the area lived on the ranches and seldom had contact with other people. Visiting with neighbors was a precious premium.

These early pioneers found they were lacking in social contacts and they also suffered a loss of religious involvement and undergirding.

In June of 1866, Charles Goodnight and Oliver Loving brought their first Texas cattle herd up the Pecos River Valley. Within three years, the valley of the Pecos held thousands of grazing cattle as other ranchers followed.

In 1867, the Pecos Valley was a sea of grass with not a single large tree for fifty miles.

In 1869, Mr. Van Smith erected the first building in Roswell, a saloon.

By 1870, the population of Lincoln County in southeast New Mexico, which contained the Pecos River valley, was 1,803, including 1,465 Hispanos, 270 Anglos, 54 children of Hispanic mothers and Anglo fathers, and 14 Blacks. Women were 41% of the population, and the sex ratio was 14 men to 10 women. There were very few children.

By 1872, the U.S. Government had created the Mescalero Indian Reservation at Fort Stanton in the mountains west of Roswell.

A stagecoach line ran through the lower Pecos Valley by 1874.

There was an increasing horde of land-hungry whites who settled along the Pecos and Penasco Rivers, beginning in the 1870's.

From 1876 through 1878, the Lincoln County War occurred between the Dolan & Riley gang and the McSween & Tunstall gang.

In 1877, Indian raids for horses were still common up and down the valley. Texas published its first list of 4,402 fugitives from Texas justice in 1878. A number of those on the list were said to have immediately moved to the New Mexico Territory, but under new names. And, gold was first discovered at White Oaks in the mountains west of Roswell.

On July 19, 1878, a five-day battle at Lincoln brought the Lincoln County War to its climax.

When families reached the country on the Penasco River, a tributary of the Pecos River, in 1881, there were two Penasco settlements: Upper and Lower Penasco.

In 1881, Generals Miles and Crook bivouaced with 1,000 Buffalo Soldiers (Negroes) at Rattlesnake Springs, west of present-day Carlsbad, during their campaigns against the Apache Warrior Geronimo.

On July 14, 1881, William Bonney, Billy the Kid, was killed at Ft. Sumner by Sheriff Pat Garrett.

Pat Garrett, ex-sheriff of Lincoln County and of "Billy the Kid" fame, came up with the idea of creating a huge irrigation complex for the Middle Pecos Valley and discussed it with Charles Eddy.

In 1884, a drought combined with overstocking caused a two-year tragedy of dying livestock and suffering animals in the Pecos River Valley, called the "Big Die."

From 1884 to about 1888, covered wagons, sometimes 20 and 30 to a caravan, brought settlers to the Sacramento Mountains to the west of the Pecos River.

The year 1886 saw the arrival of the windmill in the West, and in southeast New Mexico, which created an opening up of the *Llano Estacado* (Staked Plains) to further ranching.

A large number of Chicago people became interested in the Pecos Valley around 1888 when the Pecos Irrigation and Improvement Company began. When they first arrived in the Pecos country, there was nothing but prairie dogs, jack rabbits and wild, open country.

In 1888, the Pecos Valley Land and Ditch Company built a diversion dam on the Pecos River.

Investors advertised the Pecos Valley nationally as a veritable agricultural "Garden of Eden":

> "WATER IS KING! The Pecos Irrigation and Improvement Company is now engaged in the most GIGANTIC IRRIGATION ENTERPRISES in the West. Its canals will reclaim more than 200,000 acres of wonderfully fertile land. Limestone Soil, Plenty of

Water, Abundant Sunshine. A combination of elements
that never fails to reward the farmer for his labor."

The Pecos Valley Town Company was incorporated at this time.

Life on the early frontier required enormous tenacity in order to
survive. People in the Middle Pecos Valley, as elsewhere, made the
necessary adjustments by adapting a way of life suited to the demands
of their area and era. They maintained social traditions and practices,
such as courtship, marriage, amusements and religion, which they
had known in the east, west, north or south or from wherever they
had come. The special, big, fun social events along the Middle Pecos
Valley were rodeos, held somewhere on the range after the fall
roundup, and the shindigs or country dances.

One of the prominent social forces in the Pecos Valley was the
religious or camp meeting and the singing convention. The singing
convention in southeastern New Mexico became an institution, a
Sunday or a weekend gathering of people to sing gospel songs, visit
old friends or talk over old times. The custom had its roots in the
soil that nurtured the homesteaders, the sodbusters, the ranchers of
the wide, rich land that went beyond the limits of the Pecos River
Valley. It was a custom born of loneliness and the human need for
companionship. With its Christian faith and the love of singing, the
custom came west with the covered wagons, spreading across the
entire frontier, reaching eastern New Mexico in the late 1880's and
early 1900's.

By the end of the 19th century, Eddy and Chaves Counties in
southeastern New Mexico, were the only counties in the New Mexico
Territory in which all political candidates were Americans.

In 1891, Nathan Jaffa, a Roswell merchant, drilled the first successful
artesian well in the Pecos River Valley near Roswell.

144

By 1892, the United States entered a period of Depression.

Most of the construction work on McMillan Dam, on the Pecos River, south of Artesia, was completed by 1893, just as a series of natural disasters struck the Pecos Valley. Seemingly endless pouring rain caused the Pecos River to rise until the older Avalon Dam (near the McMillan Dam) gave way, resulting in severe damage to the canal system and flume.

Even though repairs to the Avalon Dam were completed in time for the 1894 growing season, the Pecos River Valley continued in an economic slump throughout the decade.

Many of the communities in the Pecos Valley, such as Roswell and Eddy (Carlsbad) had flood waters which raged through the streets on many occasions. Floods were recorded as early as 1894.

In October of 1894, the railroad reached Roswell from the town of Eddy.

By 1895, the Eddy *Argus* newspaper was reporting only about 300 Mexican people in the Pecos Valley. This was the closest to reality that the *Argus* had come so far, but was far from the truth.

By 1896, the larger ranches began reducing the size of their herds and by the turn of the 20th century the days of the open range were over. In February, Mr. J.J. Hagerman announced that he would soon extend his railroad northeast from Roswell to join with the Santa Fe system in Texas.

In 1899, land sales in the Pecos Valley picked up again, following the connection of the railroad from Roswell to Amarillo, Texas.

The Pecos Valley economy improved after 1900 with the completion of the Pecos Valley and Northeastern's railroad line from Carlsbad, through Roswell, to Amarillo, TX.

"The people, they came from every point on the compass, some to seek riches, some to settle, a few to evade the law . But by chance or choice, they were the people who lived their dreams or the dreams of others in a land that was rich in treasure and promise, the land that became Eddy County."

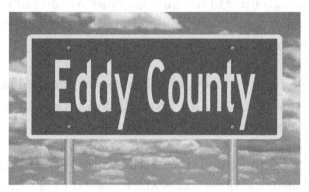

EDDY COUNTY

"Eddy County, New Mexico was among the last sections of the West to yield to settlement. Envisioning the Pecos Valley's potential took hard courage and determination to bend a stubborn nature to their will and the people persevered until the arid land was transformed into one of comfortable homes supported by fine farms, ranches and businesses. As the Pecos Valley began to develop, through the cattle ranching era then into the booming construction days of the Pecos Irrigation and Investment Company and its companion, the Eddy Town Company, many other courageous people were drawn into the scene, some attracted by the lure of frontier adventure, some by the prospect of wealth through new-found opportunities, and some only by the lodestone of good wages. As always, the jackals of civilization also came for the purpose of preying off of their fellow men and women. All of these, the men of vision, the farmers, ranchers and laborers, the business and professional men dug and hauled and built as they advanced their dreams and in the total each contributed their bit, even the gambler, and frontier harlot. The comfortable and prosperous homes and towns and lives of the present are the results of a most interesting set of circumstances that included foresight, sweat, luck and often blood and tears."

The area of Eddy County was extolled for the fertility of its soil, the climate, the never-failing water supply, and the extensive resources.

Eddy County, an area built on dreams, was a land of continuing promise. Although many sought fortunes here through grandiose schemes, it was a peculiarity of the region that none acquired wealth, nor more than a small measure of fame. What the enterprising and visionary pioneers did accomplish was to open an area where thousands of people could live in an environment of beauty and promise. The startling clarity of southwest skies, the yet untapped resources, the courage and talent of its people and the silent promise of the land identified Eddy County and the Pecos Valley of southeastern New Mexico as an area with an unlimited future.

Thus, the present-day Pecos River Valley was born. But, a dream born of hardship and struggle.

In the Spanish-American communities of the Pecos Valley, *curanderos* were even used when doctors wouldn't work. Many people would come to a *curandero*, or healer, when they couldn't be cured by doctors. Mostly, a *curandero's* work was that of being a *consejero* (counselor), and treating common ailments. Patients would pay many times with just a bowl of vegetables because they had little money. A *curandero* understood the culture and such things as *susto* (a case of spirit attack), *empacho* (stomach problems), *el mal ojo* (the evil eye), *caida de la mollera* (a baby's sunken skull), *aires* (rapid change from hot to cold or due to bewitching), *contierre*, and *encono* (spirit of ill will toward another). A *curandero* would sometimes travel many miles to get the *yerbas* (herbs) that they wanted to use with their patients. Many of the *remedios* were made up from things found at home or available without a prescription. They reacted sharply sometimes against most formal medicine. Today, some *curanderos* would say, "The AMA [American Medical Association] has taken away the people's medicine and made them pay for it." From the plants and herbs found on an Indian reservation, two-hundred medicines were derived and sold only by description. They would use *curas* and *remedios* known by the people and used by their patients. Anyone claiming supernatural powers for curing was usually a fake. "God is the only supernatural power. The *curandero* must be *muy hombre*; *un hombre honorable* (a very honorable man) and they must understand their limitations."

CURANDERO

After two years of drought, disaster once again hit the Pecos Valley in 1904 when a devastating flood struck.

The restoration of irrigation water to most of the area was completed by early 1907.

Floods again occurred in the Pecos Valley in 1908 and legalized gambling came to an end across the Territory of New Mexico.

In the early 1900's, a number of test oil wells were drilled in Eddy County.

In June of 1911, Roswell Mayor Roy Woofter was shot dead. In the 1910 Census, Roswell had a population of 6,172 and was larger than Santa Fe.

Geronimo's band, the White Mountain Apache, was to be quartered on the Mescalero Reservation, in the mountains west of Roswell.

On June 1, 1917, the new St. Peter's Catholic Church in Roswell was dedicated.

The 1930's were difficult for the populace of Eddy County. After the crash of 1929, in the early 1930's, times were particularly hard on many cattlemen who saw their cattle die on the parched ranges, or saw them shot to prevent their suffering. And then the dust came.

The final blow was the big freeze of 1932. Temperatures reached 30 degrees (Fahrenheit) below zero and a series of howling blizzards sounded the death knell for Pecos Valley fruit. Farmers turned to other crops.

The population of the Pecos Valley, chiefly Anglo-American, came from various sections of the nation "but was unified by common American values and customs." Many of the people were from Texas, while other states were well-represented — Tennessee, Missouri, Indiana, Illinois and Kansas contributed heavy quotas.

At the heart of the Pecos Valley, with its hard-working, yet cultural, educational and religious-minded people, the Artesia community expanded in all affairs and businesses. "From the beginning, Artesia was, and it has remained, the center of the oil industry in Eddy County."

In religious circles, there were early camp meetings. Ranch families from the area would come to stay a week or 10 days. They brought all their food, their tents, and personal needs and camped in a tree grove. It was a time of social involvement, catching up on the news of neighboring families and primarily a time for religious input and worship. Bloy's Camp Meeting was the grandfather of the ranchman's camp meetings of Texas and New Mexico. Nogal and Elk, New

Mexico, in the mountains to the west of Artesia, would still have annual cowboy camp meetings by the 1970's. In the 1950's, there would be some two to three thousand people who attended the week-long meeting. Four denominations were represented by teachers and preachers — Presbyterian, Methodist, Disciples of Christ and Baptist. There would be a Bible study every morning, a preaching service in the afternoon, and another at night. The time between services would be laced with visiting, discussing various points of the sermons and eating.

Camp meetings were joyous and recharging experiences. It would give attendees a whole new lease on life every year. In local church services, congregations would try to capture the spirit of the ranchmen's camp meetings in their worship services for the month. It would be a time of personal sharing, a time of informal worship, a time of joyful singing, and a time for drawing together again after the hectic pace of summer had inflicted its separating quality.

In 1951, the New Mexico Baptists planned a $4 million Camp at Glorietta, New Mexico, on the upper reaches of the Pecos River.

The Pecos River Valley surrounding Artesia grew and developed with small communities sprouting up in sparsely populated remote areas of the plains, valleys and mountains.

UPPER PENASCO RIVER VALLEY

A group of settlers occupied a town they named Badgerville in 1884, on the Penasco River, about twenty miles west of present-day Artesia, so-named because the early families dug holes, like badgers, in the banks of the stream to have a place out of the weather. It would later be renamed Hope.

By 1884, the early families settling in the Guadalupe Mountains to the west of Badgerville, were able to build log cabins. The arrival of women and children in a frontier area meant that the first written history for that area would inevitably follow. It would be family history. But, Anglo families were interested in themselves and other Anglo families. Their early histories seldom indicated that there were already Hispanic, and of course, Indian, families in the area. These would fade almost unheralded from the scene.

In 1898, a man killed a Deputy Sheriff at Hope.

In June of 1900, a Mr. Foster and friends got into a fight with a group at a Hope church. The fight left a Mr. Wilburn dead. Another big flood came down the Penasco and Black Rivers in September of 1900, doing much damage to the farms bordering on the Penasco.

In May of 1911, Rev. W.M. Beauchamp converted 22 at the first Old Time Camp Meeting at Queen, west of the Pecos. In September of 1911, Rev. Beauchamp got another fifteen converts at a Revival in Queen.

By May of 1937, the Methodist Sacramento Camp near Weed in the Guadalupe Mountains west of the Pecos Valley, was ready to open.

But, now, let's turn to the towns and cities of the middle Pecos Valley of southeastern New Mexico and the role God has played in their lives.

IN THE TOWNS AND CITIES OF THE PECOS RIVER VALLEY OF SOUTHEASTERN NEW MEXICO

Beginning from the north and heading south along current New Mexico State Highway 2, the towns of Dexter, Hagerman, Lake Arthur, Artesia and Carlsbad, just west of the Pecos River in southeastern New Mexico, form a constellation of communities that has been shaped by the historical past, but also, strangely enough, by the future, by what could have been. Obviously, it has been shaped by the climate and geography. But, it has also been shaped by religion, various circumstances and even coincidences. Most of all, however, this section of the Land of Enchantment has been shaped by its legacy of survival. For a community to survive and prosper, it must hold on to an ideal, a higher power. Throughout their histories, these communities and surrounding areas have indeed done that in many ways through future-looking investors, civic and religious leaders, and through the "keepers of the faith", the *rezadoras* (many times, women) or "pray-ers" in each community.

Dexter and Blackdom, New Mexico

An interesting fact connected with the Dexter, New Mexico area was that John Chisum, the famous Anglo cattle rancher in the Pecos Valley, had a Black "step-son", Frank Chisum, who John had bought as a black slave during the Civil War. This was to be a precursor to a very interesting chapter in the town of Dexter's history.

The town of Dexter was little more than barren range before the discovery of artesian water in the late 1890's. Around 1893, a stage stop for the Carlsbad to Roswell stagecoach line was located on an area homesteader's farm.

Then, there was Frank Boyer, a Black man, and two students, who arrived from Georgia to Eddy County in 1898, walking all the way from Georgia. Boyer's father had once visited New Mexico during the Mexican-American War.

Black homesteaders utilized the Homestead Act of 1862 to settle land several miles west of present-day Dexter where Frank Boyer and companions had come. The rest of Boyer's family came in 1901.

Boyer and his family homesteaded one mile west of present-day Dexter. The new community founded by Boyer was called Blackdom. The homesteading of Blackdom began in 1903. At the time it was settled, Blackdom was lush with artesian wells. It was advertised in newspapers back east and in the south for Black homesteaders. The fledgling white community in and near Dexter strongly discouraged the Black settlers from homesteading near Dexter and encouraged them to move further west to build their own community.

In January of 1903, three men, one from Denmark, one from Canada, and one from Iowa, filed Articles of Incorporation as members of the Dexter Townsite Company as alfalfa fields soon dotted the landscape along the line of the Pecos & Eastern Railroad between Roswell and Carlsbad in the Pecos River Valley.

A cyanide plant was constructed in Dexter.

The Methodist Church of Dexter was organized in 1905 in an old adobe schoolhouse. Thirteen people joined the church that year.

Blackdom was the first all-black settlement in the New Mexico Territory.

By 1925, Blackdom had a Baptist Church, store, schoolhouse, pumping plant, office building, blacksmith, a hotel and a newspaper. "Here the black man has an equal chance with the white man. Here you are reckoned at the value which you place upon yourself. Your future is in your own hands." The residents of Blackdom came from the post-Civil War South after the failures of Reconstruction. Blackdom was a pretty strict Baptist settlement.

By the late 1920's, the little settlement of Blackdom disappeared due to continued problems with irrigation from the distant Pecos River. The Blackdom Baptist Church was bought and moved to become the Cottonwood Methodist Church just north of Artesia in the late 1920's.

During the 1940's, Camp Orchard Park (near Dexter) was a World War Il Prisoner of War Camp. Occasionally, ministers and priests from Roswell would visit the POW and Bracero camps in the area.

The Mexican-Americans and African-Americans, who were "suppressed" like the POW's, felt some attraction to the POW's. The Roswell POW Camp had about 4,500 POW's. Religious services for the prisoners were in the gymnasium of the camp where the American servicemen enjoyed movies, dances and basketball. The Presbyterian minister from Dexter would go out to the camp and pick up four or five POW's to work around the Presbyterian Church in Dexter.

In 1945, a Catholic Mass was held at a home in Dexter. This only lasted a year, however. In 1953, Father Francis Keehn, O.F.M, a Franciscan priest, was sent to begin making plans for a new Catholic church in Dexter. A census was taken. The results were that many of the old Catholic families and their children were no longer members of the Catholic Church. After many meetings, however, between the Catholic men and the local Diocese, it was decided to build a new church in Dexter. The Catholic Extension Society came to the church's aid with very generous donations.

Half of the property for the church was donated and the other half was purchased. On May 30, 1954, the cornerstone was laid by the diocesan bishop. The money donated was just enough to buy the materials. Finally, on May 29, 1955, the church was ready. On October 16, 1955, the church was dedicated to the Immaculate Conception, since it was begun during a Marian year (a year dedicated to Mary, Mother of Jesus).

With a resident priest and Dexter serving as the parish church, Hagerman, Lake Arthur, Greenfield, Orchard Park and Flying H Ranch (west of Dexter), became the new mission field. Lake Arthur, Greenfield and Dexter had Catholic churches, but Orchard Park and Flying H Ranch had none.

This brief glimpse into the reality of Dexter's development provided the soil for finding God in the midst of life's many challenges and blessings.

Hagerman, New Mexico

The town of Hagerman was named after Mr. J.J. Hagerman, owner of the Chisum Ranch which was previously owned by John Chisum.

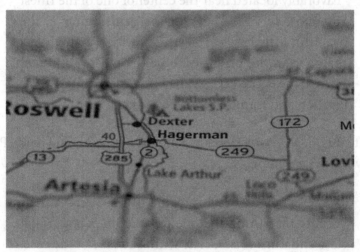

HAGERMAN, NM

The valley around Hagerman looked like a haven of rest to the people who were brought there on immigrant trains by promoters. The building of the railroad through the Pecos Valley caused an influx of settlers into the country around Hagerman.

Hagerman became one of the most important towns in Chaves County and one of the largest shipping centers for fruit, alfalfa and livestock along the line of the Pecos Valley and Northeastern Railroad.

In Hagerman, the history of the beginning of the Methodist Church was very closely related to the opening of this area to irrigated farming. The first religious services, held in the freight room of the railroad depot, brought preachers of many faiths to conduct services from time to time. Nail kegs and twelve-inch boards were used for pews. Some revivals were held in the town. In 1895, the first school building was built and regular church services began in the school. Records show that 1896 marked the organization of Hagerman Methodism.

An article in *The Hagerman Irrigator* newspaper in 1895 read:

> "Favorably located near the center of one of the finest and most fertile valleys in the arid region is the beautiful little city of Hagerman, which, though less than a year old, promises to be the most prominent town in the entire Pecos Valley, because of its favorable location and immediate surroundings."

Despite this, however, in 1895, the following was also said of the Pecos Valley near Hagerman:

> "Some people hesitate to come to the Pecos Valley, because they think that the population is of a rough class and unfit to associate with. Such is not the case. The class of people who have immigrated to the Pecos Valley are not refugees from justice, but are Christian people who have come here to make for themselves a home in a land of peace and prosperity. To make any such accusation is to cast an insult at the grandest and noblest people that ever lived and those who believe that the people of this valley are of a rough

and ignorant class have drawn a conclusion that they themselves would admit to be wrong, had they the opportunity to judge. 'By their fruits ye shall know them,' applies very well to this case and by which a satisfactory decision [about the people] could be reached."

In 1904, the Hagerman Baptist Church began. The Hagerman Presbyterian Church began in 1905.

The first Methodist church building was erected in 1905.

A statement given by Percy Hagerman, son of Hagerman founder, J.J. Hagerman, following his father's death read:

> "The last twenty years of my father's [J.J. Hagerman's] life were devoted mostly to the development of the Pecos Valley, a work which he never should have undertaken and which crowned his life with a series of disappointments in men and things. It is conservative to say that he personally put over two million, five hundred thousand dollars more into the Pecos Valley developments than he ever took out of them. As always, he was the largest owner and stood to gain or lose more than any other individual. He backed his faith with his own work and resources, and while no one can deny that his gigantic efforts resulted in great good to the valley and to New Mexico in general, it is equally undeniable that he would have been infinitely better off personally if he had let the whole business alone. I think most men would have thrown up their hands and quit in despair. He felt a great responsibility to investors and still more to the thousands of settlers and it was not in him to quit."

In 1908, a group of citizens petitioned the Town Trustees to call a special election for the purpose of stopping the sale of intoxicating beverages within the town limits of Hagerman.

In 1908, we hear of a Catholic church at Hagerman. There was never a resident priest at Hagerman, however.

In 1912, there were about eight or ten Catholic families at Hagerman. The priest would take the train from Roswell to Hagerman Saturday evening, had supper at the hotel and spent the night in a room connected with the church. After his Sunday Mass, he visited the faithful and then returned to spend the night at the church to await the train at 4:00 am Monday morning. The Catholics were Irish, German and French.

In 1923, the Hagerman Church of Christ and the Hagerman Nazarene Church began.

For some unexplained reason, the Hagerman Catholic church was discontinued in 1928.

In the national election for the repeal of the 18th Amendment (Prohibition), the churches took the lead in defeating the measure in Hagerman. The churches carried on a vigorous campaign to secure signatures that people would not vote for the repeal of the amendment. The "dry's" carried the Hagerman voter box by a majority of two to one.

The Presbyterian Church in Hagerman, during World War Il, had German POWs at a local prisoner-of-war camp make the glass windows installed in it.

The Catholic church came to life in Hagerman briefly, in 1949. Mass was offered in the home of a parishioner, but after the family moved to Texas, it was ended. Then, in September, 1961, construction of a new Catholic church began. St. Catherine Church was thus begun in Hagerman. The men of the Holy Name Society of the church were instrumental in planning the new building. The new building was completed in the spring of 1962. A Franciscan friar from Roswell was pastor at the time and would come from Roswell to say mass. The church had a 300-person seating capacity. Services were previously held in a barracks building on the same property.

And so, Hagerman relied on the land, on the water and on its faith to persevere. The neighboring village of Lake Arthur would do the same.

Lake Arthur, New Mexico

The beginnings of Lake Arthur occurred in 1885 when Arthur V. Russell, a sheep rancher, homesteaded three miles north of the present-day townsite of Lake Arthur. At shearing time each year, Mr. Russell would gather his sheep at a lake located south of present-day Lake Arthur. Over time, his first name became associated with the small lake and eventually with the town.

The town site of Lake Arthur was surveyed and platted in August, 1904.

The Lake Arthur Elementary School building began to be used in 1906. It is the oldest continuously-used school building in New Mexico.

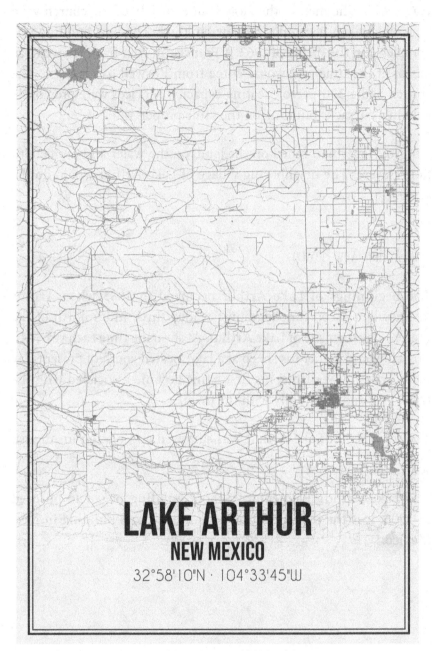

LAKE ARTHUR
NEW MEXICO
32°58'10"N · 104°33'45"W

Lake Arthur, NM

By 1906, Lake Arthur was a thriving community with many fine homes.

After a disastrous fire, however, the town was never able to fully recover.

The town was incorporated and had a population of about 400 in 1907.

Due to various uncontrollable events, the history of the First Methodist Church of Lake Arthur is very sketchy. The cornerstone of the present building is dated 1909. Ministers and Sunday School were present beginning in 1910.

Sunday School and resident ministers were discontinued at First Methodist Church in Lake Arthur in 1934.

The first time a priest came to Lake Arthur was in the summer of 1939, a sick call to St. John's Catholic Church in Roswell requesting a priest at Lake Arthur, and Lake Arthur had a new missionary. The first mass was on Sunday, July 3, 1939. Fr. Lambert Brockman. O.F.M. said mass at a parishioner's house located near the Ozark Trail stone obelisk. Mass was held there twice a month until November, 1942. At this time, the parishioner's home, where Mass was being held, became too small for the people, and it was decided to use another parishioner's old home on the present church property. This was fixed into a small church and served the congregation until 1950. At this time, the parishioners, including some people from Hagerman and Dexter, had been using an adobe structure. Fr. Joyce Finnigan, O.F.M., who would come from Dexter to say mass, was pastor at the time. The existing church was begun in 1970. Heartened by the promise of $10,000 obtained by the bishop from the Extension Society and by the Franciscan Father Provincial, a slab of concrete 36 ft. by 42 ft. was laid. Then, parishioners began doing as much of the work as they could. One supplied some of the skilled labor. By Easter of 1971, the people were able to use the new church, furnished with new benches and altar donated by the Flying H Ranch. Then, in 1972, the exterior of the church was painted and the church was ready for the official dedication. It was called Our Lady of Guadalupe Church.

In 1977, the face of Jesus Christ appeared on a flour tortilla at the home of the Rubio family in Lake Arthur. In October of 1977, Maria Rubio was rolling up a burrito for her husband Eduardo's breakfast, when she noticed a thumb-sized configuration of skillet burns on the tortilla that resembled the face of Jesus. People began to visit. Visitations were of a predominantly religious nature. Despite the braying of scientists and skeptics, the Holy Tortilla quickly developed a solid pilgrim base. By 1979, over 35,000 people had visited, bringing flowers and photos of sick loved ones. Mrs. Rubio quit her job as a maid to attend full-time to the hastily constructed "Shrine of the Holy Tortilla" in her home. When away, she'd leave the door unlocked so that no one would be denied access. The tortilla became a relic of pilgrimage to the tiny town of Lake Arthur.

THE FACE OF JESUS

And so, the tiny village of Lake Arthur added its legacy to the development and history of the Pecos Valley and the forming and maintaining of peoples' faith. But, it was Eddy/Carlsbad, about thirty miles south of Lake Arthur, that began and remained the principal town in Eddy County in this part of southeast New Mexico.

Eddy/Carlsbad, New Mexico

The following historical information pertaining to Eddy/Carlsbad (from 1889 to 1954) was taken directly from newspaper articles and reports from the following sources: the *Eddy Argus* (the first local Eddy newspaper which, later, became the *Pecos Valley Argus,* and then, the *Carlsbad Argus*), the *Eddy County Citizen,* and the *Eddy Current* (which became the *Carlsbad Current*).

Lincoln County was enlarged in 1878 to include all of eastern Dona Ana County, including the present-day Carlsbad area. This made Lincoln County in New Mexico the largest county in America.

In 1880, Joseph and Susan Edwards became the first settlers on Rocky Arroyo (12 miles due west of the future Eddy/Carlsbad).

CARLSBAD, NM

Fourteen-year old Lillian Greene, the daughter of Charles Greene, christened the new Eddy town site with a bottle of champagne at the local ford across the Pecos. The town site was to be on a flat beside the Pecos that had long been used by John Chisum as a roundup ground. Construction began on the first structure on the Eddy town site, a small hostelry for potential investors that was called the Eddy House. R. W. Tansill became one of the most significant investors and promoters of the Pecos Valley projects.

In 1889, the city of Eddy, today called Carlsbad, was officially founded. The first edition of the weekly *Eddy Argus* newspaper was published. This paper was owned and published by the P, I & I Company (Pecos Irrigation & Investment Company). There were virtually no subscribers available in Eddy at this time, but the company sent out hundreds of copies across America and English-speaking Europe in pursuit of possible investors and land buyers. Because of this purpose, readers would never read about anything being wrong in Eddy or the Pecos Valley. This astonishingly early appearance of a newspaper and a Territorial law that required courthouses to keep copies of all newspapers of record, would give Eddy, New Mexico one of the best documented early histories in the United States.

By 1890, the Methodist Circuit Rider Rev. Jackson B. Cox began preaching at the adobe school in Eddy on the 1 st and 2nd Sundays of each month. On the other Sundays, he would alternate between Upper Dark Canyon, Seven Rivers, Lookout, Plowman (on the middle Black River) and Slaughters (on the upper Black River). By this time, there was a drug store, a real estate and insurance business and a lawyer's office in Eddy, and, an estimated 40 women in town. A lime kiln was started near the Pecos River just northwest of Eddy for the purpose of making concrete. It seemed the Eddy Town Company erected early buildings without giving them concrete foundations. A half a dozen cowboys, ending their Christmas spree and heading back to their ranches, fired their guns in the air as they rode out of town. This was a fairly common occurrence in the early years of Eddy.

In the Census of 1890, the town of Eddy had a population of 278. A thousand workers and 300 teams spent nine months excavating the ditches for the Eddy irrigation system. A Jesuit priest, E.A. Antoine, of the El Paso Diocese, began monthly visits to the Pecos Valley to offer Mass for the Catholics, virtually all of whom were Hispanic. The Baptist circuit rider, Rev. J. Midd Hill, visited Eddy in January of 1890. In February, influenza struck the area. It would take several lives. Also, terrible sand storms started to occur. There was now a

Mexican Quarter of about a dozen families living in holes in the bank of the Pecos River, a little northeast of the downtown area of Eddy. A subscription drive was started for a Methodist church building.

Episcopalians began to circulate a subscription paper for a building of their own. The Eddy Missionary Baptist Church was organized by J. Midd Hill. The Episcopalians held their organizational meeting at the adobe school. The Episcopalian Bishop for the Territory of New Mexico was in attendance.

At the end of April of 1890, 10,000 sand bags were being used to stop the seepage at Rock Dam.

Eddy dubbed itself "The Pearl of the Pecos."

A small group of makeshift huts that several Hispanic families were erecting beside the Pecos River was dubbed "Little *Chihuahua*".

In October of 1890, the new Episcopal Rector, Rev. Forrester, arrived in Eddy.

Photos showed hundreds of Hispanic workers in the Pecos Valley at this time, but the *Argus* newspaper never acknowledged their numbers. Instead, the paper continued to stress the idea that "this part of the Territory of New Mexico was different because this was the American part."

The *Argus* newspaper predicted that four national railroads now being built would meet at Eddy shortly. It was also predicted that the Pecos Valley was destined to become the finest vineyard and orchard area in America.

In December 1890, the Pecos Valley Railroad reached Eddy from Pecos, Texas to the south.

PECOS VALLEY RAILROAD

This brought immigrants from Europe and Mexican laborers from Texas and Mexico into the Pecos Valley. The Mexican families built adobe huts on the east side of the Pecos River and it was known as "Little *Chihuahua*."

Catholic Carmelite priests from Marienfeld (now Stanton), Texas, visited the area to ascertain the need for Catholic services. The Diocese of El Paso did not as yet exist and the territory was under the jurisdiction of the Vicar Apostolic of Tucson, Arizona. In 1890, Fr. E.A. Antoine, a Jesuit priest, came from San Elizario, Texas (near El Paso). A foundation was started for a church in 1891, but it failed for lack of money.

By the end of January, 1891, a large spring near Eddy provided more water than was used by Denver, Colorado, which had 25,000 people at the time. It was later called Carlsbad Spring.

In February of 1891, the foundation of the Episcopal Church in Eddy was about completed. The church would be made of rock. The Rev. M.S. Stamp moved to Eddy to become the Baptist minister.

166

In May of 1891, Henri Gaullier, a Swiss immigration official, visited the valley at the invitation of Mr. Hagerman. Gaullier would recommend the Pecos Valley to the Swiss government as an appropriate location to place Swiss settlers. At the end of June, 1891, the foundation had been laid for a Catholic church. Also in June, the Eddy Baptists baptized their first two candidates.

A stone mason would soon start construction on the Episcopalian rock church.

By the end of October, 1891, eight of the adobe cottages being built for the soon-to-arrive Swiss Colony had been finished. A group of 94 Indiana newspapermen visited the valley in two Pullman cars. An article in the newspaper promoted the valley as a good place to grow sugar beets.

Eddy's colored population numbered about 50. It was reported that they were sober, intelligent and industrious. No such compliments were ever paid to the Hispanic community. Part of this distinction possibly came from the fact that so many of Eddy's citizens came here from the South. The foundation of the Methodist church of Eddy was laid. Methodist Elder Crutchfield and Baptist Rev. Stamp both preached impressive sermons against dancing.

By December of 1891, Eddy had a 10-student colored school. Many raisin growers from Fresno, California were relocating to the Pecos Valley.

The Argus newspaper referred to the fine article about the Pecos Valley in the current issue of Mr. R.W. Tansill's *Punch* magazine. To promote his 5-cent cigar, Tansill bought the rights to republish the London *Punch* in America, which he gave away at cigar stores. He used it often as a means to promote the Pecos Valley.

167

The First District Court of the Fifth Judicial District was held in the new Eddy Baptist church.

Local saloons and gambling houses in Eddy were open on Sundays, in violation of New Mexico Territorial Law.

By February of 1892, Eddy's Mexican population was about 10-15% of the total population of the town (something the *Argus* newspaper would never admit). Its Chinese population was about 3%. The nearest Native American Reservation was that of the Mescalero Apache 150 miles away. This ethnic group (Native-Americans) would never have a significant presence in Eddy/Carlsbad.

The bell tower on the Baptist church was completed, and the bell was hung. The Episcopal church would have its first services and its dedication in 1892.

In March of 1892, Jay Gould, the robber baron railroad developer and speculator, in his private railroad car, visited Eddy. Standing on Hagerman Heights, Gould suggested that both he and J.J. Hagerman would both be putting large homes there. Gould's two daughters attended the Baptist church in Eddy while their father was in town.

The Eddy Baptist church was dedicated, free of debt. It cost $2,300 with furnishings. Work was resumed on the Catholic church.

The Episcopal church members subscribed $78 for a 205 pound bell. The Methodist parsonage was being landscaped.

The Eddy Women's Christian Temperance Union (WCTU) signed a petition urging the County Commission to grant no more liquor licenses inside the town of Eddy.

The Methodist Church's foundation had to be taken out and redone. This was because of the shallow underground water.

In June, 1892, the Colored People of Eddy met to plan a June-Teenth Celebration. The Southern Methodist church was ready for its roof. The local Baptist church was also a Southern Baptist church.

Methodist Rev. Crutchfield gave his farewell service. The Pecos Valley Railroad management took possession of their new headquarters building. It was a two-story building. It was eventually going to be moved several blocks across town to become the St. Francis Academy and then the first St. Francis Hospital. The Masons organized in Eddy with their first Worshipful Master.

The stretching of necks without the formality of law (vigilante hangings), by September of 1892, was a laudable industry that was rapidly on the increase in Eddy. If they were happening, neither Eddy newspaper was reporting them. The Methodists held their first services in their unfinished church. The church cost $7,000. The colored people of Eddy had their first religious service, at the Rock School. Previously a butcher shop, and then the location of the "Punkin" Store, this long rock structure was acquired for supplemental school space in the fall of 1892.

Towards the end of September, 1892, G.C. Davis, a colored man, was engaged by the School Board to take charge of a school for colored children.

The people of Vaud (near Eddy) formed a church association.

The colored community of Eddy organized a Methodist Sunday School.

In 1892, another priest came again from San Elizario, Texas (near El Paso) to the town of Eddy. During his visit, he offered Mass in the new Mexican settlement south of Eddy called Phenix, which replaced the settlement called "Little Chihuahua" that had been ordered vacated on the east side of the Pecos River. The regular Missionary Priest from San Elizario who visited the Catholic congregation in Eddy said that most of the Mexicans were now living in Phenix. He stayed for a week, christening babies and performing other needed rites.

A little later, another Jesuit priest, Fr. Carlos Pinto, came to administer the sacraments to a seriously ill Irish Catholic man who had just moved from Nebraska to Eddy. Fr. Pinto saw the need for regular Catholic services in Eddy. This need was conveyed to the Bishop of Tucson, Arizona, who in turn petitioned the Carmelite Fathers of Stanton, Texas, to take charge.

During 1893, there was a fairly constant reporting of violence within the Hispanic-American community in Eddy. A killing seemed to be occurring about once every two months.

The Northern Methodists in Eddy were putting up a Tabernacle, a small weatherized octagonal tent. Reverend Stamp baptized six in the Pecos River behind Hagerman Dam, in the presence of an immense audience.

By April, 1893, the Silver King, the largest saloon in Phenix (a notorious area of Eddy), planned to hold regular Sunday sacred concerts. Proceeds would go to charity. No alcohol was to be sold.

Four Blacks were united in a double wedding by Rector Bennett at Grace Episcopal Church. Both grooms were employed at the Hagerman Hotel. This was the first church wedding in Eddy.

It was being said that ten acres around Eddy, properly worked, was more productive than 160 acres in Iowa or Nebraska.

In July, James Barrett killed two men at the McMillan Dam construction camp. He would later be hanged in Eddy County's only legal hanging.

In August, the Episcopal Church Women's Guild set up Eddy's first public Hospital. They would run it until August of 1894, when the Eddy Hospital Association would be set up to take over its operation.

The original adobe school in Eddy was being changed into a Charity Hospital. Joseph Hayman started a dry goods store in Eddy. A Jewish-American, he appeared to be the first Jewish businessman in Eddy.

By the end of 1893, Catholic Mass was offered monthly in an old adobe school. By November of 1893, a cornerstone had been blessed and laid for a Catholic church. By Christmas, the church was completed and dedicated to St. Edward the Confessor.

The altar was an old packing case. A cedar tree with a curtain thrown over it served as a confessional. The congregation knelt on a dirt floor. Planks over carpenter "horses" served as pews or benches. An open fire of mesquite branches burned on the dirt floor for heat in the winter with the smoke drifting out through unfinished window openings.

The Eddy Presbyterian Church was organized in 1894. In April of 1894, the Colored Methodist Church organized in Eddy. It had eight members.

In May of 1894, the Eddy County Hospital Association was set up to take over the running of the Eddy Charity Hospital.

In June of 1894, Rev. William Lee Lawrence became the first Presbyterian minister in Eddy. The church was not finished until May of 1896.

On September 14, 1894, James Barrett was hanged at 1:30pm on a scaffold near the cemetery. Old timers would later remember that the town of Eddy turned out in force, many with picnic baskets. School was dismissed at Florence town south of Eddy so the students could attend the event. It drew better than a circus. Sheriff Kemp pulled the lever.

Rev. Uriah Tracy was the new Rector of Grace Episcopal Church in Eddy.

The Eddy Hospital closed because there were no patients. Plans were afoot to erect a $1,800 stone Presbyterian church in Eddy. Mrs. Harry Hart of Eddy died at the age of thirty-one during childbirth.

Rev. M.C. Stamp of the Eddy Baptist church died of consumption (tuberculosis).

The railroad Gospel Car "Emmanuel" arrived in Eddy in April, 1895, for a month-long revival. A bad windstorm took out the windows of the Methodist church.

In June of 1895, young Tommy Carson died of strychnine poisoning. He was herding sheep in Johnson Canyon.

In July, the small Piontkowski son was scalded to death in a wash day tragedy.

Colored minister W.P. Roberts left town fast over charges that he had been playing around with a young girl.

A Mexican woman committed suicide at Phenix with morphine.

Bids were out for a 28 foot by 45 foot First Presbyterian Church, to be of stone.

In 1895, the first resident pastor of St. Edward's Catholic Church in Eddy was installed. He learned to speak Spanish and labored zealously for the Spanish-speaking people living in the Phenix settlement south of Eddy. Phenix was a rough settlement of huts, frame shacks and five saloons. Gambling and vice one could easily find in Phenix. Hardly a Saturday night passed without someone being injured or killed in fights. To save many good people forced to live there, the Catholic pastor bought 10 acres of land, the present San Jose section of Carlsbad, and had it laid out in lots. He invited the people to leave Phenix and move to this new section of Eddy. When, in 1896, three men were shot to death in Phenix, the end of Phenix occurred and the beginning of the Eddy area named San Jose. When the priest/pastor arrived, he found only four or five Mexican children attending school. So, he petitioned the school board for a school for the Mexican children, but was refused. So, on opening day, he presented himself to the teachers with 28 Mexican children. They were not admitted. The following day, the padre came again, but with 40 little ones. While teachers seemed willing to allow the Mexican children to attend along with the Anglo children, the parents of the latter objected. Finally, the school board established a school for the Mexican children in an old adobe building south of town.

In 1896, the Eddy Methodist Church was wired for electricity.

In January, political candidate William Jennings Bryan spoke at the Eddy County Courthouse in Eddy on bi-metalism [a system of allowing the unrestricted currency of two metals, gold and silver, as legal tender, at a fixed ratio to each other]. He spoke for 3 hours. Only about a hundred people attended. He was taken on an outing to Eddy Reservoir.

Reverend Father H. Kempker arrived in Eddy from Prescott, Arizona to lead the local Catholics.

The Reverend J. Mid Hill committed suicide, drowning himself in the Penasco River.

In May of 1896, St. Edward's received its first organ and held its first sung High Mass.

The rock work on the Presbyterian one-room Austin limestone chapel was finished. The church would not be enlarged beyond this until 1917.

St. Edward's Catholic Church in Eddy had the Catholic missions of Artesia, Hope, Dayton, Lakewood, the Mexican parish of San Jose near Eddy, and, south of Eddy, Loving, Malaga and Ojo Azul.

In 1896, the Bishop of Tucson, Arizona secured the services of a young priest from Iowa, whom he appointed first resident priest of Eddy County. This was the Rev. Herman Kempker, who spent most of his time among the Mexicans.

The Presbyterian church was being roofed.

Helen Calvani was born in Eddy. She would be the first Anglo baby baptized at the new St. Edward's Church.

In October, Father Kempker was giving one sermon in English and one sermon in Spanish each Sunday.

The Eddy Town Trustees repealed the anti-gambling ordinance, letting gambling houses back into Eddy town. It was decided they could be better controlled by town ordinance than by letting them float, uncontrolled, out at Phenix. The local public schools closed for lack of moneys to pay teacher salaries. These shortened school years would occur frequently over the next few years.

The Eddy Town Trustees, in February of 1897, under great pressure from the churches, again made gambling illegal in Eddy. Newly-installed Sheriff Les Dow (age 36) was shot before the Eddy Post Office. He died hours later. Two men, Mr. Kemp and Mr. Kennon, were arrested for the shooting. They would ultimately be acquitted the following year.

A local chapter of the Women's Christian Temperance Union was reorganized in Eddy with 17 members. It quickly became a significant force in the town fights with the saloons.

In May, the Research Circle had its first meeting in Eddy. It would later become the Literary Club in February of 1898 and then the Women's Club in May of 1904. It began as solely a group of Episcopal women meeting.

In September, the Mexican Community of Eddy put on three night performances, in costume, of *Los Pastores* at the Opera House to help raise money for St. Edward's Church.

In November, a Baptist church was organized in Florence, south of Eddy. Actually, they just moved the charter of the defunct Lookout Baptist Church to Florence. In December, Bishop Kendrick gave Episcopal Confirmation to 4 women.

African-Americans Miss Willie Jones and J.M. Summey wed at her parents' place. Eddy opened the first office in New Mexico for enlisting volunteers for the War with Spain. Two Sisters of Our Lady of Mercy were in town to consider Eddy for a School for Girls. At the end of May, Thomas Roger hung himself from a cottonwood tree. Augustin Lerma killed Senior Marianna in a Phenix brothel.

On July 4, 1898, Eddy had a Fourth of July Rodeo. Constable Dee Harkey later said that Will Rogers, an area cowboy (yes, that Will Rogers), participated in this rodeo. Will Rogers was not mentioned in the newspaper coverage, but only a few persons were.

The citizens of San Jose celebrated *Diez y Seis* (Mexican Independence Day) with a mimic bull fight and numerous kinds of games.

In February of 1899, the Eddy County Hospital incorporated. A residence was turned into a 4-room Hospital. About 1900, this Hospital would shift to a two-story frame building.

In 1899, the name of the town of Eddy was considering changing its name to Carlsbad after the mineral springs in the city of Karlsbad, Germany. In February of 1899, Eddy hit a temperature of one degree Fahrenheit above zero. A genuine colored minstrel show played to a packed house at the Tansill Opera House.

The Eddy schools closed for the year (after a 6-month term). An Eddy newspaper lauded the Eddy Sugar Beet Factory as the greatest manufacturing institution in the Territory of New Mexico.

Fr. Herman Kempker died in Eddy in May of 1899. Two Mormon missionaries visited Eddy. This was treated as a very unusual event for Eddy, so it may have been the first such visit. Mrs. Nannie Robb died at the age of 52. The first local member of the Methodist Congregation, she was given a huge funeral by her fellow members. Prairie schooners from Texas passed through Eddy regularly. By a vote of 83 to 43, the town name of Eddy was changed to Carlsbad. Carlsbad was the largest cattle shipping point in the Southwest. It was now the ranchers who were running Carlsbad.

In August of 1899, the Eddy Missionary Baptist Church voted to change its name to First Baptist Church. The death of Emma Hardcastle (age 11) led to the suicide of her friend, Beulah Bryant.

In October of 1899, Catholic Sisters Berchman and Mary Angela of Ft. Stanton, Texas were in Carlsbad to explore the possibility of placing a Sanitarium and Female Academy in town.

In 1900, thousands of acres of apple orchards were in the Pecos Valley, but nearly all of them would be gone by 1916. It was later said that nearly half the farms in the valley had been abandoned by the year 1900. A major influenza epidemic hit the Pecos Valley. Grandma Anderson took care of 60 influenza patients and did not lose a single one.

In the 1900 Census, Carlsbad had a population of 962. A newspaper in Carlsbad warned not to boom Carlsbad for health seekers. Probably no other town in the U.S. had been so persistently boomed as was Carlsbad, and there was probably no place where the evils of such booming were more apparent. Sixteen-year old Florence Hunt committed suicide, which was thought to have been caused by an infatuation with Jerome Edwards.

Fr. Elias Mayer arrived to take charge of St. Edward's Catholic Church. Henry Jones, who attempted suicide with a knife across his throat, was sewn up. He suffered from something resembling epilepsy.

In July of 1900, Fr. Patrick dies in La Huerta, north of Carlsbad.

The discovery of large deposits of guano [bat excrement] was being mentioned in one of the Carlsbad newspapers as something destined to become a major new New Mexico industry. This appeared to be the second reference in the newspaper to the Bat Cave [Carlsbad Caverns].

The local saloons agreed to close on Sundays.

In February of 1901, the results of the official 1900 Census figures gave Eddy County a population of 3,229 and Carlsbad a population of 963.

Six unfortunate women each contributed $9 to the Carlsbad Court, charged with waywardness. Three were Anglo, three were Hispanic.

In June of 1901, seven girls of ill repute were jailed overnight. Flitting about the streets in negligee costume became common in Carlsbad. Sheriff Stewart was fining the prostitutes every day. In August, a

Mexican Baptist Church began forming in Carlsbad. Mrs. Traynor from Carlsbad sang at the local memorial service for President McKinley after his assassination.

In October of 1901, Ed Collins, in delirium tremors, injured himself jumping from the 2nd story gallery in front of the Mullane Building in Carlsbad. A house of prostitution was at this second-story location.

In 1901, Negro Tom Harvey got 100 days in jail for assault with words on a white woman. The *Current* newspaper commented. "The law-abiding colored population of Carlsbad owe it as a duty to take this fellow, with his beastly attitude, and give him a good sound whipping with five minutes to leave town. They may well regard his action as a menace to their future peace and prosperity here. Had he chosen some well-known woman, rather than one almost wholly unknown, he would now be in his grave. If the negroes do not take some action the white citizens may give Harvey a dose too strong for his constitution." The editors of the *Current* at this time were two brothers out of the Deep South.

Carlsbad was hit by typhoid fever. C.H. McLenathen was confirmed in the Episcopal Church.

From 1899 through 1902, Catholics in the town of Carlsbad again came under the care of the Carmelite priests of Stanton, Texas. Mass was first offered in Loving (south of Carlsbad) in 1900. In 1901, the first Catholic mission was preached in Carlsbad. The mission priest preached twice daily at the Eddy County Courthouse. From 1901 through 1902, this famous Texas missionary preacher, who lived in Pecos, Texas, served Carlsbad. The first San Jose Parish church was built in Carlsbad. It was an adobe church.

The Mexicans organized a second Baptist Church in Carlsbad.

In 1902, the schools closed for the rest of the year. They ran out of money.

In May of 1902, the Carlsbad Schools had a graduating class of three (all girls). A nine-mile long fire in the Guadalupe Mountains destroyed much fine range land.

In August of 1902, the Carlsbad Town Council was upset by the prostitutes on Mulberry Drive going up to Hagerman Heights. Black ranch cook Dick Jackson died. The 25-year servant always wore women's clothing (and went barefooted) while cooking. Ranchers from across the Southwest came to his funeral, which was said to have had the longest cortege ever-before seen in Carlsbad.

In October of 1902, Mexican-Americans were excluded from the Democratic Primary. Rev. E.S. Goodson became the new Methodist minister in Carlsbad.

There was a new town ordinance forbidding spitting on sidewalks and requiring cuspidors in all businesses. Five women were indicted for keeping bawdy houses and were given 30 days to move outside the town limits.

The original adobe Catholic Church of San Jose was built, giving its name to that community.

There was no resident priest at San Jose Catholic Church until 1905.

In February of 1903, the Carlsbad Sugar Beet Factory burned to the ground. The Carlsbad Railway Depot burned down. This was the original Depot. The fire occurred on a bitterly cold night, and one of the volunteer firemen caught pneumonia, which ultimately led to his death.

In June of 1903, the Methodist Parsonage was relocated to face the same direction as the church. In August, the new Colored Methodist Church was dedicated.

In October of 1903, Elmore Freeman (age 32), the son of Judge Freeman, committed suicide. All local Ministers refused to marry a well-known divorced couple. An Episcopal Parsonage was being built just west of the church. The first local Official Board for the Christian Church was organized in Carlsbad. In December of 1903, the first Catholic High Mass was said at San Jose Catholic Church.

E. McQueen Gray, from Carlsbad, was considered the finest amateur Shakespearian actor that ever appeared in England. According to Lord Tennyson, he was the only man who knew how to read Shakespeare.

Excavation began for a rock Christian Church. The Episcopalians were planning to have services in French on the 1 st and 3rd Sundays of each month to serve the French and Swiss Colonies in Carlsbad. In March, the Colored Methodist Church, just west of the San Jose Catholic Church, burned down.

A priest usually made a monthly visit to both the San Jose and St. Edward's Catholic Churches.

In May of 1904, an ordinance was passed regarding spitting in Carlsbad, over worries that consumptives (those who were suffering from consumption) might do this (spitting) and spread their disease. J.H. Johns was named the first (unpaid) sexton of the Carlsbad Cemetery to stop the practice of people who drifted onto the grounds and dug graves most any old place, often in the streets.

In July, E. McQueen Gray, from the Carlsbad area, was ordained an Episcopal Minister in El Paso, Texas. He was one of only 6 surviving scholars who received the Degree of Master of Literature from Oxford University in England.

The Mexican Baptist Church formed in San Jose in August of 1904.

In October of 1904, a mighty flood swept down the Pecos Valley. It was the biggest ever.

Eusebio Pompa married Sebastina Griego at San Jose Catholic Church.

In November of 1904, Etienne Bujac, Ill, was christened at Grace Church in Carlsbad. In a violation of all tradition, Col. Bujac, his father, served as his Godfather, and Mary Robinson of Colorado Springs, not the child's aunt, served as his Godmother.

With the coming of the Franciscan Fathers from Roswell in 1903, a new era of Catholic growth began in Carlsbad. A priest began residing at San Jose Church in 1905. The first Mass was said at San Jose church in 1903. A Franciscan Father attended the faithful both of Carlsbad and Artesia, from Roswell, until 1905.

Fr. Juvenal Schnorbus became the first resident priest at San Jose Catholic Church in Carlsbad. The St. Edward's Catholic Church planned to erect a Parsonage (Rectory).

Rev. E. McQueen Gray was now the District Missionary for the Episcopal Diocese.

In April of 1905, the Territorial Attorney General voided the Carlsbad city election because voters had to select ballots from two piles, in public view. The Eddy County artesian water belt was the best in the world according to the newspaper.

In July of 1905, the Catholic Sisters of Wichita offered to establish a non-denominational boarding school in Carlsbad if the citizens would provide a location and building delivered to them furnished. The Sisters would maintain it. Roswell got a Catholic Sisters Hospital. In August of 1905, a committee planned to buy the old Pecos Valley

Railroad General Office, now unused, for the Catholic Sisters' School. A Mr. Stevens from New York donated a piece of land for it. The physical moving of this large building was considered by all to be one of the most impressive things accomplished in Carlsbad in years.

In September of 1905, Sister Superior Ursula and Sisters Florentine and Virginia arrived in Carlsbad. Tuition in their new school would be $1 per month at the primary level, $2 per month for the higher grades. In October, the Sisters' School had 32 students.

Four cases of diphtheria closed the public school.

In 1906, a baptistry was built in the Carlsbad Baptist Church. Before this point, their baptisms had taken place in the Pecos River. The bell tower was added to Grace Episcopal Church.

In February, 1906, the Sisters of the Most Precious Blood moved into their handsome new home. The Presbyterians were now building a Parsonage just north of their church.

Carlsbad was the only town left in Eddy County that still permitted legal gambling. There were already some 60 professional gamblers in the area.

On Halloween (October 31, 1906), Carrie Nation spoke at the Eddy County Courthouse in Carlsbad, both afternoon and evening. But, according to the newspaper, she sadly failed to physically attack any of the local saloons. In December, it was reported that 8 sheepherders died in the recent blizzard. The regional press reported many more.

In January, 1907, Grace Episcopal Church received a new walnut wood altar, a tribute to Grandma Anderson. Rev. E. McQueen Gray was now a General Missionary of the Episcopal Church. The Epworth League organized in Carlsbad.

In March of 1907, work on the memorial tower at Grace Church continued. A 1,040 lb. bell for Grace Episcopal Church arrived. The Tenderloin District of Carlsbad had a fire. Two more buildings burned in the Tenderloin District. Both buildings were tenanted by prostitutes. The newspaper said, "If you permit licensed gambling, you cannot do away with prostitution."

The Grace Episcopal Church tower was completed.

In September of 1907, the Carlsbad City Council approved a license for an in-town house of prostitution.

In June of 1909, the Rev. E. McQueen Gray of Carlsbad was appointed President of the University of New Mexico. In September, William Jennings Bryan gave his Prince of Peace speech to 800 people in the new high school auditorium. He was in Carlsbad as a Chautauqua speaker. In November, the Sisters of St. Francis purchased the property of the Sisters of the Most Precious Blood. The Sisters of St. Francis would later convert the school to a hospital. The Father Abogast rock tower on San Jose Catholic Church was almost completed.

In February of 1909, the name of the Carlsbad Missionary Baptist Church was officially changed to that of the First Baptist Church of Carlsbad.

In March of 1910, the Women's Temperance Union organized in Carlsbad. Carlsbad now had a National Anti-Saloon League chapter. In June, the St. Francis Xavier Academy closed its doors for lack of patronage. Carlsbad saloon owners agreed to close on Sundays.

In July of 1910, the *Circulo Catolico Mexicano* was formed among the men of San Jose. The name was soon changed to that of *Sociedad Mutualista Mexicano*. The San Jose Church bell tower was completed. A cross had been placed at its top.

E.T. Carter of Carlsbad was escorting a second group of Mennonites who were looking over the Pecos Valley.

Blondie Holland, a young colored woman and cocaine addict, committed suicide.

In May of 1911, Tansill Farm, most recently the Benson Farm, was sold to the Mennonites, who moved to the Carlsbad area from Oklahoma, where they had been since 1901. The farm had 602 irrigated acres. The Sisters of the Most Precious Blood returned in May of 1911 to open a Sanitarium in what was previously their boarding school.

Mr.'s Joe Walker and John Hart shot it out in a duel at 40 paces. Both survived.

In July, 1911, the Mennonites, who had purchased 1,320 acres around Loving, south of Carlsbad, moved in. Flooding occurred again in Carlsbad. Rampaging Dark Canyon melted many of the San Jose adobe buildings and severely damaged the San Jose Church. The Mennonites paid $53,000 for the Benson Section of Carlsbad.

In August of 1911, Rev. E. McQueen Gray, from Carlsbad, President of the University of New Mexico, was to deliver a speech at the First Methodist Church and another at the Hotel Schlitz. In September, Father Florian took charge of St. Edward's Catholic Church. Fr. Arbogast was reassigned to San Jose Parish.

In November of 1911, the Sisters of St. Francis bought out the property of the Sisters of the Most Precious Blood. Mother Ann & Sisters Francis, Rufina and Boniface came to Carlsbad to set up a sanitarium, the forerunner of the St. Francis Hospital.

Rice Memorial (Colored) Methodist Church was founded in Carlsbad by Rev. John Rice. In January of 1912, the Territory of New Mexico became a State of the United States.

In March of 1912, prominent area rancher Roy Burnett (age 31), owner of the D Ranch, killed himself at his Carlsbad home in a one-person game of Russian roulette. In April, the *Titanic* sank. It would later be said that the chief investor for the Artesia-to-Hope-to-El Paso railroad died in this tragedy, bringing those railroad plans to an untimely end. The Franciscan Fathers were at St. Edward's Catholic Church in Carlsbad.

In July, Dr. E. McQueen Gray, past President of the University of New Mexico, was advanced to full Episcopalian priesthood.

Father Arbogast sought to have San Jose annexed to Carlsbad to get rid of the new saloon that was in San Jose.

In November of 1912, the Presbyterians voted to enlarge their church, adding a Sunday School on the north. In December, the big wedding of Anita Hernandez to Susano Baca occurred in Cuba (west of Otis, south of Carlsbad). Father Arbogast performed the ceremony. A large pavilion was built for the occasion. There were 100 guests for the three-day feast.

The State of New Mexico passed a law restricting saloons and brothels near schools, churches and public buildings.

In March of 1913, the Methodist Church at Loving was dedicated.

The *Los Angeles Express* newspaper announced that the Carlsbad Chamber of Commerce had invited two California Japanese to take up land around Carlsbad. The *Argus* said that this was not so. According to the newspaper, "Carlsbad did not want the Japs. No cheap little brown men would be asked to come to Carlsbad." The *Argus* said that "It was the Artesia Chamber of Commerce that invited those Japs." The *Argus* added, "The deceitful lying Jap is not wanted." It was reported that Carlsbad had more flies than anyone else. Father Gilbert Schults was the new Pastor of St. Edward's

Catholic Church, replacing Fr. Florien Bricae. The Methodist Wesley Bible Class Sunday School building was almost finished.

In January of 1914, there were recent big doings among the colored population over the wedding of Miss Zelma Smith and Jesse Stephens. Rev. John Rice performed the ceremony at the residence of Clarence Penn.

In February of 1914, Rocky Arroyo School got a new organ for its church services. According to the newspaper, "Faggot parties were in vogue". In April, a 20 by 26 foot Sacristy was erected on the west side of San Jose Church by Father Arbogast. In July of 1914, there was the first known reference in a local newspaper to a tourist.

In February of 1915, St. Edward's Catholic Church had a passion-vine motif painted around the main sanctuary. St. Edward's now has a chandelier donated by two parishioners. In November, two attempts were made to burn down the Mexican School in San Jose.

St. Francis Hospital opened as a Tubercular Sanitarium. It would become a General Hospital in 1917. The St. Edward's 2-room parochial school opened. Run by the Sisters of the Most Precious Blood, it started with 18 students.

In March of 1916, the Carlsbad National Guard (Company B-Cavalry) was called together and ordered to Columbus, New Mexico to pursue Pancho Villa. They would not return to Carlsbad until April 5, 1917. The Carlsbad Guard Unit was said to be the only such Unit that saw active duty (briefly) in Mexico (one weekend). The Carlsbad Regulars, as they were called, headed for the Mexican border, without the man who organized and commanded them, Maj. Bujac, who the Army refused to call to active duty. There were rumors in town that he had a drinking problem.

An African-American band was brought to Carlsbad to play for the Commerce Club, but was pelted with rotten eggs. It left without playing.

In May, 1916, there were only 8 Carlsbad High School graduates, all girls, because the boys were in the National Guard and were out pursuing Pancho Villa.

The Public Utilities Company discovered that the Chinese Laundry had sleeping accommodations for about 40 underneath the floor in a windowless and unventilated cellar with an open sewer, like the 1 st century. The new St. Francis Hospital, being conducted by the Sisters of the Most Precious Blood, opened for the reception of patients.

In January of 1917, the Presbyterians started a 30 foot by 30 foot addition on the south of their existing church. The Mormons withdrew from Northern Mexico. The Presbyterian Guild was organized in Carlsbad.

In March of 1917, the Presbyterian Church had a cornerstone ceremony. They included a sealed box. In April, St. Edward's Catholic Church acquired the 40 acre Tucker place for a Catholic Cemetery. The Catholic School in Carlsbad graduated its first three 8th Grade students.

In July, 1917, Carlsbad's Christian Scientists raised $135 for War Relief.

In August, the Rev. Uriah Tracy, Grace Episcopal Rector, 1894-1898, died in Carlsbad at the age of 88.

In September, the Methodist youth re-established the Epworth League. Forty children in the local Loyal Temperance League marched while singing Temperance songs and gave Prohibition yells.

In October of 1917, the Crawford Theater showed *The Birth of a Nation*. The Editor of the *Argus* newspaper applauded its portrayal of the Ku Klux Klan as the salvation of the Post-Civil War South. In November, the salaries of New Mexico's rural teachers were the lowest in America.

Henry Lange was taken from his home and tarred and feathered as a pro-German sympathizer. In May, the Methodist Young People held a Japanese Lawn Social to raise money.

In June of 1918, the city of Carlsbad had a new Anti-Vagrancy Law.

In July, Carlsbad prided itself on having led the State of New Mexico in providing men for the War [WWI].

In August, 1918, Maj. Dean Smith surprised Carlsbad by landing his military plane in the Irv Osborne alfalfa field. The plane was swarmed, and the alfalfa was ruined. When Mr. Osborne objected, he was denounced as un-American. Boys poured yellow paint on his buggy. Fr. Arbogast, the priest for eleven years at San Jose, was shifted to Roswell. A new 30 x 50 open-air roofed Tabernacle was erected at Queen, in the Guadalupe Mountains. Rev. William Beauchamp of Lovington, New Mexico held the first camp meeting there.

Carlsbad High School was requiring 30 minutes of military drill per day for all boys and girls. The Carlsbad paper said "This is no time for people who speak with a German accent to make remarks that are not thoroughly understood."

In October of 1918, the Spanish Influenza Epidemic spread across Carlsbad. Sister Osmunda died of influenza. The churches and school closed because of the influenza epidemic.

Albert Givens (age 17) died of influenza. A Carlsbad High School Senior, he was the only boy remaining in the Senior Class. All the others had left for the military. In December, bootlegging seemed to be flourishing in and around Carlsbad.

In January of 1919, Elena Quinones was the only Mexican-American student in Carlsbad High School. In February, Rev. Arbogast Reisler, who was responsible for building the San Jose Catholic Church tower, died in Roswell at the age of 44. He came to Carlsbad August 20, 1907 and was there 11 years. In June, the Christian Scientists of Carlsbad were meeting every Sunday morning at 11am in the Women's Club Building. The foundation was laid for a $5,000 Baptist Church at Loving.

In February, the Eddy County Health Board forbade all public gatherings because of influenza.

In April, the Baptists in Carlsbad completed their 2-room Sunday School building behind the church. In July, a new priest's residence was constructed at San Jose Catholic Church. It was of concrete and had six rooms. In November, the foundation for the new Sisters Hospital went in. The new Sisters Hospital would have three stories.

In January of 1922, the First Baptist Church of Carlsbad was damaged by fire. In October, the new concrete Catholic Church at San Jose was dedicated.

The year 1923 saw the San Jose Catholic Parochial School opened in Carlsbad, staffed by Franciscan Sisters from Indiana. The Catholic Sisters' Hospital announced its grand opening on March 13th. In March, the third floor of the Sisters Hospital was for the Sisters only. It was divided into seven individual rooms. In July, the local Baptists, by resolution, took positions against the game of bridge, modern dance, pool halls and a number of other local problems.

In December, the old Carlsbad Methodist Church was razed.

In February of 1926, the foundation was laid for the new Carlsbad Methodist Church. In April, the Carlsbad Church of Christ organized. In October, the Methodists were meeting in the basement of their new building.

January of 1927 saw giant girders for the roof going up on the new Carlsbad Methodist Church. In March, the first church service was held in Carlsbad Caverns. In November, St. Edward's Catholic Parish planned to build a new concrete church.

In March of 1928, while in California, Bob Dow of Carlsbad visited western movie star Tom Mix. Dow gave Mix the gun that killed Billy the Kid. Dow said that Tom Mix, at one time, worked for him as a Deputy Sheriff in Eddy County. His pre-stage name was not known. Roswell saw three burning crosses recently. Their Ku Klux Klan group, however, denied responsibility. In April, the final service was held in the old Carlsbad Christian Church. In May, the Presbyterians added a Sunday School room. In August, the Carlsbad Christian Church began construction of a $16,000 building. In November, the local (and regional) Presbyterian Church went from being Southern Presbyterian to being United Presbyterian.

In 1929, the superiors of the Franciscans from Cincinnati, Ohio, decided to withdraw their priests from the parishes and missions of Eddy County. Their withdrawal brought a new group of Franciscans of the Friars Minor Conventual (Conventual Franciscans) from Louisville, Kentucky to Carlsbad. The first of the new Franciscans arrived in Carlsbad in 1929. One of the Franciscans was assigned to live in Carlsbad as an associate pastor with care of the faithful in Artesia. We see the spiritual work in Eddy County being handed on from priest to priest, from one group of religious priests to another. St. Edward Parish in Carlsbad was the first church serving especially the English-speaking Catholics. Assistance was to come from it for the parish of St. Anthony in Artesia. San Jose Mission, now San Jose Parish in Carlsbad, was seen growing alongside St. Edwards to serve the Spanish-speaking of Carlsbad, Malaga, Loving and then finally, also, Our Lady of Grace Church in Artesia.

The cornerstone was laid for a new Carlsbad Christian Church in March of 1929.

In October, the Knights of Columbus were organized in Carlsbad. On December 30, the First Assembly of God Church in Carlsbad burned down.

In 1930, the African-American Mt. Olive Missionary Baptist Church was organized in Carlsbad. It would later move. In June, it was noted that many Carlsbad women had taken up smoking in the last six months. The women said, "The movie stars all do it." A Lucky Strike cigarette ad that appeared in Carlsbad said that smoking helped women control their weight. In December of 1930, Negro Dan Palmer was shot to death in the Doc Vest sheep pen in Carlsbad. Charges were never filed, nor explanations printed. In 1931, local Baptists helped provide materials to build a Spanish Baptist Church in Carlsbad. In March of 1931, the Methodists completed their new church. In April, the formal dedication of the new Methodist Church happened. In September, the Methodists established a Sacramento Summer Assembly four miles west of Weed, in the mountains west of Carlsbad. In November, it was reported that H.E. Hubert, the Eddy County Welfare Officer, handled 1,618 welfare cases during the year of 1931. He mainly gave out old clothing from his office. J. Henry Yates (age 59), owner of the D Ranch and D Camp killed himself in a game of Russian roulette at his home on Greene Heights. The town of Loving was feeding 31 children who came to school each day without lunch.

In March, Fernando Ruiz was sent to jail for selling marijuana, probably, a first for Carlsbad. In April, work was started at the Methodist Sacramento Camp in the mountains west of Carlsbad.

In 1933, a minus 31 degree Fahrenheit freeze killed the remaining orchards of the valley. Fourteen children of poor families in and near Carlsbad died from lack of proper diet and housing in the last three weeks.

In March of 1934, a Negro Boy Scout Troop was organized at the Colored Methodist/Episcopal Church of Carlsbad. In May, Clyde Barrow and Bonnie Parker (Bonnie and Clyde) were killed. The comment of Bonnie's local aunt, Mrs. E.M. Stamp was: "I'm glad she's dead at last."

In January, Carlsbad High School offered a course on New Testament History. The Presbyterians added a north addition that gave them a larger auditorium and a basement with a kitchen. The City Council also announced that liquor sales would be restricted to two blocks downtown.

First Baptist Church of Carlsbad was planning to build a new $45,000 church where the parsonage was presently located. In December, work was about to start on the new Baptist Church.

In January of 1936, Mr. Hoffman opened a Night High School for Negro adults in Carlsbad. In March, Rev. Bill Dando from Flagstaff, Arizona agreed to accept the Presbyterian pulpit in Carlsbad. The new St.Edward's Church was designed by Robert Turk. In May, St. Edward's Church construction began. The Presbyterians were erecting a new manse. Construction began on the new Carlsbad Church of Christ. In October, the new St. Edward's Catholic Church was dedicated. In November, the cornerstone was laid for the new Lutheran Church in Carlsbad. It was made of native stone.

In January of 1937, Rev. Wiggins opened the new Carlsbad Church of Christ building. In March, the new Lutheran Church in Carlsbad was dedicated. In April, the Kiwanis Club organized in Carlsbad. Rev. Dando was elected their first local President. The Mexican Episcopal

Church of Carlsbad, with its 35 members, was seeking funds for remodeling. The church was a converted business building.

In July, Joe Johns of Bonnie and Clyde fame became the new Carlsbad Chief of Police (after Craddock Rule resigned).

In July of 1939, Carlsbad had been dumping raw sewage directly into the Pecos River since 1909. The new Carlsbad Sewage Plant had just begun operation.

In 1940, First Baptist Church of Carlsbad organized two Missions, one for Mt. Olive Baptist Church (Black), the other, the West Side Mission, which would later become the Hillcrest Baptist Church. In March, Father Divine, the famous Negro religious leader, visited Carlsbad.

The Nazarene Church in Carlsbad started a church building in 1940.

In 1941, the results of the 1940 Census showed that Eddy County was the 3rd largest county in the State of New Mexico. In May, a major flood swept through Carlsbad. Six hundred were left homeless, particularly in San Jose. It was estimated that 1,000 had been left homeless from the flood. At least twelve were missing. In the end, only one body was found.

An even-worse-than-the-May flood swept through San Jose. Hundreds were left homeless. Ten drowned, seven of them were African-Americans. In October, Gladys James of Carlsbad was named head of the El Paso Diocesan Catholic Women.

In February of 1942, there was a Pentecostal Mission in Carlsbad. In March, Mt. Olive Baptist Church (Colored) received a new pastor, Rev. O.E Dixon. Also receiving a new pastor was the Carlsbad Church of God in Christ (Colored), Rev. S.W. Williams. The new concrete Church of Christ in Carlsbad was completed. In April, Gladys James of Carlsbad was elected a Director of the National Council of Catholic Women. In May, the Knights of Columbus held a High Mass in the Carlsbad Caverns, the Most Reverend Father Metzger (future Bishop Metzger) of El Paso presiding. The Carlsbad Army Air Base Chapel was dedicated in October of 1942. The Rev. Sidney Metzger was named Bishop of El Paso, Texas in 1942.

In February, the new Rice Memorial Church was dedicated in Carlsbad. In June, the *Sociedad Hispano-Americano* (for both men and women) was organized in Carlsbad. In December, the Hillcrest Methodist Church formally opened.

In 1944, the National Park Service was ordered to stop the Rock of Ages religious ceremony in Carlsbad Caverns. Rev. L.B. Trone replaced Rev. C.E. Jameson at Carlsbad First Methodist Church. A High School was established for Carlsbad Negroes. In December, Rev. Constant Klein died.

In January of 1945, Carlsbad First Christian Church burned its 20-year-old mortgage. In February, the new rector for Grace Episcopal Church, R.H. Cannon, arrived. In March, the Cavern Theater in Carlsbad began showing a Spanish language film every Tuesday and Wednesday. The theater continued with its English language films on all other days.

In August of 1945, the first services were held in the new Hillcrest Baptist Church auditorium in Carlsbad. In September, Fr. Gabriel Eilers succeeded Fr. Clement Orth at St. Edward's Catholic Church. Orth, who had been in Carlsbad for six years, was being moved to Kentucky. Dr. W.J. Dando resigned his pastorate at First Presbyterian Church. Spanish classes were being offered to all students in Carlsbad, 4th grade through 6th They were not compulsory, however. In December, Rev. Joseph S. Willis replaced Rev. Dando at First Presbyterian Church.

In February, the Rev. A.L. Goodwin resigned at First Baptist Church of Carlsbad. The Otis Baptist Church was dedicated.

The old Mexican Methodist Mission in Carlsbad, built in 1908, came down, along with its bell tower. The Mexican Methodist Church would be moved. The new Church of God building was completed. The Methodists were awaiting the arrival of their new $11,000 pipe organ.

Catholic Bishop Metzger blessed the new Our Lady of Grace Catholic Church in Loving. The building had been the Carlsbad Army Air Base Chapel.

In April, work started on the new St. Edward's Elementary School. Construction began on the Hillcrest Church of Christ in Carlsbad. An architect's drawing was completed for the proposed new First Presbyterian Church.

The Carlsbad City Police arrested 13 boys and girls caught in a raid on a club. Whiskey and beer were confiscated. Those involved were ages 14 to 19. Four days later, the Police arrested 8 boys and girls, ages 15 to 19, in a raid on a house. Whiskey was confiscated.

In January of 1949, the new Minister of the First Baptist Church of Carlsbad was Rev. J. Melvin Ray. In February, students moved into the new St. Edward's Elementary School. In April, the newly remodeled Mt. Olive Baptist Church (colored) was dedicated. Rev. Edwin V. Byrne, Archbishop of Santa Fe, conducted a Mass in the Carlsbad Caverns. May marked the formal dedication of the new First Methodist organ and chimes. The San Jose Knights of Columbus Council (the first indication that they existed separately from the Carlsbad Knights of Columbus) received the State of New Mexio Efficiency Trophy. The First Methodist Minister, L.B. Trone, was appointed Superintendent of the New Mexico Conference. He would, soon after that, move to Pecos, Texas.

The Presbyterians had a Masonic cornerstone ceremony for their soon-to-be $90,000 sanctuary. Several men were arrested for operating a prostitution ring in Carlsbad with the assistance of certain taxicab drivers.

In September of 1949, the Emmanuel Lutheran Church was building a new parsonage. Carlsbad Police investigated a gang fight between local teenage Anglos and Hispanics. Catholic Bishop Metzger of El Paso, Texas dedicated the St. Edward's Parochial School. The Carlsbad City Council discussed the large flocks of chickens presently being kept inside the City Limits, drawing flies.

The West Funeral Home burned down after an explosion. All Municipal Cemetery maps and burial records were destroyed in the fire. Because of the potash strike, 2,300 were out of work in Carlsbad.

In 1950, Rev. Hershel Drake began building the Church of God in Carlsbad. In January, the Presbyterians dedicated their new $75,000 building. Rev. J.A. Davis of the Pentecostal City of Carlsbad Mission posted a sign which read "We don't rent to scabs." There were charges of continuing violence related to the potash strike. A striker was fined for concealing a deadly weapon. By the end of January, the 73-day Potash Strike had come to an end. The Union agreed to return to work without a pay raise. The newspaper labeled it a total defeat for the Union.

In March of 1950, an unemployed 25-year-old traveling through Carlsbad offered to sell one of his eyes for $3,000. In April, the St. Francis Catholic Hospital planned a $600,000 addition that would double its size. In its recent Revival, 116 persons joined First Baptist Church in Carlsbad.

In June, 300 attended the funeral of Roy Jennings (age 56), local African-American leader, at Rice Memorial Church. He was buried in Carlsbad Cemetery. He was apparently the first African-American since roundup cook Dick Jackson was buried there in 1902 to be placed in the basically segregated cemetery. He was buried in the southeast corner, and this would become the only area where other African-Americans were buried for the next 10 years.

In August, the First Methodist Church of Carlsbad launched a Building Fund for a new $75,000 parsonage. The Hillcrest Methodists were planning to build a new Sanctuary.

In September of 1950, the Pecos Valley Baptist Association admitted the Carlsbad Thayer Baptist and Calvary Baptist Churches to its membership. A visiting New Mexico A&M University Professor said that the Carlsbad Schools were rated among the best in the nation. In November, more and more babies in Carlsbad were forcing the St. Francis Hospital to double the size of its nursery. In December, a Chapter of Hadassah, the national Jewish women's organization, was formed in Carlsbad. The new First Methodist parsonage was completed. Largely untreated sewage was being dumped into the Pecos River.

The Negro women of the new San Jose Church of Christ formed a Homemaker's Club. In March, Carlsbad community leaders denounced the telephone service as the poorest of any city the size of Carlsbad in the United States.

Both local hospitals in Carlsbad were so crowded that cots were being set up in the halls.

In June, Fr. Zeitler announced plans for a $40,000 addition to San Jose Catholic School. It does not appear that this was ever built.

In July of 1951, 44 of the 195 privies in New San Jose were labeled a health menace. Discarded watermelon rinds were causing a major fly problem in Carlsbad. The State of New Mexico Department of Education said that Carver High School (Black) cannot be accredited because its facilities were inadequate. The new First Methodist Educational Annex held its first classes.

In August, 1951, seventy-seven persons joined the First Christian Church during its recent three-month Crusade. Carlsbad had its sixth polio victim of the summer.

In September of 1951, the Sisters of the St. Edward's Parochial School moved into their new residence. Carlsbad participated in the privately-sponsored Crusade for Freedom, dedicated to fighting Communism. Fr. Hugh Rochkes arrived from Hobbs to replace Fr. Gabriel Eilers as pastor of St. Edward's Catholic Church. St. Francis Catholic Hospital opened its 4th floor to patients. Originally built as the Sisters Residence, the 16 sisters were now living in a separate Sisters Residence behind the Hospital.

In November of 1951, Leo Sandate was arrested for possession of one pound of marijuana. In the first nine months of 1951, 35 infants died in Carlsbad, which gave Carlsbad the 4th highest infant death rate in the State of New Mexico. Ten more infants would die in Carlsbad in the remaining three months. The new Full Gospel Church of God opened. 70 mph winds toppled the west wall of the Cavern Baptist Church which was under construction.

The St. Francis Catholic Hospital had 13 sets of twins born in 1951, setting a record for Sister Benedict. The Latter Day Saints Church was completed.

The new Seventh Day Adventist Church was dedicated. Almost 50 years later, it would become the first Jewish Tabernacle in Carlsbad (2001-02).

In February, 1952, Methodist Bishop Angie Smith said he preached the first church service ever held in the Carlsbad Caverns when he was an El Paso minister in the early 1920's. Carlsbad had four different

Sunrise Services scheduled for Easter. The Latter Day Saints Church in Carlsbad was dedicated.

In August, dog poisoning had become an epidemic in Carlsbad.

The Methodists organized a Men's Club and got their Charter.

In January of 1953, Carlsbad Sheriff High lamented that with a Juvenile Ward that could only hold 5, he currently had 15 in his jail, and had to place 10 of the 15 with the adult prison population. Carlsbad got only 5.45 inches of rain during the entire year of 1952, the driest year in the last 25 years. In February, a new Baptist Church was being organized in Carlsbad.

In May, 1953, Carlsbad First Baptist Church crowned a Queen Regent of the Girls Auxiliary. Fire destroyed the old Cavern Baptist Church. It was being used as a Sunday School facility. Rev. Joe Emanuel returned to Carlsbad as Minister of Hillcrest Methodist Church. Groundbreaking was held for the new Riverside Assembly of God educational building. An architect's drawing was revealed of the new home about to be built for the Sisters of the Most Precious Blood.

In June of 1953, the Blodgett Street Baptist Church was dedicated. The Seventh Day Adventist Church started a $15,000 Education Structure. In July, Eddy was one of 26 Counties in New Mexico declared to be a drought area.

In August, 1953, a juvenile gang was uncovered in Carlsbad. They marked their foreheads with a cross. The West Side Assembly of God broke ground for a new 50 foot by 70 foot cinder block church. A campaign was launched seeking $600,000 to help with further construction for both the Memorial and St. Francis Hospitals.

A local gang fight resulted in a 9:30pm teenage curfew, except for the weekly sock-hops at the High School gym.

In April, the First Baptists opened a new $50,000 Educational Building. The Happy Valley Baptist Mission held a groundbreaking ceremony.

Four First Methodist Sunday School teachers resigned, charging that the International Sunday School Lessons were pro-socialism/communism. In September, the City of Carlsbad heard a report on growing racial troubles between teenage groups in the city.

But, so much for some of the very interesting history of Eddy/Carlsbad, which became the county seat of Eddy County, an older town named Seven Rivers stood near the Pecos River decades earlier.

Seven Rivers, New Mexico

The first known documented reference to "Seven Rivers", located fifteen or so miles south of present-day Artesia, on the Pecos River, was a designation on a 1710 Spanish map showing the location of a branch of the Faraoan Apache Indians known as the *"Apaches de los Siete Rios"*.

Somewhere between 1767-1778 (the date is not exact), Governor of the New Mexico Territory of New Spain, Pedro Fermin de Mendinueta first mentioned Seven Rivers when he described how inadequate the Spanish settlements of the New Mexico Territory were arranged to withstand the incessant inroads of raiding hostiles, chiefly Apache and Comanche Indians. The Indian pueblos, or towns, he said, were compactly built and easily defended, whereas the villas of the Spanish were not properly built for defense against the enemies and were so scattered they could not help each other. So, the frontier *presidios* (Spanish forts) were rearranged.

Spanish soldiers built forts or *presidios* in the borderlands. When the Spaniards established a settlement, soldiers built a *presidio* or fort. The *presidio* began as a wooden or stockade fence where the settlers could have protection from attack. Later they built stone walls around the wooden fort.

A *presidio*

"This would [also] make it easier for the clergy to administer to the people and educate them in the most important mysteries of the Holy Faith, since the people heard the ceremony of mass hardly any day of the year, and would come together only on feast days to implore Divine aid."

Military campaigns against the Indians were directed toward Seven Rivers by the Spaniards. At Seven Rivers (*Siete Rios*), Indians met in the early days to rest after a raid into Chihuahua, Mexico and points south. When the Comanches pushed the Apaches westward, the Apaches "holed up" at Seven Rivers until all was quiet again.

Seven Rivers was a watering place for travelers along the Gila, Los Castillos and Elizario Trails. The Jicarilla tribe of Apache Indians took possession for a time but later moved north. The Mescaleros made it the trading center for their tribes, exchanging captives, stolen horses, mules and weapons from Mexico, Texas and New Mexico. It was an advantage point for raids on El Paso to the west. Seven Rivers was referred to by Spaniards in 1722, as being in the Province of Natagees. It was mentioned in old Spanish history as a place that should have been colonized because of its water, good grass and game in abundance. Comanches were reported to have ridden by Seven Rivers on horse stealing forays. Settlers heard rumors of terror in Seven Rivers and hesitated even to pass through that way. When General Nicholas de la Fora passed through in 1766, he wrote: "the spring is very dangerous. Seven Rivers is a favorite meeting place of the Apaches." Seven Rivers was once a prosperous little village. At one time, there were seven lively little streams dancing their way to the Pecos River. When the Indians moved to the Sacramento Mountains, to the west, sheepherders from near El Paso and San Elizario, on the Rio Grande River, began grazing their flocks at Seven Rivers.

From 1850 to 1870, the *Comanchero* trade (trading with nomadic Indian tribes) was at its height on the Staked Plains (*Llano Estacado*). *Siete Rios* (Seven Rivers) was apparently one of the trading grounds. The name appeared on very early maps of the area.

During the Civil War, a number of sheepmen made their permanent residence near Seven Rivers. After the war, Charles Goodnight and Oliver Loving, and other cattlemen from Texas passed by with beef herds, on their way to parts north and west. More Texans came to know of the water and the savannas near Seven Rivers. Dick Reed, a cowboy, set up a trading post in the fall of 1867 to cater to the travelers.

In 1867, the first Anglo settlers arrived at *Siete Rios*, calling it "Dog Town" because of all the prairie dogs. In 1870, Hugh Beckwith established the first ranch at North Seven Rivers.

Captain Sam Samson established another trading post and a saloon near the confluence of Seven Rivers with the Pecos River. Cow camps were scattered about in the area and the cowboys referred to the upper, lower and middle Seven Rivers country. As wagon trains and cattle herds passed through Seven Rivers going west, cowboys started cattle spreads of their own. When Texas law pushed criminals and hardened characters out of the state to the west, they settled at Seven Rivers and/or hid away in the rugged Guadalupe Mountains to the west. Cavalrymen and Apaches, ranchers and homesteaders, miners and gamblers — bad men and good, and bad women as well, began to appear in the colorful tales of the country around Seven Rivers as it was then.

By the mid-1870's, the frontier ranchers and farmers of the middle Pecos Valley were involved in what was to be known as the Lincoln County War. The locality of Seven Rivers was often mentioned in accounts of this civil disturbance. The Beckwith Ranch, near Seven Rivers, was a particularly important locality in that dispute at that time. Ranches in the area and marginal businesses were established, making Seven Rivers a local trade center catering to the cattle trade.

Seven Rivers had a reputation for toughness where 10 men "who died with their boots on" were placed in the little cemetery. Several of the early settlers of Seven Rivers had been involved in the Lincoln County War that had climaxed with the battle between the McSween-Tunstall-Chisum faction and the Dolan-Murphy-Riley faction in 1878. They became members of the notorious "Seven Rivers Warriors", headquartered at the Beckwith Ranch near Seven Rivers.

In 1878, "Dog Town" was renamed Seven Rivers. The Corn Family settled west of North Seven Rivers. In 1879, the Mart Fanning Family arrived at Seven Rivers and Charles Slaughter and his herd settled on South Seven Rivers.

In 1880, Charles B. Eddy made his first trip to Seven Rivers to buy cattle for his Colorado Halagueno Ranch. Captain Samson built the first store at the future village of Seven Rivers. In September of 1880, a train of 16 wagons arrived from Texas, carrying nine families. They settled in Seven Rivers, which seemed to mark the end of the wildest times there, and began a shift toward a more stable farming and ranching economy.

In October of 1880, the Mescalero Apaches staged their last significant raid in the Seven Rivers area.

By 1882, there was one store in Seven Rivers. It was a general merchandise store, post office and saloon combined. The name Seven Rivers came from seven springs, each forming a stream that emptied into a main channel and then into the Pecos River. The main stream ran right by the store. Along the several streams were a number of settlers. Each had a small ranch and owned either sheep or cattle.

In 1884, a Seven Rivers Real Estate Company was engaged in immigration work to help attract settlers from the mid-western states of the United States.

In the 1880's, the town of Seven Rivers moved farther north and was called "Henpeck". Later, it was moved still farther north and called "White City". The town was moved because of a water shortage due to increased artesian well activity.

Seven Rivers was a ranching center that provided goods and services to the cattle industry and its existence depended a great deal upon the growth and decline of that industry. The town supplied basic services: two saloons, a hotel, two general stores, a schoolhouse and a cemetery. The town had several freighters, a blacksmith, retail salesmen, and even a jeweler.

The town of Seven Rivers, by 1890, had become the economic and social center of eastern Lincoln County.

In 1885, the town of Seven Rivers had two general merchandise stores (one included the post office), an eating house, a saloon and a small adobe building. Seven Rivers had its larger population around the schoolhouse in what was called the "Rock Schoolhouse District". The Rock Schoolhouse was also used for church and Sunday school.

Regular stagecoach service to and from Seven Rivers was established in the late 1880's.

Frederick Hodson would later say that when he arrived at Seven Rivers in the Spring of 1888, it had 2 stores, 1 cafe, 1 saloon, a bootmaker and one blacksmith shop.

By the 1890's, there were indications that the stores at Seven Rivers were losing their business to surrounding areas.

In April, a young alligator was seen on the banks of the Pecos River just below Seven Rivers. There was a major construction site 4 miles east of Seven Rivers at the new Reservoir, with hundreds of resident workers there.

A detailed description of Seven Rivers in August of 1893 included one general store, two boarding houses, two saloons, twenty families and about one hundred people.

When the Pecos Valley Railroad bypassed Seven Rivers in 1894 for Eddy, there was a definite shift of economic activities from Seven Rivers to other communities including Miller (now Artesia), Penasco, Hope, Mayhill and Weed.

The railroad bypassed Seven Rivers in 1894 as it was extended from Eddy to the north to Roswell, which essentially stopped any future development around Seven Rivers and the Post Office was closed in 1895.

In January of 1895, the Seven Rivers school was closed temporarily because of diphtheria. In March, Martin Marose of Seven Rivers skipped town after being indicted for cattle theft.

In March of 1898, Henry Jones and Henry Lemons fought at Seven Rivers, rock versus pistol.

By the turn of the 20th century, the town of Seven Rivers was considered a ghost town.

In May of 1902, Seven Rivers produced an egg with golden lettering which said, "Prepare to meet your God!" It was put in a hen house where it was found. It sparked a very emotional, if brief, revival period in Seven Rivers.

In June of 1950, there was an article in the newspaper on the memories of Aunt Fannie (Slaughter) Lucus, who arrived at Seven Rivers with her parents on May 28th 1879, when she was 9 years old. She remembered the buffalo herds passing to the east.

The ruins of the Rock Schoolhouse still stood in the 1960's.

Thus, the rise and fall of Seven Rivers was a product of many things. Just north of Seven Rivers, the town of Lakewood had its own history.

Lakewood, New Mexico

As early as 1870, individual families of settlers came to the Rio Penasco and North Seven Rivers area south of Artesia, along the Pecos River, south of where Lakewood stands today.

In March of 1894, Mr. J.J. Hagerman chose the name of McMillan for the future railroad station near the big reservoir. This name would not stick. The citizens who soon accumulated near that siding first referred to their community as White City, which really had been an early name for Seven Rivers. Later, after a short move, they christened it Lakewood, because of its proximity to Lake McMillan.

So, the town of Lakewood was originally known as McMillan. It was just a siding placed at the time along the railroad which was built from Eddy to Roswell in 1894. The next building put up was a saloon. This was followed by a drug store.

In July of 1897, the Rheinboldt Brothers built a small cannery for tomatoes on their farm five miles south of Miller Siding (Artesia). This area would be called Lakewood. In November of 1899, the Rheinboldt Canning Factory near Lakewood would be moved to Roswell.

The Lakewood community, 10 miles south of Artesia, sprang up largely as a result of the influx of settlers seeking the easily available artesian water and because of extensive real estate promotion. "At one time there were two different school districts there." A number of settlers moved to Lakewood from their farms and ranches in the Pecos Valley, especially from Seven Rivers to the south.

The first church to be established in the town of Lakewood, with its population of 500, in about 1902 or 1903, was a white frame building known as "The Community Church." This church was built by people of different denominations, many who were not affiliated with any denomination. It had no regular pastor, but pastors from other churches of different denominations preached on a fairly regular basis. Many two-week long "Revivals" were conducted. One man in particular is remembered who walked from town to town in the rural area preaching the Word of God.

In 1904 a post office was established in Lakewood. In August, the new township of Lakewood replaced the town of McMillan. This township was on the railroad, almost 3 miles west of McMillan. Two hundred acres of town lots, streets and parks were laid out. In December, Lakewood got a saloon.

LAKEWOOD, NM

In 1905, a town site company was organized, land purchased and the town was laid out, being called Lakewood. The discovery of artesian water was certainly the motivating factor in laying out the town. In March, twelve Polish families started a 2,600 acre colony near Lakewood. In May, the Lakewood Oil Company was organized. In September, Lakewood began calling itself "The Oil City".

In 1906, George Truitt, son of the first permanent settler on the present site of Artesia, helped to build a schoolhouse in Lakewood, which used to be North Seven Rivers. The schoolhouse was later used by the Baptist Church. In July of 1906, oil was discovered five miles west and one mile north of Lakewood.

In January of 1908, oil was hit eight miles northwest of Lakewood on Four Mile Draw.

An early-day resident of Lakewood, a Civil War army veteran, wrote from his home in Lakewood in 1909: "I have here in New Mexico lots of old [Civil War] friends." In 1909, the Franciscans began visiting Lakewood. Having no Catholic church there, mass was sometimes said at the home of the town banker and sometimes at the D'Autremont general store. Besides the banker's family and the

D'Autremont family, there were about a dozen Spanish families and one Italian family in the Lakewood area.

In March of 1911, a new Lakewood Tomato Cannery was under construction.

In December of 1911, two Japanese, Kawa Moto and Ben Akaida, successfully raised 40 acres of cantaloupes, 30 acres of tomatoes and 5 acres of truck produce near Lakewood. They were looking for an additional 40 acres near Carlsbad to raise cotton. They apparently returned to Lakewood. They were never mentioned in the newspaper again.

Francisca Rodriquez was born at Fort Davis, Texas in 1888. When Francisca was a small girl, her family moved to Mexico where they lived until they had to flee across the river to the United States to safety from Pancho Villa, who was shooting at them. They came to Lakewood in the early 1900's where her husband worked on the McMillan Dam. She attended the First Assembly of God Church in Lakewood.

In May of 1917, the *Lakewood Progress* newspaper folded.

When the town of Dayton (just south of Artesia, between Artesia and Lakewood) was abandoned, the Methodist church in Dayton was moved away and a rumor reached the people at Lakewood that their church building was also to be moved away. Even though the people of Lakewood were still worshiping in the church and keeping it in good repair, without a word to the community people, a wrecking crew was sent in to tear down the building. Some of the members of the Community Church were Methodist, but some quickly changed their religious affiliation. Thus ended "The Community Church" that served the people for over 30 years in Lakewood.

On Sunday afternoon, September 1, 1940, a council was called to meet for the organization of a Baptist Church in Lakewood. The first church was built across the street from the store.

The Lakewood school closed its doors in 1940.

"Christians were baptized in the Pecos River by the Baptist churches in the area such as the Lakewood Baptist Church." The Lakewood Baptist Church got its start in 1940. One woman remembers being baptized just below the head-gates of the former McMillan Dam in a rocky area where fishermen liked to fish. She also believed her daughter, who was born in 1940, was baptized in the Pecos at age 9 or 10 (1949 or 1950). Her son was baptized at an old swimming hole in the South Seven Rivers, near the point where the South Seven Rivers joined the Pecos River.

In October of 1950, the greatest claim to fame for Lakewood was that it had not had a single crime committed there since 1923. In 1951, the one-room church building for the Lakewood Baptist Church was moved to the Morningside area on the north side of Artesia as a mission of the Baptist Church. It became the Grace Temple Baptist Mission. The County School Board sold the Lakewood church for $700.

The artesian wells and springs began to dry up around Lakewood, and most of the people moved out.

Today, Lakewood proper is little more than a general store and post office, the old school building and a few neighboring houses that reach out from the Santa Fe Railroad.

This was Lakewood. But, just east of Artesia, about 20 miles, was a very small community called Loco Hills with its own unique story.

Loco Hills, New Mexico

OIL PUMP JACKS

Some say the hills were termed "loco" (crazy) because of the mirages seen from their tops during the spring and summer months. Others say the word "loco" was used to describe the people who lived among the small, barren sandhills east of the Pecos River and twenty or so miles east of present-day Artesia. And then there were those who contended that the community was named after the locoweed, which they say grew abundantly in the vicinity. Loco Hills was not founded as a town, per se. The people who made it their home never had a mayor, city council or even a town sheriff. The community simply sprouted with the coming of the oil industry to southeast New Mexico in the early 1920's and has grown slowly ever since. The settlement actually started about 10 miles west of the present location of Loco Hills, near the old Illinois Oil Camp. At that time, the community, called Old Loco, consisted of a few shacks to house the oil field workers, a supply store and a cafeteria which also served as a temporary school. A man named Smith built a post office and a store in the early 1930's and also erected several houses. J.L. Briscoe, one of the first oil field workers in the area, went to work in the oilfields in 1925 and moved into a small shack north of Loco Hills in 1936. The things remembered most about living in Loco Hills at that time, were all the rabbits and rattlesnakes.

There was no electricity and no telephones or refrigeration. Everybody had gas lights. There were a lot of good people. They used to say you could hear anything in the world at Loco Hills except the truth and meat-a-frying. Water was another problem for the early residents of Loco Hills. The people had very little drinking water available and only went to Artesia once a week for supplies. Almost everybody made a little home brew. And, since there was no refrigeration, it was drank hot. The population of the Loco Hills community always consisted of oil field workers — drillers, truck drivers, roustabouts, location builders and some chemical company employees in later years. But, the oldest inhabitants of the area were the ranchers, including the owners of the Turkey Track Ranch, who held surface rights to much of the valuable oil land. As the oil industry continued to pick up in the Loco Hills vicinity, the oil companies began to move in, bringing a few trailer houses with them for their employees. The population of the community leveled off as more and more workers commuted from Artesia to their jobs in the oil fields near Loco Hills.

In 1939, the Loco Hills pool of oil, reportedly the second largest in the country, was discovered.

WELCOME TO
Loco Hills
New Mexico

LOCO HILLS, NM

The Sherman Memorial Community Methodist Church of Loco Hills included all Christian denominations and was organized by a Presbyterian Sunday School missionary. The first church building was dedicated on Easter of 1940.

Some years later, part of the Baptist constituency withdrew and organized a church of their own. For several years, the Sherman Community Church of Loco Hills was without pastoral care.

Preachers of different denominations came intermittently and held services.

In 1952, the formal opening services were held for a new church. The church in Loco Hills was serviced by local preachers through 1978 and beyond.

Along with Loco Hills, another community developed some twenty miles west of Artesia called Hope. Its history brings with it another unique story of struggle, perseverance and faith.

Hope, New Mexico

HOPE, NM

Pioneers, weary of Indian fighting and longing for peace, found and settled the verdant spot they named Hope, New Mexico, located twenty miles west of present-day Artesia. This was around the early 1880's, even though earlier settlers had occupied areas of the upper Penasco River to the west.

Cattlemen herded their cattle through the Penasco River Valley. One of these cattlemen camped on the banks of the Penasco River, decided to build a home there, and thus became the first settler of Hope. In 1886, he was joined by two families.

All of the early settlers of Hope built their homes along the banks of the Rio Penasco. They built them from sun-dried adobe bricks. Because of these dugouts, as they were called, since they were built of sod mud and into the ground itself, the first name of the community was Badgerville. Although the entire village later moved north of the Penasco River, most of the early dugouts and the school, were on the south side of the river. Badgerville was not only isolated from other white communities, but was located near Indian country. But, there was no problem with the Indians. As the settlement grew, more families moved from the adobe dugouts to houses made of lumber. A post office was established in Badgerville on October 10, 1890. When this happened, it was said, two men who had expressed "hopes" for a raise in their salaries and the building of a post office had their "hopes" fulfilled. Since both men had received their "hopes," the townsfolk decided to change the name of the community from Badgerville to Hope. Of course, this was just one of several stories about the naming of the town of Hope.

According to early records, the Hope Baptist Church, which began August 12, 1891, was affiliated with the American Baptist Home Mission Society and was known as "The Baptist Church of Christ at Hope."

In 1893, the Rev. John C. Gage and his family settled in the town of Hope.

Despite continuing supply problems, expansion of irrigation continued at Hope. In 1908, Pete L. Loving came to Hope, which at that time, was a more thriving and prosperous community than was Artesia to the east. People of kindred faith met together to worship.

In many areas, it was customary to attend worship services only when a preacher happened to pass by.

There were some shootouts and killings near Hope. The house in which the Wake family had first lived had bloody men's clothing in the closets. They learned that a man had waylaid to kill an enemy, but he killed the wrong man — his own son. There were many feuds and fights, for many years, among the women, too. After 1909, times and conditions were better, however, as law and order came to the town, with sheriffs, justices of the peace and town officials.

All early settlers' churches were among the first buildings constructed in Hope. There was the Methodist Church and the Church of Christ. These churches served the spiritual needs of the people through many decades. Music recitals, school plays and graduations graced their sanctuaries, marriages were performed and funerals were held, all within their portals.

The First Baptist Church of Hope was completed April 5, 1908. During the early years, the church showed strong doctrinal practices and withdrew fellowship from church members for heresy, dancing or attending dances, preaching contrary to Baptist beliefs, holding the church in contempt, quitting one's wife, using profanity and being guilty of non-Christian conduct. People could, however, ask for forgiveness from the church body. It was strong faith and practices that caused the church to endure through the many years of hardships.

At one time, a Catholic priest was found visiting the community of Hope. The priest went there once a month and said mass in the homes of his parishioners.

There was also a Hope Water Users Association.

Hollis G. Watson came to the Artesia region through Amarillo, Texas in 1913, his destination was Tucumcari, New Mexico, and in the minds of his friends back in Chattanooga, Tennessee, sure death. At Hope, New Mexico, however, he became a pharmacist and his distinguished career was launched.

Today, a virtually waterless ghost town, Hope, in the early part of the 20th century, had irrigated orchards - apples, peaches and grapes - shipped far and wide, hauled to the Artesia railhead in wagons pulled by four horses. "Hope still had good land, if it only had water."

The Hope Methodist Church had no found historical records. It was a preaching appointment in 1913.

In the fall of 1917, there was a lot of water for irrigation and many acres of fruit trees grew in Hope, including apple, peach, pear, plum and some grapes. There were also fields of alfalfa, corn and all sorts of food stuffs. The soil was deep and rich and it was a farmer's paradise. Hope was a happy community with three prosperous churches, each with its own full-time preacher. There was a drug store, two furniture stores, two millinery shops, a blacksmith shop, hotel, post office, bank, meat market, two grocery stores and a theater. There was a new First Methodist Church, a First Baptist Church and a Church of Christ, and then, there was the Chautauqua, which was an "everybody show" that came to Hope every year, a combination of education and comedy. In Hope, "We worked hard and played hard and had some sad times, but mostly we were very happy. We helped our neighbors spray their orchards, and fight their forest fires, and sat with the sick and divided our fruits and vegetables with the preachers." Hope grew to a community of about 2,000 farmers and ranchers.

With the orchards in and around the town of Hope, it became a fruit-producing center. Hope was great fruit country, known for its apples.

In July of 1918, the Hope Methodist Church and parsonage were destroyed by fire.

The population of Hope began to decrease for various reasons: the banker, Hugh Gage, absconded with the capital funds, and, shortly after this, the Penasco River went dry. As a result, many residents of Hope moved to Artesia. Among them was A.J. Cox, a preacher of the gospel.

In 1949, the Penasco River went dry, leaving the farmers around Hope with no way to raise a crop.

As the water supply declined, the Baptist Church of Hope declined and finally disbanded in the early 1960's, with the membership absorbed into the First Baptist Church of Artesia. In 1969, the church building was sold.

Today, Hope lies as an almost-ghost town on the plains west of Artesia. As Hope rose and fell, another small community developed along the railroad line between Artesia and Carlsbad, some miles south of Artesia, called Dayton.

Dayton, New Mexico

Farming and ranching were taking place south of present-day Artesia in 1897.

Dayton, eight miles south of Artesia, near the confluence of the Penasco and Pecos Rivers, on the line of the Pecos Valley Railroad, was named for J.D. Day, founder of the town in 1902, and plotted in 1904. In May of 1903, the Dayton townsite was incorporated. In July of 1903, ground was broken for the first house in Dayton. In August of 1904, Dayton got a new school, and a hotel was planned. In November, the Dayton townsite, having suffered major damage in a big flood, was moved from north of the Penasco River to its present location.

Dayton grew rapidly, and by 1907, the place had two churches, a public school, a good hotel, a weekly newspaper, and all the business and social accessories of a flourishing community. It was located in a very productive artesian water belt.

In September, there was a new gas and oil well at Dayton with a strong flow of natural gas. By October, Dayton had a 75-barrel-a-day oil well.

DAYTON. NM

The town was built around a town square. On the square, there were two livery stables, a dry goods store, three grocery stores, a drug store, a blacksmith shop, two feed stores, a bakery, a real estate office, a weekly newspaper, a two-story hotel with 20 rooms, two saloons, a barbershop, and a lumber company. The north end of town was the Spanish-speaking area. Dayton had an adobe Catholic Church. There was also a Methodist, Presbyterian and a Baptist Church. A school house was built. In the very early days they built a steam-operated, two-stand cotton gin in Dayton which was the first gin in this part of the Pecos Valley.

In 1909, Franciscan friars built a new Catholic church at Dayton. The church soon began to grow with the town.

Eddy County claimed its first oil wells in 1909, when two wells with good oil shows, and one indication of gas, were drilled in the Dayton area.

By November of 1912, Dayton had a saloon.

In 1913, Eddy County got another oil well, the Brown Well, two miles northeast of Dayton, which delivered 52 gallons per day. The oil boom started as a discovery well came in about nine miles east of Dayton. A small oil refinery was built. A land development company came in. The West and North Dayton Town Site Companies were formed. A cafe was moved from Lakewood to Dayton. The North Dayton Townsite Company built a bridge across the Pecos River for traffic from the oil field.

With time, Dayton's population began to thin. Desperate farmers put in centrifugal pumps to lift water from beneath the ground. When pumps failed, pits were dug and pumps lowered. Still, the water level fell and Dayton's doom began to loom. The town's population went down as the water level went down. The Bank of Dayton moved to Artesia. The Artesia School District took over the schoolhouse of Dayton. Carlsbad got Dayton's Methodist Church. At one time, the town had a population of some 300.

A small 1,000 barrel-per-day refinery was built at Dayton in 1925, but was shut down that same year.

In August of 1927, an old Baptist church was acquired to be used as a Catholic church in Dayton.

A priest would come from Roswell to say mass every first Saturday in this old Baptist church for the Mexican settlement at Dayton.

However, the Spring of 1928 saw an exodus of many Catholic families so that by July, Mass was no longer celebrated in Dayton.

The Dayton post office closed in March of 1944.

The Dayton Catholic Church was torn down in 1949.

Dayton disappeared from the map. Another small enclave of people existed just north of Artesia called Cottonwood.

Cottonwood, New Mexico

According to the 1884-1885 Census of Lincoln County, Territory of New Mexico, the community of Cottonwood, just north of Artesia, was named for a grove of cottonwood trees near a spring. The grove was located on land first settled, with government script, by the Holt Cattle Company during the 1880's. The company was settled on land up and down both sides of the Pecos River. Two brothers in the area raised turkeys and drove them, like cattle to market in El Paso. The drive would take two weeks, and was the only turkey drive known in the Pecos Valley. There was a Cottonwood School. Cottonwood never became a town as such. Early day residents say it was a combination of two communities situated along the spring-fed Cottonwood Creek. Both upper and lower Cottonwood at one time provided their own schoolhouses and a "smattering of general stores, none of which remain in use today." After graduating from the eighth grade, Cottonwood students had to travel or board themselves in either Lake Arthur or Artesia, if they planned to attend high school.

The Cottonwood community was located in rich fertile farm land. The farming families that made up this community were strong and dedicated to their Christian beliefs and family values. In 1921, the Cottonwood community purchased the Baptist Church building from Blackdom, New Mexico, near Dexter, when the Blackdom

220

community disbanded for lack of water. This building became a community church in Cottonwood where all denominations could come together for worship. Its pastor also served the Hagerman, Hope and Lake Arthur community churches. The church developed a very active Sunday School. It was decided that the Methodist Conference would supply the pastor.

In 1933, the Upper Cottonwood School was closed down altogether and consolidated with the Lower Cottonwood School.

The Cottonwood Community church had difficulty in keeping pastors. Some just didn't work well in this small community while others were moved up to serve larger congregations. This and the extra work placed on the members to maintain the grounds and the building led the group to disband and drive into Artesia to the various churches there for worship and other activities. This took place in the early 1950's.

Cottonwood exists today as a group of properties and houses north of Artesia. As Cottonwood survived north of Artesia, another small enclave of people called Atoka existed a few miles south of Artesia.

Atoka, New Mexico

Atoka was listed as a place or community on the AT & SF (Atcheson, Topeka and Santa Fe) Railroad, some five miles south of Artesia. The word, "Atoka," is said to have meant "in or to another place," and was thought to have been a Choctaw Indian word found in Oklahoma, Tennessee and Virginia. Atoka, like Cottonwood, Dayton, Lakewood, Artesia and Hope, became recognized as a community (though perhaps not a town) in the years around the turn of the 20th century. An Edward D. Kissinger came to Atoka in 1904 for land and the abundant water, and to escape the bitterly cold Nebraska winters. Many emigrants from the Eastern and Midwestern region were attracted to the Pecos Valley in those early years by land, water and a healthy climate. Crops raised on farms from Atoka south to Seven Rivers were tomatoes and cantaloupes. Alfalfa hay was perhaps the most stable crop. The "Red Top School" was built in Atoka in the very early 1900's, possibly in 1902, where a few children who lived in the Artesia area went to school.

Mr. and Mrs. Joe S. Torres, and Joe's brother, Cleto, came to Atoka in 1903, to operate a farm. In addition to their own six children, the Torres family raised six other children from Mrs. Torres' two sisters. All the children attended school at Atoka.

Mrs. J.H. House, who had lived near Atoka since 1904, remembers that children went to school in summer and picked cotton in the fall. "The school children carried water in a bucket from an artesian well just across the railroad tracks west of Atoka. They all drank out of the same dipper, and all appeared to be healthy."

In 1904, Rev. Juvenal Schuerbus, a Franciscan missionary from Carlsbad, found three Mexican Catholic families near Artesia. In 1905, he celebrated his first mass at the George Wetig place about 3 miles southeast of Artesia in Atoka. Eight persons were present. By the next month, 22 people attended mass in a small schoolhouse. By the next month, there were 40 people in attendance. Two months later, mass was celebrated in a large frame schoolhouse which in 1907 became the Baptist church in Atoka.

In April of 1949, the contract was let for the new Atoka school and gymnasium.

The Atoka School closed in 1970.

And so, another small community in the Pecos River Valley started, thrived for awhile and then declined. It was a familiar pattern. But, not so with the town, and later, the city of Artesia.

Artesia, New Mexico

The history of churches, regardless of doctrines and beliefs, had great impact on the growth and development of a community called Artesia.

"Religion, morality and knowledge, being necessary to good Government and the happiness of humankind, schools and the means of education shall for ever be encouraged." In these words did the drafters of the Ordinance of 1787 seek to inspire the people of the new commonwealths to be formed "beyond the Mountains" in the western parts of the new United States of America, including the future state of New Mexico.

Settlers to the Pecos River Valley of southeastern New Mexico and the Artesia area came over mountains, across plains and rivers. They came in ox carts, covered wagons, on foot or horseback, driving their herds before them. They came with an ax in one hand and a Bible in the other, and began at once to clear the land, build homes and places of worship.

Churches came to Artesia with these settlers. Isolation and the hardships of frontier life drew them together more closely. Union services (several churches together) were held chiefly in homes and brush arbors or tents, until schools were built where the services could be held. When church denominations were "numerically and financially able," they built their own churches which, even then, were shared with others. From the very beginning, the churches in Artesia had great influence on the growth and development of the community.

The first record of actual permanent settlement on the present site of Artesia was that of John T. Truitt, a union soldier, who filed a homestead claim in about 1889.

Between Lake Arthur and Artesia, some of the early settlers lived in Indian caves or "dugouts" (made out of the side of a hill of dirt or rock) dating around 1890 and for the next thirty-five years. These were frequently referred to as Anglo homesteads, although there were Hispanics inhabiting dugouts as well. Families would live in these dugouts for an average of nine months.

Sallie L. Chisum was one of the first to reside on the town site of Artesia. She was the niece of John Chisum, the famous cattle rancher. This was around 1889.

J.C. Gage was a preacher circuit rider for the Methodists who located at Hope (20 miles west of Artesia) in 1892 and purchased the Artesia Hotel as well as organized the Bank of Artesia.

In 1894, the townsite of Artesia consisted of a framed shack housing a country store, post office, and a Pecos River Railroad station. The siding was known simply as "Miller". In 1895, Sallie Chisum Robert Stegman named the new Post Office at Miller Siding, Stegman, after her second husband. It was later changed to Miller-Stegman. She established a homestead there.

In May of 1896, John Richey (known as the "father of Artesia") staked out a desert claim and began farming near Miller-Stegman.

According to John Gage, Jr., son of Rev. J.C. Gage, "I came down here to Artesia from Hope country in 1896 or 1897 with my father. I went with my father over to Sallie Chisum Robert's (her first husband's last name was Robert) place about where Roselawn Avenue now crosses Eagle Draw. The place was called Miller then."

The town of Artesia opened excellent artesian water wells, "of which the yield was so good that the town became the center of a prosperous agricultural belt known widely for its dependable supply of fresh, cool and pure artesian water."

Artesia, NM

In 1902, a group of God-fearing people banded together in Artesia to form a Union Sunday School.

In January of 1903, the town of Artesia was laid out. The post office was named Stegman, and later, Artesia. In 1903, Artesia got its first school house, fire department, newspaper, drug store, library and bank charter.

The first babies born in Artesia were triplets.

What was called the world's largest artesian well came in three miles east of Miller Siding.

The town of Artesia was first called "Miller", named after a railroad employee. For a brief time, it was known as "Stegman". With the discovery of artesian wells in the area, however, the town was renamed "Artesia" in 1903.

George Truitt, son of John T. Truitt, the town's first homesteader, wrote in later years:

FATHER BRIAN VINCENZO GUERRINI, SS.CC.

"We used to go to church at the schoolhouse in Miller sometimes, but I don't remember the preacher's name nor the teacher's name either."

In 1902, there was only one little store and a house in Artesia. Previous to 1902, Artesia was used as a range for cattle and antelope. With water, however, farming developed and alfalfa became a big crop.

Rev. J.C. Gage, a Methodist minister, was preaching wherever he could get a few people together. He and his family were in Artesia when the first train on the Pecos Valley Railroad arrived. Rev. Gage organized the First Methodist Church of Artesia in 1903. The First Presbyterian Church of Artesia was also organized in 1903.

Times were very hard during the beginning of the 20th century, but the Methodist congregation in Artesia was determined to continue its efforts through prayer, sacrifice and hard work.

The First Christian Church in Artesia began when, at the turn of the 20th century, several groups of people, already active as church groups, came together without a church home, worshiping only as a group of common believers. Among these were members of the Christian Church who had moved to Artesia in the latter part of 1902 or early 1903. In 1903, the Christian Church began holding services in the school where a union Sunday school was organized.

Artesia grew very rapidly and even before the close of 1903, there was a bank, drug store, a doctor's office, "Shorty's" Cafe, the Gage Hotel, the Owens Hotel and a section house to shelter the railroad laborers, to name only a few of the buildings.

The first Sunday School in Artesia, organized early in March, 1903, met in an attic over a drugstore located on the corner of Fourth and Main Streets.

226

The pre-organization of the Methodist Episcopal Church South, of Artesia, dates back to 1903. Brother J.E. Ray and Brother J.R. Chisholm, with their families, were the first ones to meet together in private homes for worship. J.R. Chisholm was in Artesia engaged in constructing a water project on the Penasco River, south of Artesia, after which, he went on from there and did a lot of preaching and established several churches.

The First Baptist Church of Artesia was organized in 1904.

The Artesia Church of Christ (originally First Methodist Church) was founded in 1904.

In 1904, the Territory of New Mexico issued incorporation papers to the First Christian Church of Artesia. The pioneers had the need of Christian fellowship and began weaving then, what through the next 80 years, was the thread of love, compassion, fortitude and sacrifice and the golden thread of faith in God and prayer, continually forming the design of Christianity in Artesia.

A synopsis of a regular meeting of the Artesia Church of Christ went something like this: "Nothing sensational in the preaching or Bible study, just a plain statement of Bible facts and an earnest appeal to get men and women to be doers of the Word and not hearers only. Come, hear, understand, obey and be blest." Another went like this: "Brother Worley would just read a full chapter from the Bible. He couldn't comment or sermonize." A division occurred between members of the Church of Christ of Artesia over having or not having Sunday school. An observation was made: "We had a time with the anti-Sunday school bunch. We refused to let them meet in our building in the afternoon because of their factious spirit, so a few of them finally rented the First Christian Church building. They also tried to get us to let one of their preachers hold a meeting in our building, but we couldn't hear to it, for fear it would cause division within the congregation."

By 1904, Artesia had grown substantially.

There was only one educational building standing in Artesia at the time, however. In August of 1904, several young men of Artesia were charged with disturbing the peace in an attempt to drive a Negro man out of town.

The first baptisms at the First Baptist Church of Artesia were in October of 1904. The people of First Baptist first met in the Gore Building downtown. The Christian Church then invited them to share their building. They also shared the Methodist Church which is now the funeral home.

Artesia quickly became an important railroad stop. There was an attempt by the San Diego, El Paso and St. Louis Railway Company to build a line between Artesia and Hope and on to El Paso.

The first services held at Artesia's First Christian Church were held in 1905. For many years, Artesia's Spanish-speaking people attended church at St. Anthony's Catholic Church, a frame building which was built in 1905. Artesia was incorporated as a town in 1905 with a population of 1,003.

In 1905, St. Paul's Episcopal Church of Artesia was started.

In March, the village of Artesia banned gambling. In April of 1905, Artesia's town election was voided because it took place in the wrong year.

An ice cream social was conducted in 1905 by ladies from the Presbyterian Church in Artesia.

Three early Spanish-American families came to Artesia around 1905: the Villas, the Hernandez's and the Torres'.

The Ernest Almanza family, who settled in Artesia, was from Spain with some Navajo Indian blood. They fought the Apache Indians over the water problem. They were a very religious Catholic family. In one fight with the Apaches, when they saw they were losing, they fell on their knees and prayed. The family patriarch finally stretched his arms wide in the form of a cross and cried out, "St. Francis, help us to kill this Indian Chief!" The Mexican-Americans of Artesia had a strong devotion to the United States.

In the early 20th century, influenza was on the rampage in Artesia and persons were asked to stay out of public buildings, especially the post office except to attend to business required.

In 1906, Holy Mass was celebrated at St. Anthony's Catholic Church in Artesia once a month for the growing congregation. The parish was named after St. Anthony of Padua.

In 1906, an Artesia College was built.

A railroad grade was prepared from Artesia westward to Hope and was to be extended further west to El Paso, Texas. However, the money to complete the Artesia-to-El Paso railroad project was coming from an English capitalist, who was on board the ill-fated Titanic. Portions of the unfinished roadbed may still be seen today.

The first sung Mass at St. Anthony Catholic Church was in 1907.

The Artesia Christian Science Society was started in 1907 by three ladies meeting in each other's homes Wednesday afternoons to read the lessons together. Later, Sunday services were held in a private home and a Sunday School started with six students, but was discontinued later, most of the students having moved elsewhere.

The Don Pablo Alvarez family moved to the Artesia area in 1907. Don Pablo was a *curandero* (herb practitioner, healer) for over fifty years in Artesia and the Middle Pecos Valley.

Artesia's quest for higher education continued with the establishing of Artesia Western Methodist College in 1908.

The life of St. Paul's Episcopal Church in Artesia concerned itself with survival. St. Paul's history and life began around 1908 with meetings in the homes of a core of Episcopalians who found themselves in Artesia. The church, at the time, held mission status.

The magic word "oil" did more for Artesia's growth and prosperity than any other factor, although agriculture and potash contributed extensively. Since 1908, when drillers noticed traces of oil in water from new artesian wells, the magic word has flowed through the veins of the community, town and city.

In the early days of Artesia, the big event was the annual Alfalfa Day Celebration.

The Joyce-Pruitt General Store was the "Heartbeat of Artesia".

In 1909, the Hammond oil well came in near Artesia, the first dependable producer in Eddy County, although only at 6-10 barrels a day.

In the 1910 Census, the Artesia population count was 1,883.

In 1910, a second monthly mass was added at St. Anthony's Catholic Church.

In 1910, the first Church of the Nazarene of Artesia was founded.

A Mr. Cyril Stone, whose parents came to Artesia in 1910, made a profession of faith somewhere about the age of 10 or 12 years of age.

He recalls that there was a city-wide revival when he was 12 and it was there that he made his acceptance of Christ and his own profession of faith in response to an altar call. He also felt the call to be a missionary. He attended Sunday School regularly and lived on a small farm west of Artesia. He remembered his Sunday School teacher who instilled in him much of his early knowledge of the Christian faith and established his prayer life.

On July 24, 1910, the First Baptist Church changed from the Northern Baptist Convention to the Southern Baptist Convention.

From the *Artesia Advocate* newspaper, June 24, 1911:

"The Artesian district of the Pecos Valley has been more maligned than any other region of the United States. People have come here and being carried away with the possibilities of the developed irrigated land have brought more than they had capital to develop and very naturally they became discouraged and have blamed the country. Others have been ensnared by unscrupulous land sharks and have been located upon poorly watered land and they have cursed the country and left it. Still others have thought by the glowing accounts they have read of the returns made on this irrigated land that one could raise crops and sell produce with ease. They, too, have joined the discontented. The real facts remain about the Valley, namely: There is good land and poor land; there are poor water belts and good water belts. The soil varies and in all these respects the Artesian belt along the Pecos River is just like all farming countries."

"Whatever is put in the ground and cared for can be raised profitably in the Pecos Valley near Artesia" it was said. "The Artesia district has passed by the speculative period and now is in need of men who want to build up homes and enjoy the fruit of their industry as they advance in years. We believe that there is no other farming community where so much return can be secured with the same outlay of time and energy as that in the vicinity of Artesia. Neither is there another place with which we are familiar where the moral sentiment and intellectual standard is as high as it is here in Artesia and surrounding country."

"People came to Artesia with the idea that it was a growing town and that whatever business they were in would grow too if they worked hard. It really was the land of opportunity and the prettiest little town I ever saw," said Lillian Spitz, reminiscing about Artesia.

Artesia was described thus, "The houses were new and freshly painted. A flow of Artesian water helped produce green grass and an abundance of beautiful flowers in the yards. The relationship of school, teachers, parents and the community is a friendly cooperative effort and the social contacts, pleasant. Aside from school - picnics, family get-togethers, church affairs and games - formed the basis of community life. Children assisted their parents with seasonal work. Among the most pleasant of these tasks was the gathering of luscious red apples. [Also,] a favorite pastime was the excursion trains that arrived frequently bringing prospective new citizens from throughout the country [to Artesia and the Pecos Valley]. Many of these excursion passengers returned to Artesia as permanent residents."

At this time, the churches of Artesia tried to outdo each other in attendance and growth.

From the *Artesia Advocate* newspaper, September 26, 1913:

"During a revival service in Artesia, a general spiritual uplift [was] noticeable and the evangelist [would] be remembered for a long time to come." A Pecos Valley Holiness Association participated in the Revival.

The beginnings of Trinity Temple Assembly of God of Artesia began in 1913 when J.A. 'Pegleg' Perkins migrated to New Mexico from

Nebraska with his family. They settled near the oil boomtown of Artesia in Cottonwood where Brother Perkins farmed.

There were only five self-supporting Baptist churches in New Mexico in 1913 and Artesia First Baptist Church was one of them.

By 1914, Artesia was known as the "Home of Abundance". The area was known for its alfalfa, fine fruit and vegetables.

The entire J.A. 'Pegleg' Perkins family of Cottonwood returned to Arkansas. There, during the summer of 1914, the Perkins family attended a Pentecostal Revival and the entire family experienced the infilling of the Holy Spirit. That fall, Brother Perkins had an urge to move, loaded up his family and returned to Cottonwood. The evangelist N.R. Nichols and Brother Perkins launched a campaign with meetings at the Cottonwood schoolhouse, north of Artesia. After the success of these meetings, they shifted their efforts to the town of Lake Arthur.

In 1914, the new Catholic Diocese of El Paso, Texas was erected by Pope Pius X and included the lower Pecos River Valley of New Mexico and the town of Artesia.

Lutheranism traced its beginnings in the Pecos Valley around Artesia to 1915, when Rev. Carl Schmid conducted his first service in the Pierson family home in Cottonwood, on the northern outskirts of Artesia.

Immanuel Lutheran Church, Missouri Synod, was founded in Artesia in 1915 when the Lutherans in Artesia and the surrounding area banded together.

Don Callentano Saiz came to Artesia in about 1915, possibly from Hope. He and his wife lived northwest of town in an adobe house. Don Callentano drove a team of mules hitched to a wagon, as a sort of taxi, for the Spanish-speaking people of Artesia who had no way of conveyance in those days.

In 1916, the First Methodist Church of Artesia was founded.

After meeting in a number of temporary locations, the church building for the Artesia Methodist Episcopal Church South was begun in 1916. A period of depression came to the valley at that time, however, and this delayed the building of the church.

Word of the discovery of commercial-grade oil near Artesia during the years 1917-1918 received near-sensational reporting all over the nation, particularly in Oklahoma City, where a now defunct newspaper, the *Western Oil Derrick*, promoted interest in the discovery with a series of articles and sections written by Artesians.

In 1919, the Continental Oil Refinery was established in Artesia.

In 1919, the *Artesia American* newspaper made its first appearance. It later merged with the *Artesia Advocate* newspaper.

After World War l, the town of Artesia suffered a recession which also affected the Christian churches. But, that didn't hamper the future of Artesia churches. And, it seemed that every time a new church building was completed, it was followed by a revival meeting.

Artesia was an agricultural oasis until the early 1920's when many of the area's artesian wells began to dwindle because of twenty years of unchecked flow.

The Spanish Baptist Church of Artesia was organized in 1920, when a group of interested people met in the home of De Anacio Elaez.

Typical immigrants from Mexico to the area included Mr. and Mrs. Julian Ochoa, Sr., who came from Mexico to Presidio, Texas, then moved to Artesia in the 1920's.

In 1922, a church was built named the Gospel Tabernacle.

The growth in Artesia, like many other southeastern New Mexico communities came at a time when oil and gas exploration and recovery were on the upswing. In 1923, the discovery well of Eddy County's Artesia field was drilled and the town's growth hit an all-time high.

In 1924, Artesia was described as a quiet little town of some 1,900 residents. The people were mostly farm families, with some merchants and businessmen. The town still shared the tradition of the Old West. There was still a cattle industry in the area as well as farming and trade. The yield of crops — alfalfa, fruits, grain and cotton — was consistently good, and the presence of artesian water in abundance "gave Artesia and its environs an advantage denied to most Western communities. The raising of beef cattle and sheep, as well as stock farming, added profits to the local economy."

Agriculture in the fertile Pecos Valley, oil and gas from the oil fields to the east and ranching to the west formed the basis for Artesia's economy. The people still treasured good solid American traditions of family and country.

In May of 1924, the D'Autremont Brothers of Artesia were suspected of the October 11, 1923 train robbery in Oregon that left four dead.

In 1925, Artesia got a six-story brick hotel and its first refinery. Within a few years, there were two refineries. Ultimately, they combined. In June of 1925, the Navajo Oil Company of Artesia incorporated.

In 1925, the Artesia First Assembly of God Church was founded. That same year, the congregation voted to affiliate with the national Assemblies of God.

At St. Anthony Catholic Church in Artesia, a second Mass at 10am was added for the "Mexican Catholics" in 1925.

Artesia had now gone from a dusty settlement to a well-established city.

In 1925, the marketing of apples became big business in Artesia when the community of Hope, west of Artesia, was flourishing with orchards and alfalfa farms.

The Catholic parish of St. Anthony was well enough established by 1927 that the Roswell priest extended the Artesia mission to include Dayton, south of Artesia, during the oil boom that took place there.

The first two decades of the First Christian Church in Artesia were years in which spiritual strength seemed to be far ahead of the physical strength. These years, however, were a prelude to rapid growth and development in the church. The Providence of God was indeed a wonderful service rendered to humankind. Probably during those early years of struggle, the First Christian Church did not always realize the fact that providential care was being exercised over them. However, it was made manifest to them as time went on. One meeting in 1927 consisted of talks on different Bible characters, also good congregational singing, followed by a round table talk on the Bible. A weekly meeting prayer service was held on Wednesdays. There was also Bible school.

In 1927, the first Spanish mission was begun for the Spanish-speaking parishioners at St. Anthony's Catholic Church in Artesia.

The Salvation Army began in Artesia in about 1927, when "Baron" Arianno, an Italian, came to Artesia to raise funds for needy people. People who passed through the town and became stranded or in need, often went to the police department for help. There they were usually directed to the Salvation Army group, who provided food, clothing, medical care or a night's lodging. Money or other need was often given to help them on their way. A collection was taken up for the needy at Thanksgiving in 1927, but there was no one to take charge of the funds for the town. Finally, Mr. Bullock, owner of the feed store, did it when no one offered to do it. Mr. Bullock and his son, Charles, continued this service until the State of New Mexico Welfare Department came into existence. Then, for more than 40 years Mr. Bullock was Chairman of the Salvation Army activities in Artesia. When other organizations were tied up by red tape, which sometimes took longer to get through, the Salvation Army was authorized to act immediately.

Within the first two decades of the 20th century, Artesia became the first town in New Mexico to prohibit, by local option, gambling and the sale of intoxicating liquors. There were no longer low dives, bar rooms, or places of ill-repute in Artesia.

Following the discovery of oil, Artesia's population more than doubled.

In 1929, the Conventual Franciscans took charge of St. Anthony's from the previous Franciscan missionaries.

First National Bank of Artesia was one of few area banks to survive the 1929 stock market crash.

St. Anthony's was a mission taken care of first by Franciscan Fathers from Roswell and then, beginning September 15, 1929, cared for by Conventual Franciscan Fathers from Carlsbad.

The first houses for the Negro people of Artesia were built on the northside of Artesia in the 1930's. They were all Negro servants' quarters.

Members of the Church of Christ in Artesia believed that the first Pentecost marked the establishment of the church. Members of the Churches of Christ believed that the whole structure of Christianity rested upon the divinity of Christ and his resurrection and that the New Testament was true and contained the final and complete revelation from God to man. Members of the church believed that their very salvation was measured by loyalty to his name. As a creed book, the Churches of Christ used the New Testament as the only authority for faith and practice. It revealed that God had vested 'all authority in Christ.' They believed that the Old Testament was also inspired, but that it was only a preparation or a 'tutor to bring us to Christ.' The Church of Christ had no county, state, national or international headquarters. Christ was the head of the church in a general sense and He was the head of each individual congregation. Every congregation was an independent unit selecting its own local officers and having Christ in heaven as its head. These people believed in worshiping after the pattern revealed in the New Testament. They met upon the first day of every week and believed that their worship must be in spirit and truth, and from the heart. The worship consisted of preaching or teaching, prayer, the contribution, singing and the communion. They believed that obedience to the following scriptural items constituted obedience to God's law of pardon to the unsaved: hearing, believing, repenting and confessing faith in Christ at baptism. They believed that baptism was for the remission of sins and that it consisted of a burial or immersion. Members of the Church of Christ believed that the New Testament made no distinction between 'clergy' and 'laity'. The leadership of individual congregations was given into the hands of elders who in turn were aided by deacons. The people believed that members of the church should be good citizens of established government, and also that they should keep Christ's law of divorce and remarriage.

In 1933, an evangelical meeting of two weeks duration was preached in Artesia at the Church of Christ. The church was obligated to aid the poor and needy and started a benevolent program. In order to raise the money for shoes and to aid in clothing, some of the ladies of the congregation picked cotton at a local farm. A truck from an orphanage came through Artesia twice per year to gather whatever necessities the congregation could provide. The church helped needy persons in the Artesia area as well by distributing baskets of food to families in the area. Other beneficial works included a good influence among the young people, the distribution of tracts to every home in the city, compilation of the first membership directory and publication of the first news bulletin for the church. Members were most thoughtful in sharing their vegetables, poultry and other eats. 'Stay with the truth that will strengthen the church, and growth will follow as a natural consequence,' was a common phrase at the time.

The first attempt to organize a formal ministerial association in Artesia was in 1934 with three ministers: A.C. Douglas, pastor of First Methodist Church; Rev. W.B. McCrory, pastor of First Presbyterian Church; and Rev. John Briece, pastor of the Church of the Nazarene. The Artesia Ministerial Alliance is still in existence today.

In 1936, there were two Sunday masses at St. Anthony, one with an english sermon and the other with a spanish sermon.

A visiting evangelist conducted a series of gospel meetings at the Artesia Church of Christ in 1936. The congregation felt compassion for the fatherless and needy and sent a contribution to the Tipton, Oklahoma, Orphan Home. A small donation was also sent to the small congregation meeting at Mayhill, New Mexico.

For many Artesia churches, civic affairs, sometimes, conflicted with the regularly scheduled services of the church.

In 1939, the *Gethsemani Iglesia Methodista Unida* (Spanish Methodist Church) was started by a man who came from Cuba, New Mexico (south of Carlsbad). The members first met in the homes of interested persons.

In April of 1940, the Santa Fe Railroad Depot in Artesia burned down.

Lutherans started meeting in the early 1940's.

A growing oil industry was the basis for a population boom during the 1940's in Artesia.

Until the 1940's, periodic services were held at Immanuel Lutheran Church.

Mr. and Mrs. Porfirio Sosa of Artesia were born in Mexico. They had an exciting and interesting contact with Pancho Villa, the bandit, whose real name was Doroteo Arango. Porfirio's son relates his parents' story: "Pancho Francisco Villa crossed the Rio Durango to a little place called Parral and went into Torreon. He was dressed as an old man the first time he came to Ojinaga, Mexico. He was planning to look over the entrance to Pajarito with his *tropa* (troop). Villa and his *tropa* had been on a long journey and were tired and hungry. It was about 1916, when they stopped at the hacienda of my father, Porfirio Sosa, and Senor Blas Soso, where the *tropa* and Pancho Villa rested. There were only old men, women and children at the hacienda. Villa ordered my mother, Manuela Pena, to roast meat for them, but she was frightened and didn't know what to do. She told Don Andres Vargas, of the hacienda, that these people wanted her to roast the meat, and Don Andres said to her, 'Tell me how and I will fix it for them. You women must hide in the cellar.' My mother knew by the way he talked that they might be in great danger, for they had heard very bad things about the guerrilla leader Villa, who was called a general but could hardly be told from his own guerrillas. The women who went into the cool meat cellar were Senora Vargas, who was blind, Angelita Gallegos, Manuela Pena (my mother), and my older sister, who was nine years old. I was not born at that time. The women who helped to feed Villa and his *tropa* were Agapita Jimenez and Gallantin Rubio. They were all very frightened and expected to be killed any moment, for they had heard Pancho Villa was a ruthless killer and bandito and full of tricks. He often laughed uproariously as he watched his victims die. Others, of course, said that he was a kind man who only robbed the rich to give to the poor. When Pancho Villa was ready to leave, he ordered the women to hold out their aprons. They did so, thinking this was only some kind of trick to kill them on the spot. Villa then took heavy filled bags of money from saddles of the *tropa* and poured the money into their outstretched aprons. There were several bills of paper money and cinco pesos de Plata. Then, he told his *tropa* that from there on they were all on their own. This all happened after Villa and his *tropa* had already crossed the border into the United States, and had been to many places, such as Chihuahua and Juarez, Mexico and El Paso, Texas. He had already made his raid on Columbus, New Mexico. General John J. Pershing was sent into Mexico after Pancho Villa to capture him, but he had not succeeded. One night when Villa and one of his men were returning to his hacienda from nearby Parral, in Mexico, his car was ambushed, and both Villa and his companion were badly wounded. They tried to climb Sierra Madre Mountain but were captured by some of Villa's own men in ambush and killed. The two dead men [Villa and his companion] were brought down from the mountain and hung in a plaza for all the people to see. Villa's story has become a legend. Some Sierra Madre mountain people of Mexico say they can still hear him laughing in a big roar that actually shakes the mountain and causes the great landslides that come during the rainy season. This is only a legend, of course, but many people from Mexico believe it. My parents moved to Presidio, Texas, where I was born on August 25, 1916, the year Villa was killed. I grew up there and was married and moved to Artesia in the 1940's. At that time, there were no houses in northside Artesia, only mesquite bushes everywhere, and bear grass. We built a small shack and lived there."

Mrs. Porfirio Sosa worked at the Artesia Hospital starting in 1940, and for the next ten years, and helped put her children through school.

Two additions were added to the original building of St. Anthony's Catholic Church, as the church building was now too small to accommodate the combined English-speaking and Spanish-American Catholics of the Artesia area, who totaled over 260 families. The Spanish-American Catholics were actively preparing to build a new church on La Loma Hill, on the north side of Artesia. The English-speaking Catholics were planning a new church to replace the original St. Anthony church building, located in the southwest part of Artesia. There were in the Artesia area about twenty-five English-speaking Catholic families and about 237 Spanish-American Catholic families. In order to take care of the large congregation in one church building, two to three Masses were celebrated each Sunday forenoon. The Catholic work at Artesia was in the charge of the Franciscan Fathers at Carlsbad, but a resident priest for Artesia was expected soon, and it was hoped that two resident priests would be stationed at Artesia, to care for the spiritual needs of both the English-speaking and Spanish-American congregations.

In 1941, construction of the first church for the Spanish-speaking Catholics of Artesia was begun on the northside.

In 1942, the Thompson Chapel of the Christian Methodist Episcopal Church (Black) started.

Frequent rains hampered construction of the Our Lady of Grace adobe church for the Spanish-speaking Catholics of Artesia. The new church was blessed in 1942, and dedicated to Our Lady of Grace. A priest from San Jose Mission, Carlsbad, was assigned to Artesia at that time.

Our Lady of Grace was opened on May 4, 1942. Outside of Mass and the Sacraments offered at the church, the people of God nurtured their faith in other ways. People united together in prayer in different homes. Dona Fidela Barrera built a small chapel on her property to gather people to pray the rosary, especially children who offered flowers to our Blessed Mother Mary. Dona Julianita Almanza directed performances of the "Appearance of Our Lady of Guadalupe." The Jose Alvarado, Sr. family opened their home to teach children about their faith. The Gonzalo Gomez family hosted novenas in honor of *El Santo Nino de Atocha* in their home and accepted *milagritos* ("little miracles") from the faithful for petitions granted. The Cayetano Saiz family hosted *Las Posadas* and Christmas fiestas for the children. For funerals, the men got together to help build the coffin, dig and cover the grave, and, if it happened to be *"un angelito"*, a deceased infant, Mr.'s Prajedes Navarrette, Hilario Brito and Matias Heredia would get together to play their violins during the wake.

The Sister Adorers of the Most Precious Blood of Wichita, Kansas operated Artesia General Hospital beginning in 1942 and continued for ten more years.

Several organizations began and flourished in the parish of Our Lady of Grace: the Daughters of Mary for single girls, ages 12 years and over, the Cordliers for children under 12 years of age, the Boy Scouts of America for boys and the Fraternity of San Jose for women. The Daughters of Mary helped with teaching catechism, singing in the choir, cleaning of the church and in fundraisers. The Boy Scouts helped in serving as altar boys and helped to maintain the grounds. The ladies of the Fraternity of San Jose helped in maintaining the linens for the altar and sewing.

In the spring of 1942, a few African-Americans met together in the homes of two families for Sunday School and worship services. In October of that year, about 11 members organized the Black Christian Methodist Church of Artesia. The church was called Phillips Chapel.

By 1943, no longer did a Catholic priest arrive by train or motorcycle from Carlsbad or Roswell. The old Catholic church at Dayton was torn down.

During World War Il, there was an Artesia sub-camp for POW's from WWII. At the end of WWII, Artesia was still a small community filled with energy but not yet realizing its potential.

In 1945, Fr. Stephen Bono, a Franciscan, was instructed to construct a small rectory at Our Lady of Grace and live among the people. The people responded, and money was raised so that the resident priest began living in a new small rectory.

The local Artesia mission of the Reorganized Church of Jesus Christ of Latter-Day Saints started in 1946.

The KSVP AM radio station in Artesia first took to the air in November of 1946. The Artesia Broadcasting Company was later formed.

There was a need to establish a church congregation for the benefit of the African-American population of the city. In 1947, several African-Americans began meeting with the Seventh and Grand Christian congregation.

Ed Mitchell, future astronaut, graduated from Artesia High School in 1948.

A fund was established to build a new church at Our Lady of Grace Catholic Church in 1950 since the existing church was becoming too small for the growing congregation.

For almost the entire year of 1950, the Lutherans freely shared St. Paul's Episcopal Church's building. There was a long period when there was no rector at St. Paul's. However, the people strongly desired to keep the church alive.

The Calvary Baptist Church of Artesia was organized in 1950.

The Church of Jesus Christ of Latter-Day Saints in Artesia was organized in 1950.

On June 12, 1950, Artesia had its worst fire in ten years. The Midwest Auto Store burned down.

In 1951, Emmanuel Baptist Church of Artesia was organized.

The Seventh and Grand Christian Church congregation conducted some mission work in Mexico in 1951.

In 1951, a group of people designating themselves as Jehovah's Witnesses began to meet in homes of interested persons, then in rented buildings. They formed the Congregation of Jehovah's Witnesses in Artesia.

In February of 1951, the Sheriff's Department raided the Artesia Elks Club and seized six slot machines.

In 1952, Immanuel Lutheran Church was built.

In 1952, the Sister Adorers of the Most Precious Blood left Artesia and Artesia General Hospital for Kansas.

In January of 1953, a flu epidemic forced closure of the Artesia schools. In February, a new $200,000 Presbyterian Sanctuary was dedicated in Artesia.

The summer of 1953 saw an expression of interest in the Spanish-speaking Christian residents of Artesia, with the result that a Mexican preacher was secured to commute from Carlsbad each Sunday afternoon and conduct Christian services for those interested in worshiping in the Spanish language.

There was a local radio program five days a week called 'Your Bible Study Program' on KSVP radio AM.

In 1953, the old Presbyterian church was given to the Bethel Baptist Church (Black) and moved across town. The Church of Christ congregation in Artesia began offering a Bible correspondence course in 1954. The evangelizing work of the Church of Christ among the Spanish-speaking people of Artesia was greatly enhanced when a man was secured to carry on full-time work, giving some attention also to Spanish-speaking people in the Dexter area. He would conduct the services in the Spanish language in his home.

"The existence of two or more congregations of the same religious group in a city may at times indicate that there is division existing within the group, due to differences over doctrinal matters or matters of opinion. On the other hand, a plurality of meeting houses may indicate that the leaders have seen the need of better serving the people of the community by placing the physical facilities for worshiping in new areas as the city expands with growth. Among the Artesia Churches of Christ, there was strong feeling about the individuality of congregational autonomy, which meant that each congregation should be free from control by any other congregation or system." Thus, the existence of several churches of the same denomination was justified.

In 1954, the name of the Christian Methodist Church (black) of Artesia was changed to "Thompson Chapel of the Christian Methodist Episcopal Church."

The *Templo de la Cruz* was formed in 1954 as a Spanish-speaking mission in Artesia.

On June 2, 1954, the first issue of the *Artesia Daily Press* newspaper appeared.

In August of 1954, involvement of a 13-year old Carlsbad boy in an Artesia melee led to the death of an Artesia boy. In September, Artesia was once again turned down in its request for air service.

In 1955, the Sister Adorers of the Most Precious Blood from Carlsbad were conducting weekend religious education classes for the children in Artesia.

Early in 1956, the Menefee family donated land for a new Methodist Church on Artesia's west side, to be called Clark Memorial Methodist Church.

In 1956, land was purchased in Artesia for a small convent across from the Our Lady of Grace rectory to house Catholic religious sisters.

In 1956, the young mothers of Our Lady of Grace Catholic Church banded together to sponsor a kindergarten for their children. They called themselves the Christian Mothers' Organization.

A new church congregation was established in the city in 1956 which was called the Hermosa Drive Church of Christ.

The *Iglesia de Cristo* was organized in Artesia in 1956. At first, there were only cottage meetings (in the homes).

The Clark Memorial Methodist Church of Artesia was founded in 1956 as a mission church.

The opening service for the Clark Memorial Methodist Church was in 1957.

In 1957, a building program was started at Immanuel Lutheran Church for a new church building. The Primitive Baptist Church was organized in Artesia in 1957. They used the Cottonwood Methodist Church, then rented a building in Artesia.

Discovery of the Empire Abo Oil Pool, southeast of Artesia, in 1957, was proclaimed the major oil discovery of the year in the United States and marked an exciting new era for the oil industry in southeastern

New Mexico. A new church building at Immanuel Lutheran Church was completed in 1958.

Here are some 1950's remembrances of Mr. and Mrs. Joe Torres of Artesia:

"There were mornings that Mrs. Joe Torres found very trying when she tried to fix breakfast and feed all the little ones. They would be crying and calling for help with dressing or for food, and Mrs. Torres would only sit down and cry with them. Then the neighbors began to come in and help with the 12 little ones and times got better." Mrs. Joe Torres of Artesia was elected Artesia's Woman of the Year in the late 1950's. Ninety-year old Joe Torres recalled that he was not so old after all. "I have a friend right here in Artesia, Mr. Candelero Villa, who will soon be one hundred years old!" Joe Torres attributed his own good health and long life to hard work and God's will. "I work in the yard and garden each day," he said, "and I pray to God each night."

The present *Gethsemani Iglesia Methodista Unida* Spanish Methodist church building was constructed in 1959

The *Iglesia de Cristo* church was built in 1959.

By 1960, there were more than 12,000 people in the city of Artesia with nearly 6,000 more in rural areas. There were in excess of 3,300 oil wells in the area. Three quarters of the farm and ranch income was derived from Acala cotton.

In 1960, a new sanctuary for the Artesia Methodist Episcopal Church South was opened for worship by Bishop Angie Smith, who told the group assembled: "Only when it has become a part of every member's heart, through such events as the baptizing of babies, marriages of sons and daughters, daily worship of the Lord and the comforting of the bereaved — then and then only will it really become the House of God."

By the 1960's, because of the lack of young people in the St. Paul Episcopal Church, there was no longer an active Girls' Friendly Society and no Young People's Group. Sunday School was discontinued because of the scarce attendance and the lack of Sunday School teachers.

The Victory Baptist Church of Artesia was built in 1960.

The parish hall at St. Anthony's was erected in 1962.

Abo Elementary School in Artesia was the first public school in the United States constructed entirely underground and equipped to function as an advanced fallout shelter. Designed at the height of the Cold War and completed in 1962, the school had a concrete slab roof which doubled as the school's playground. It contained a large storage facility with room for emergency rations and supplies for up to 2,160 people in the event of nuclear warfare or other catastrophe.

In 1963, the Abo Baptist Church was formally organized. It eventually became the Hermosa Drive Baptist Church.

There was a Hermosa Heights Children's Home, started by the Hermosa Drive Church of Christ, that existed northwest of Artesia, founded in 1966, where 40 foster children lived through the years of its existence.

A large, new church was completed and dedicated at Our Lady of Grace Catholic Church in 1967 in Artesia.

The Our Lady of Grace kindergarten came to an end in 1967 when the Head Start program for pre-schoolers opened in Artesia.

In 1968, the convent at Our Lady of Grace became occupied by two Immaculate Heart of Mary sisters.

In 1969, Continental sold its refinery, and a new group known as the Navajo Refining Company was formed, which also included Holly Corporation of Azusa, CA. During the 1960's, the Navajo Refining Company became the largest employer in the City of Artesia and the largest petroleum refinery in the State of New Mexico.

By 1972, the Hermosa Heights Children's Home of Artesia had a total of 34 children in their care. Some children adjusted better than others and as much as would have been liked, the staff never felt like they were their parents. Most of the children were wards of the state, from in or near Artesia. They were all from broken homes. The Artesia Evangelistic Center was organized in 1972.

There were some significant and long-lasting effects from the City of Artesia's municipal strike from 1972 to 1974. Although it began as an ordinary worker walkout, the strike was later split down racial lines, Anglo versus Hispanic. According to Fr. Charles Zengel, "It was the most un-Christian thing I ever saw." There were two Catholic churches in Artesia and, unfortunately, St. Anthony's was often thought of as the Catholic church for Anglos while Our Lady of Grace was considered the Catholic church for the Spanish-speaking people.

In 28 years, from 1947 to 1975, the records of Our Lady of Grace Catholic Church showed the following:

4,672 Baptisms (averaged 166 Baptisms
per year, 3 Baptisms per week)
3,524 Confirmations (averaged 125 Confirmations per year)
2,432 First Communions (averaged 86 First Communions per year)
611 Marriages (averaged 21 Marriages per year)
285 Funerals (averaged 10 Funerals per year)

Faith Baptist Church of Artesia was organized in 1975. It was an independent fundamental church that, for the most part, stood alone from the other Baptist churches.

Other churches organized in Artesia were: Immanuel Full Gospel Church, Zion Temple Church of God in Christ, First Free Will Baptist Church, *Tabernaculo Del Amor Asambleas Evangelicas, Inc.*, Gospel Chapel Church, United Pentecostal Church and Congregation of Jehovah's Witnesses.

The number and varied choice of denominations demonstrated the large part religion played and continued to play in the growth and development of Artesia and the surrounding area.

In October of 1975, Artesia Christian College received official nod from the state office of the Board of Educational Finance to hold classes and begin operation.

The Reorganized Church of Jesus Christ of Latter-Day Saints became a mission in 1976 which meant they were large enough to have local ministers, elders and priests.

A statement of faith by the Hermosa Church of Christ was mentioned in the *Artesia Daily Press*, June 19, 1977. The article stated: "God is a spirit and we are called to worship in spirit and truth. In order to be saved, one must hear the gospel, believe it, repent, confess and be buried in baptism. Baptism is by immersion. In order to become a church member one must confess Jesus is the son of God and be baptized."

In 1982, Ricardo Ramirez, CSB, was named Bishop of the newly-created Catholic Diocese of Las Cruces, New Mexico, to which Artesia and the Pecos Valley from Roswell to Carlsbad now belonged.

The Immaculate Heart of Mary Sisters from Tucson, Arizona ministered to the parish of Our Lady of Grace for 19 years, from 1968 until 1987. Two Artesia women from Our Lady of Grace became Catholic religious sisters: Sr. Leticia Gomez and Sr. Alice Martinez, IHM.

In 1986, the St. Vincent de Paul Society was organized at Our Lady of Grace Catholic Church to serve the poor and needy in Artesia with food, clothes and financial help. Twenty years later, it was to form its own non-profit organization, called the St. Vincent de Paul Society of the Pecos Valley, Inc., become incorporated in the State of New Mexico and operate out of its own building.

A native son of Our Lady of Grace parish, Miguel Briseno, was ordained a Catholic priest of the Conventual Franciscans in 1990. Also, in 1990, the parish of Our Lady of Grace held its first Mexican heritage fiesta.

In 1991, the Good Shepherd Mission began its ministry to alcohol and drug addicts in the former Our Lady of Grace sisters' convent.

A long-standing tradition of helping people by setting up bank accounts to help families in times of crisis or catastrophe continued in Artesia and the Pecos Valley and continues to this day.

The oil and gas industry continued to flourish in the Artesia area along with farming, ranching, dairies, small businesses and the building and operation of the Federal Law Enforcement Training Center - FLETC (where Department of Homeland Security U.S. Border Patrol Agents from all across the United States are trained).

And so, Artesia's destiny in the heart of the Pecos River Valley of southeastern New Mexico continued to parallel the lives of its inhabitants, their challenges, their triumphs and their faith.

But, so much for the past. How do present inhabitants of the Pecos Valley see God and their faith through the eyes of their lives?

Southeast New Mexico Pecos River Valley: The Present

——————————— INTRODUCTION ———————————

The people who currently live in the Pecos Valley of southeastern New Mexico are a mixture of immigrants. In keeping with its history, the Pecos River Valley continues to attract settlers to this day.

In response to interviews conducted in English and Spanish at four of the southeastern Pecos Valley's Catholic churches: St. Catherine Mission in Hagerman, Our Lady of Guadalupe Mission in Lake Arthur and Our Lady of Grace and St. Anthony Parishes in Artesia, over a period of several days in August of 2014, answers to the following question were gathered and are presented here.

"How do you find God and where?"
"¿Cómo encuentras a Dios y dónde?"

—————— PERSONAL INTERVIEWS ——————

HAGERMAN, NEW MEXICO

1. *Hispanic female, age (70's):*

"Dios es en cielo, en la tierra y en todo lugar, en todos sacramentos, especialmente en la comunion y esta en mi corazon y en mi mente y en todos mi Vida. Amen."

[Translation: God is in the heavens, on the earth and everywhere, in all the Sacraments, especially in Communion and is in my heart and in my mind and in all my life. Amen.]

2. *Hispanic female, age (70's):*

"La presencia de Dios mira en la sonrisa de un nino. Cuando un nino sonrie ve la presencia de Dios."

[Translation: The presence of God is seen in the smile of a child. When a child smiles, I see the presence of God.]

3. *Hispanic male, age (70's):*

"Hallo Dios a dentro de mi corazon y en mi Madre Santisima."

[Translation: I find God inside my heart and in my Most Holy Mother.]

4. *Hispanic female, age (late 30's):*

"Well, my earliest memories of being introduced to God were actually from my grandmother. She had a Bible. And, in the middle of the Bible were several pages, and I can still see the Bible clearly, the cover and the gold, the fancy gold edges on all the paper. But, what I loved most about her Bible was that in the middle of the Bible she had probably about ten or fifteen pages of beautiful illustrations of various scenes of, you know, famous Bible stories. And so, I can remember going to her house and she would have the Bible on her lap and she would open the Bible to those pages and she would tell me the Bible story that went along with the illustration. As I got older, I realized that those colorful pictures that I loved to look at were actually oil paintings that hung in some of the most, you know, famous museums. I'm sure all of these paintings are at the Louvre, or something like that, in France, but they were scenes from Bible stories that various artists had painted on canvas and, whoever put my grandmother's Bible together, that company, had just taken some pages from the middle and put all these paintings in there, and that's what I looked at for so long and I can still remember some of the images like Jesus calming the storm. I also remember some of the ones that kind of, that I found kind of scary, like Lot running. I remember that one. That one kind of scared me. And, I also remember, of course, you know, things like the Agony in the Garden, kind of a sad-looking scene. But, then there are also happy scenes like when, of course, Jesus was born. I remember loving to look at that image because he was such a cute little baby, that little cherubic face. But, that is a real pleasant memory that I have and I credit my grandmother for introducing me to very loving and sweet images of God and Jesus in my life and really all of the saints. My grandmother taught me a lot of Bible Stories that way. And, it seems like my family has always been involved in church in one way or another, but mostly through music, so I grew up in the church choir, became an official member about the age of twelve. I play the piano, organ and guitar and I'm still a church choir member to this day, even though I'm almost forty. So, I've been in the choir about thirty years, off and on, even when I went off to college. And so, in preparing the music liturgy for the week, I look at the gospels and readings and I look for themes in the readings and I try to pick songs that are reflective of those, and sometimes the lyrics of songs can be very direct and when you listen to the music that goes along with them, there's something about the melody that's very beautiful and it kind of enhances the meaning and it really, really draws out those lyrics into just a lovely, lovely prayer. But, sometimes I struggle with the idea of God because throughout my life I've had just some challenges, most notably, a few years ago, I went through a terrible episode of what I found out later was depression and then it returned even worse than the first time. I wasn't real happy with anything and the easiest thing to rebel against was the thing that had no human voice to talk back to me and so it turned out to be God himself, not so much God himself, but mad at the obligation of serving him, which wasn't good, but fortunately, God was patient with me and I let that anger burn out and as I turned back and found my journey back those same songs that I found joy in have returned and it's very nice, its comforting to know that God was patient and forgiving with me when I was still serving but I felt so spiritually empty about it."

5. *Anglo male, age (mid 40's):*

"Well, I guess like so many, I was born into a Christian family and I don't really ever remember like a conversion experience or anything like that because all of my memories my whole life included at least knowing about God and being taught about Jesus and heaven and angels and so on. My mother was, without a doubt, my biggest influence in my spiritual life. When I was growing up, we kinda had a mixed situation in my house because my mother was very faithful to church, attending every week, and she would take myself and my brothers, whereas my dad, his idea of church was going to the cafe and waiting until we were out. And so, as I got older, and you begin to make your own decisions about where your life's going to take you, I remember thinking, well, this is kind of uneven because, in a way, I got two different messages, one very strong from my mom that God should be important and that, one, very strongly from my dad that he really wasn't because of the practices that they were involved in in terms of either praying or reading the Bible or going to church or any of the things that we associate with the Christian life. When I was in high school, I actually went to a Christian high school and was fully immersed, I guess that's one way to put it, in, we're talking having chapel every day and our classes started with prayer and God was interwoven into the lessons, those kind of things, which was different, completely different, from my experience when I was in public school where, at that time, it wasn't like it is now, necessarily where God was absolutely not welcome at all, but still there was a large contrast between my experience in a Christian school versus a public school. I think like so many when I graduated at eighteen and I started to live on my own it's really easy to kind of put religious or spiritual things aside. I've always thought of myself I guess as a "good person". I mean I wasn't out robbing banks or doing anything like that or drugs or anything like that, but I would say that I feel like I kinda lost my way for awhile there. I pretty much wasn't mad at God or anything like that but there really wasn't a lot of interest either. But, when I got into my mid-twenties and especially into my late-twenties, I got married and, I can honestly say that one of the biggest influences now, as I see myself at forty-five, has been my own wife. She's of a different faith than I am, but there's still a concert between us, there's still a common ground, and that common ground is Christ, and, one of the lessons I've always taken with me my entire life is that, really, your spiritual journey should be centered around a personal relationship with Jesus and I believe that you accomplish that by reading through his Word, the Bible, by praying, by interacting with other Christians, and by contemplating some of these things, and that contemplation is something I never did when I was younger and I guess maybe it's just, when we get a little older, we spend more time doing that, but, thinking about the larger questions of life, you know, why are we here, what is, what really is God's will, why, I always think of St. Paul, why do I do the things that I know I shouldn't and I don't do the things that I know I should, and so. But, overall, I definitely always identify myself, when I think of myself and my identity, I definitely think of myself as a Christian, and I think of myself as being blessed by the sacrifice that Christ made at Calvary. I do believe that it was through that sacrifice that I am saved and given eternal life and so I feel very comfortable at this point in my life to say that I love my Lord and Savior and I know that He loves me."

LAKE ARTHUR, NEW MEXICO

   1. *Hispanic female, age (70's):*

"*Para mi, Dios esta siempre conmigo porque es mi alma y ha hecho muchos, y mucho misericordia a mi. Dios esta alrededor de mi, en la gente, en las personas. El responde con entusiasmo, en el espiritu adentro.*"

[Translation: For me, God is always with me because He is my soul and has made many things and shown me much mercy. God is around me, in the people, in persons. He responds with enthusiasm, through the spirit inside.]

   2. *Hispanic female, age (70's):*

"*Encuentro Dios en mi corazon, en la Iglesia, y cuando visito los enfermos. Hay la presencia de Jesucristo con los enfermos.*"

[Translation: I encounter God in my heart, in the Church and when I visit the sick. There is the presence of Jesus Christ with the sick.]

   3. *Hispanic female, age (80's):*

"*Dios esta en todas personas. Dios esta en todas partes del mundo.*"

[Translation: God is in all persons. God is in all parts of the world.]

   4. *Hispanic female, age (50's):*

"*Yo creo que Dios esta en todas partes, con todos nosotros, todas personas, en los enfermos, en los que tienen cancer. Dios es todopoderoso, en oracion. Yo doy gracias que estoy aqui. Estoy triste cuando Dios no respuesta mi oracion y las oraciones de los enfermos. Yo tengo mucho miedo de la enfermedad. Creo que el poder de Dios es todopoderoso con los enfermos.*"

[Translation: I believe that God is everywhere, with all of us, all persons, in the sick, in those that have cancer. God is all-powerful, through prayer. I give thanks that I am here. I am sad when God doesn't respond to my prayer and the prayers of the sick. I am very much afraid of sickness. I believe that the power of God is all-powerful with the sick.]

ARTESIA, NEW MEXICO

1. *Anglo male, age (17):*

"Now, as a cradle Catholic, I've grown up with God present in my life for a very long time. I've had seventeen years of seeing God daily and in weekly Mass, going pretty consistently. But, the first time I really, actually, laid eyes on God, when I actually found Him, was at the center of the Blessed Sacrament during Eucharistic Adoration. That's when I found God and that's kinda where I found God. I found God basically at the heart of the Mass, during the consecration and also during the Exposition of the Blessed Sacrament. That is when I can see God, that is when I can find Him, and that's where I have found Him. It's just that awe and wonder. Here He is, exposing Himself to you, a little piece of Heaven on earth. I don't think there's anything that can truly dissuade me from continuing my life as a Catholic. There's nothing that can make me convert to any other religion in the world."

2. *Hispanic male, age (50's):*

"I always knew He was there because I've had a very good life. I've been blessed, very blessed, and I've always had work and very good health. But, I've always wondered what's next, what's out there. I answered His call, but I think He came looking for me because it was my time. Does that make sense? I've been here since 2001. In the fall of 2007, I met another who got me involved in Boy Scouts and church. I picked up on it right away. I now can't stop learning about Christ, about God. The more I look, the more I find, the more I find myself reading more and learning more. I'm a cradle Catholic, but in the middle part of my years, sometimes I would go to Mass, sometimes I wouldn't, and then we would go a lot, but that was it, just Mass, and then, WOW, He always had a plan for me. So far, this is what it is and we're learning more. God is definitely there pushing me. Now, I can't stop finding Him. I have to learn more. My brain is asking me to learn more."

3. *Hispanic female, age (50's):*

"The way I found God was initially through my parents, who were Catholic, and I was baptized early on. And, then we were school age, my parents made a lot of sacrifices to put us through Catholic, parochial, schools. And, all my elementary years, I went to a Catholic school in El Paso, TX, and I was really intrigued by the nuns. And, the convent was right next to the school and I would tell my mom, "Don't pick me up today. I'm going to go with Sr. Joann." And, they taught me a whole different thing. I was impressed by the way the nuns lived. I saw their relationship, the way they were. I was really interested in how they helped each other. It's almost like they had their own language. One can finish the other's sentence and one knew what the other one needed. I don't know. It's just like what I consider our marriage to be now, my husband's and mine. I did, of course, enter into my rebellious teenage years. Of course, a lot of kids do that. I went through the motions because a lot of times we went to church because mom said so and I wasn't going to Mass whole-heartedly. Then, I got married and then I realized that, you know, life is hard, it's hard and it's a struggle. I didn't have internal peace. That's mainly what it was. Going back to church brought me peace as did my marriage. The greater reality was God. I have always worked in the medical field and I've loved that self-rewarding feeling that you helped someone, where you give of yourself and that's where I was running through my troubles. When you're in the medical field, you have that, say, monkey on your back called administration where it's money, where it's show me that you can pay or you won't receive services, where I was doing patient education on the side, during my breaks, and I would get in trouble for it. You know, this person needs help and that's when I started seeing the ones who couldn't afford the health care. When I had that struggle, I knew God needed me, but I just didn't know where and I know you want me to give. I asked God to tell me where to go and that's when somebody told me, I think it was a sister, that, don't ask God to open doors, but ask God to close doors. Then, I asked God to close these doors and that door closed on me. I have so much more to learn about God. I think it's a life-long learning. I think till the day we go meet Him."

4. *Hispanic female, age (60's):*

"My mom was the main person in my coming to church and doing everything I had to do. At first, mom was very strong in her faith and she taught us everything we needed, but after my husband passed away was when I really did find God. And, He's in my heart now and He lives with me all day and all night. He's my main person in my life and I pray that my sons will head the same direction. I'm praying for them and the members of my family. God is awesome. He is always there for you. He helps you in everything you need. Just keep praying and have faith that He's there with you and He'll take care of you. Thank you."

ANALYSIS OF INTERVIEWS

Introduction

Upon reflection on the content of these candid interviews, what strikes me about them are the differences and similarities among cultures, age groups, genders and locations. Based upon the history of this area, they all seem to be hauntingly similar to responses one might get if they were to ask the same question of those who settled in these parts over hundreds of years ago.

The interviews can be broken down like this:

Interview Respondents (Total number of Interviewees = 13)
(number in parentheses is the number of Interviewees)

31% Hispanic Females in 70's (4)
15% Hispanic Females in 50's (2)
7.7% Hispanic Female in 80's (1)
7.7% Hispanic Male in 70's (1)
7.7% Hispanic Female in 60's (1)
7.7% Hispanic Male in 50's (1)
7.7% Anglo Male in 40's (1)
7.7% Hispanic Female in 30's (1)
7.7% Anglo Male in teens (1)

The composition of the interviewees, by location, culture, age and gender broke down like this:

Location

38% Hagerman
31% Lake Arthur
31% Artesia

Culture

84.5% Hispanic
15.5% Anglo

Age

38% 70's
23% 50's
7.7% 80's
7.7% 60's
7.7% 40's
7.7% 30's
7.7% Teens

Gender

69% Female
31% Male

The interviews were conducted randomly after services or functions at four Catholic churches.

Out of the thirteen interviews, about one-third were with Hispanic females in their seventies, about one-sixth with Hispanic females in their fifties and the remaining half with Hispanic and Anglo males and females ranging in age from the 80's to the teens. It would seem that these percentages might be somewhat indicative of the composition of the congregations of these churches in general.

It would also seem that the cultural group composition of these interviewees, 84.5% Hispanic and 15.5% Anglo, would also be an approximate composition of the church congregations in general.

Seventy percent female and thirty percent male with respect to the gender of the interviewees would also seem to be consistent with church-going representations of these gender groups in general.

As far as age groups of the interviewees go, it seems that thirty-eight percent of the respondents were in their seventies, twenty-three percent were in their fifties and the remaining thirty-eight or so percent ranged in age from the eighties to the teens. Again, this is probably consistent with the percentages of these age groups who attend services and/or functions at these churches.

These interviews were conducted in the year 2014, however, one could possibly find the same percentages of the faithful well over a hundred years ago in these communities. I don't think that the numbers have changed that dramatically over time from a century or more ago.

When one looks at the specific results of the answers to the question asked in the interviews, "How do you find God and where?", one discovers some interesting results. I will break down the results into the following four categories: by location, by culture, by age and by gender.

By Location

In comparing responses to the question, "How do you find God and where?", from the three towns of Hagerman, Lake Arthur and Artesia, there are some similarities and differences. I will address the similarities first.

Respondents from Hagerman and Artesia both found the following to be part of their journey of finding God:

. . . . that they were blessed by God
. . . . that the person of Christ was central to their faith
. . . . that attending Mass*/Eucharist was crucial in their spiritual life
. . . . that their faith was very important to them
. . . . that their family was very important to them
. . . . that they believed in the existence of heaven
. . . . that God was a co-equal partner in their marriage
. . . . that their mother was a big influence on their spiritual life
. . . . that other Catholics/Christians were a big influence on them
. . . . that sacrifice played a big part in their faith

(* Note: For Catholics, the Eucharist is the main form of worship service, also called the Mass, which contains prayers, Bible readings, changing of the bread and wine into the Body and Blood of Jesus Christ (the Consecration) and the receiving of the Body and Blood at communion)

In addition, there were elements common to all three communities:

. . . . that church played a big role in their faith
. . . . that God was found in their heart
. . . . that God was found through prayer

In both Hagerman and Lake Arthur, the importance of forgiveness also played a role in the respondents' finding God.

In looking at these inter-community interviewee responses, despite Artesia and Hagerman being further apart distance-wise than Artesia and Lake Arthur, Artesia and Hagerman seem to be more similar in their responses than Artesia and Lake Arthur or Hagerman and Lake Arthur.

There were a number of responses, however, that were unique to each of the three communities. Here is a list of these.

For Hagerman interviewees, it was important in finding God:

. . . . that sometimes it was through anger that I realized God in my life
. . . . that the Word of God, the Bible, Scripture is very important in my faith
. . . . that when I am challenged in life, I find God is there
. . . . that when I see the smile of a child, I see God
. . . . that when I have time for contemplation, I can experience God
. . . . that when I get depressed, I can depend on God
. . . . that God can be found in the earth, in the land
. . . . that when I am feeling emptiness, God will fill me up

. . . . that through the promise of eternal life, I find God

. . . . that through my grandmother, I have a great teacher of Godly things

. . . . that when I question life itself, God is there to answer me

. . . . that through love, I find God

. . . . that God is in my mind

. . . . that through music, playing and singing in the choir, God becomes more alive to me

. . . . that when I am patient, I find I see God more clearly

. . . . that when I am rebellious, God calms me down

. . . . that through the lives of the Saints of the Church, I see God

. . . . that knowing that I am saved, helps me experience God

. . . . that through my spouse, I have found God

So, for Hagerman interviewees, a number of things were important in finding God, from human feelings to divine revelations.

For Lake Arthur, finding God was...

. . . . in knowing that God is all around me

. . . . in knowing that God is all-powerful

. . . . through the trauma of cancer

. . . . in all of creation

. . . . through discovering

For Lake Arthur interviewees, again, like in Hagerman, human as well as divine elements played an important role in how people found God.

For Artesia, finding God was...

. . . . in knowing that God is here all the time

. . . . in knowing that God is awesome, a God of awe and wonder

. . . . through my Baptism

. . . . when God calls me

. . . . when God takes care of you

. . . . in my time in Catholic schools

. . . . during the Consecration* at Mass

(* Note: For Catholics, the Consecration is when, at Mass, the priest holds up, at the altar, the bread and wine before the people and the moment when, for believers, the bread and wine become the Real Body and Blood of Christ)

. . . . through the examples of others in my life
. . . . when God finds me
. . . . knowing that God will be in the future
. . . . through the wishes of God
. . . . knowing that I am in good health
. . . . in discovering all the good in my life
. . . . when I am aware of a greater reality in my life
. . . . when God helps you
. . . . when I am not at peace but aware of God's presence
. . . . in the process of learning more about God
. . . . through life's struggles
. . . . in the example of the Nuns* I met
. . . . through my parents
. . . . when I petition God
. . . . when I know that God has a plan for me
. . . . through experiencing the presence of God
. . . . through God pushing me
. . . . through my work

(* Note: Nuns are Catholic women who consecrate themselves to God by taking vows of poverty, chastity and obedience and live, usually, in a community of other like-minded women)

For Artesia interviewees, finding God derived from several different things: from church things, from personal things, from community things, from divine things and from human things.

By Culture

When we look at the cultural backgrounds of those interviewed, the following similarities were found between Anglos and Hispanics concerning answers to the question, "How do you find God and where?":

I found God...

. . . . in knowing that God is here all the time
. . . . in knowing that God is awesome, a God of awe and wonder
. . . . in the Bible/Scripture/Word of God
. . . . when I realize that I am blessed
. . . . in the person of Christ
. . . . in the church
. . . . in being a cradle Catholic
. . . . in the Eucharist (Mass)
. . . . in my faith
. . . . in my family
. . . . knowing that there is the existence of heaven
. . . . in my marriage
. . . . from my mother
. . . . from other Christians/Catholics
. . . . in prayer
. . . . through sacrifice

In looking at these cultural similarities between Anglo and Hispanic interviewees, we find, again, that God is found through knowledge, the written word, institutions (both human and divine) and actions.

But, there were some unique answers given for each cultural group as well.

God was found...

For Anglos:

. . . . in the presence of angels
. . . . when I am aware of the bigger picture
. . . . at the moment of the Consecration at Mass
. . . . in contemplation
. . . . in knowing that there is eternal life
. . . . in spending time in Eucharistic adoration
. . . . in getting to know God
. . . . through love
. . . . through being aware of the presence of God
. . . . in knowing that I am saved
. . . . from my spouse

For Hispanics:

. . . . knowing that God is all around me
. . . . knowing that God is all-powerful
. . . . knowing that God is all you need
. . . . knowing that God is always there
. . . . in times when I am angry
. . . . through my Baptism
. . . . when I feel called by God
. . . . when God came looking for me
. . . . through the illness of cancer
. . . . knowing that God will take care of you
. . . . through the Catholic schools I attended
. . . . through the challenges in my life
. . . . through a child's smile
. . . . in creation
. . . . when I am depressed
. . . . when God gives me direction
. . . . in the earth
. . . . in emptiness
. . . . in my enthusiasm for things of God

. . . . in everybody

. . . . everywhere

. . . . through the examples of others in my life

. . . . in finding myself

. . . . through forgiveness

. . . . in the future

. . . . in giving

. . . . in good health

. . . . through a good life

. . . . from my grandmother

. . . . when I am aware of a greater reality

. . . . in my heart

. . . . when God helps you

. . . . in discovering the idea of God

. . . . when learning of God

. . . . through the experiences of my life

. . . . through the struggles in my life

. . . . knowing that God is my main person in life

. . . . in finding meaning in my life

. . . . in my mind

. . . . through music, playing and singing in the choir

. . . . through knowing Nuns

. . . . from my parents

. . . . through patience

. . . . through the peace that I feel

. . . . in knowing that God has a plan for me

. . . . in experiencing the power of God

. . . . when God pushes me

. . . . when I am rebellious

. . . . through the Sacraments

. . . . through the lives of the Saints

. . . . when I serve others

. . . . when I or someone else is sick

. . . . in my soul

. . . . through the Spirit

. . . . when I give thanks
. . . . when I am working

For the cultural differences between the Anglo and Hispanic interviewee responses, we see that most of the Anglo responses could be classified as being more qualitative than quantitative, whereas, for the Hispanic interviewees, more quantitative responses were given. For example, the Anglo interviewees mentioned things like angels, the Consecration at Mass and eternal life, things less quantitative than qualitative, while Hispanics mentioned things like Catholic school, the Sacraments and specific people or things in their lives, things more quantitative than qualitative.

By Age

When we look at the age group breakdown of responses to the question posed to interviewees, "How do you find God and where?" we see the following similarities:

80's & 70's

. . . . God is everywhere
. . . . God is in everybody

80's, 70's & 50's

. . . . God is everywhere

70's & 60's

. . . . God is found in my heart

70's & 50's

. . . . God is found in the sick and when I am sick

<u>70's, 40's & Teens</u>

.... God is found in heaven

<u>70's & 30's</u>

.... God is found through forgiveness

<u>60's & 50's</u>

.... God is always there
.... God is always with you

<u>60's, 50's, 40's & 30's</u>

.... God is found in prayer

<u>60's & 40's</u>

.... God is found in my faith
.... God was found from my mother

<u>60's, 40's & 30's</u>

.... God is found in my family

<u>60's & Teens</u>

.... God is here all the time
.... God is awesome, a God of awe and wonder

<u>50's & 40's</u>

.... God is found when I am blessed
.... God is found in my marriage
.... God is found through other Catholics/Christians
.... God is found through sacrifice

50's & 30's

. . . . God is found in church

50's & Teens

. . . . God is found because I am a cradle Catholic

40's & 30's

. . . . God is found in the Bible

Looking at the above age group similarities, we can break the responses generally into three groupings: those interviewees in their 70's and 80's, those in their 60's, and those under the age of sixty. Let's look at the older age group, those in their 70's and 80's.

For those interviewees over the age of 70, they find God everywhere and in everybody, in their hearts, with the sick or when they are sick, in heaven and through forgiveness.

For those in their 60's: God is always there, God is always with you, God is found through prayer, God is in my faith, finding God was through my mother, God is found in my family, God is here all the time, and God is an awesome God, a God of awe and wonder.

Those interviewees under the age of sixty responded that they were blessed by God, God was found in their marriage, God was found through other Catholics/Christians, through sacrifice, in the Church, because they were cradle Catholics and in the Bible.

A peculiar set of responses given by the teen interviewee included responses that fell into all three of the above categories. The responses were: God is found in heaven, God is present all the time, God is awesome, a God of awe and wonder, and I found God because I was a cradle Catholic.

But, there were also responses that were unique to each of the interviewee age groups such as:

70's

. . . . God is all around me
. . . . God is found in a child's smile
. . . . God is found in church
. . . . God is found in creation
. . . . God is found in the earth
. . . . God is found in my enthusiasm for God
. . . . God is found in the Eucharist (Mass)
. . . . God is found in life
. . . . God is found in Mother Mary
. . . . God is found in my mind
. . . . God is found in the Sacraments
. . . . God is found in my soul
. . . . God is found in the Spirit

60's

. . . . God is all you need
. . . . God will take care of you
. . . . God helps you
. . . . God is my main person

50's

. . . . God is all-powerful
. . . . God is found through my Baptism
. . . . God is found when I feel called by God
. . . . God is found when God came looking for me
. . . . God is found in cancer patients
. . . . God is found through my Catholic schooling
. . . . God is found when God directs me

.... God is found through the examples of others
.... God is found in the future
.... God is found when I give
.... God is found in good health
.... God is found when my life is good
.... God is found when I realize that there is a greater reality
.... God is found when I learn more about God
.... God is found in life's struggles
.... God is found through the examples of the Nuns I knew
.... God is found through my parents
.... God is found when I am at peace
.... God is found when I am aware of God's plan for me
.... God is found in the power of God
.... God is found when God pushes me
.... God is found when I give thanks
.... God is found when I am working

40's

.... God is found in the angels
.... God is found when I see the bigger picture
.... God is found in and through Christ
.... God is found through contemplation
.... God is found when I know that there is eternal life
.... God is found when I am aware of God's will for me
.... God is found when I know God
.... God is found when I love or someone loves me
.... God is found when I know that I am saved
.... God is found from my spouse

30's

.... God is found in my anger
.... God is found through the challenges in my life
.... God is found when I am depressed

. . . . God is found when I am empty

. . . . God is found from my grandmother

. . . . God is found when I am aware of the idea of God

. . . . God is found when I am looking for meaning in my life

. . . . God is found through music, singing or playing in the choir

. . . . God is found through patience

. . . . God is found when I am rebellious

. . . . God is found through the lives of the saints

. . . . God is found when I serve others

Teens

. . . . God is found at the Consecration at Mass

. . . . God is found when I attend the Eucharist (Mass)

. . . . God is found when I am doing Eucharistic adoration

. . . . God is found when I am aware of the presence of God

Some interesting results came from the individual age groups themselves as can be seen above. If we look more closely at these responses, there are some patterns that emerge.

For those interviewees in their 70's, the responses seemed to focus on church things, on human things and on divine things, with responses like finding God in the Sacraments, in my mind and through the Spirit.

For those in their 60's, it seemed that God was sufficient, that God takes care of you and that God helps you.

Those in their 50's focused more on three kinds of action - my actions, God's actions and the actions of other Catholics/Christians - with responses like finding God when I give to others, when God directs me, and through the examples of Nuns I knew.

Interestingly, the respondents in their 40's seemed more transcendent in their answers, with responses like, I find God through contemplation, in knowing that I am saved, and through angels.

Interviewees in their 30's found God through more personal/human traits such as in my anger, when I am depressed, and when I serve others.

Finally, the lone teen interviewee responded in a very contemplative way with answers like finding God at the Consecration at Mass, through Eucharistic adoration and in the presence of God.

By Gender

Looking at the gender breakdown of responses, the similarities between male and female interviewees in how they find God are these:

. . . . God is present all the time
. . . . God is awesome, a God of awe and wonder
. . . . God is found in the Bible
. . . . God is found in Christ
. . . . God is found through the church
. . . . God is found when I go to the Eucharist (Mass)
. . . . God is found through my faith
. . . . God is found in my family
. . . . God is found in my heart
. . . . God is found in heaven
. . . . God is found when I learn more about God
. . . . God is found in my marriage
. . . . God is found from my mother
. . . . God is found through prayer
. . . . God is found through sacrifice

Both men and women interviewees responded similarly with such ways of finding God as through the Bible, in my family, and through prayer and sacrifice. The responses that were unique to males in the interviews were:

Males

. . . . God is found in the angels
. . . . God is found when I am aware that I am blessed
. . . . God is found when I am called by God
. . . . God is found at the Consecration at the Mass (Eucharist)
. . . . God is found in contemplation
. . . . God is found because I am a cradle Catholic
. . . . God is found because I know that there is eternal life
. . . . God is found when I do Eucharistic adoration
. . . . God is found in the future
. . . . God is found when I am in good health
. . . . God is found when life is good to me
. . . . God is found when I know God
. . . . God is found through life's questions
. . . . God is found when God is looking for me
. . . . God is found in love
. . . . God is found in Mother Mary
. . . . God is found through other Christians/Catholics
. . . . God is found when am aware of God's plan for me
. . . . God is found when I am aware of the presence of God
. . . . God is found through my spouse
. . . . God is found when I am working

For male interviewees, responses that had to do with finding God within myself and finding God outside of myself were 42% from within myself and 58% from outside myself. The responses for within myself ranged from finding God through my being blessed by God to finding God through my being called by God to finding God through being aware of God's love for me. Responses for finding God outside of myself ranged from finding God in angels to finding God through my spouse to finding God through other Catholics/Christians.

The responses that were unique to females in the interviews were:

Females

.... God is found knowing that God is all-powerful
.... God is found knowing that God is all I need
.... God is found knowing that God is always there
.... God is found when I am angry
.... God is found through my Baptism
.... God is found in cancer patients
.... God is found when I have cancer
.... God is found knowing that God will take care of me
.... God is found through the Catholic schools I attended
.... God is found in the challenges in my life
.... God is found through a child's smile
.... God is found in creation
.... God is found when I am depressed
.... God is found in the earth
.... God is found in emptiness
.... God is found in my enthusiasm for God
.... God is found in everybody
.... God is found everywhere
.... God is found through the examples of other people
.... God is found through forgiveness
.... God is found when I give
.... God is found when God directs me
.... God is found from my grandmother
.... God is found when I realize that there is a greater reality
.... God is found when God helps me
.... God is found when I learn more about God
.... God is found in life
.... God is found through life's struggles

. . . . God is found when I know God is my main person
. . . . God is found when I am searching for meaning
. . . . God is found in my mind
. . . . God is found through music, singing and playing in the choir
. . . . God is found from the Nuns I have known
. . . . God is found from my parents
. . . . God is found through patience
. . . . God is found when I am at peace
. . . . God is found when I am aware of the power of God
. . . . God is found when I am rebellious
. . . . God is found in the Sacraments
. . . . God is found through the lives of the saints
. . . . God is found when I serve others
. . . . God is found in the sick or when I am sick
. . . . God is found in my soul
. . . . God is found in the Spirit
. . . . God is found when I give thanks

For female interviewees, responses that had to do with finding God within myself and finding God outside of myself were very similar to male interviewees, with 43% finding God from within myself and 57% finding God from outside myself. The responses for finding God within myself ranged from finding God when I am angry to finding God when I serve others to finding God when I forgive. Responses for finding God outside of myself ranged from finding God in creation to finding God through my grandmother.

Based on these results, the differences in responses between male and female interviewees seemed to be more in the area of content than in within/outside myself differences.

Now, I would like to turn attention to a reflection on my eleven years of personal experiences of the 21st century reality of finding God in and around the Artesia and southeast New Mexico Pecos River Valley.

Southeast New Mexico Pecos River Valley: Reflections and the Future

---------------------------------- REFLECTIONS ----------------------------------

THE WONDERS

It amazes me how the past can repeat itself over and over and over again as the years roll by and, in the case of this part of the country, it is so true, probably more so than in many other parts of the country. Over the period of eleven years, I have come to believe that adversities and challenges in living our lives accompany us in all ages, past, present and future, and that, no matter who you are, the process of finding God is incorporated into our surroundings, into our families, into our communities and into the people we meet and the circumstances that accompany those encounters.

But, discovering the presence of God in the present also includes all the wonders, the awe-inspiring moments, when we take a back seat to the wonders of God and let God do the driving, let God provide. Having known so many people like those whose interviews you read here, I am amazed at how the parallels of the universe work, or, should I say, how God works. In the eleven years spent in this part of the "Land of Enchantment", "Satan's Paradise," I am in wonder at how one's faith shines forth in the simplest of ways, at how God finds a way to break through into our lives in a way that sometimes seems very effortless, while at other times, so fragile.

All of us are given opportunities to discover God in our lives through the people we meet, the events that happen to us and the awe-inspiring moments in time when even the simplest of things seem overpowering.

I witnessed people re-connecting with God through sacramental moments at church and in church gatherings such as Baptisms, Confessions, First Communions, Confirmations, Marriages, Healing Services and Ordinations. I also witnessed this re-connection through funerals, quinceaneras and times of prayer, through religious education and faith classes and workshops, talks and missions, through fiestas, pot-lucks and fundraising dinners and meals, and, in the one-on-one counseling sessions in the parish office.

But, I pay homage to the past and the ways the peoples of these parts have, over the centuries, lived their lives with a faith in God, in a Supreme Being or in a pantheon of native deities. Connections abound between the past and the present in the faith journey of southeastern New Mexico Pecos River Valley inhabitants. People still find God in much the same way, from the way a neighbor helps a neighbor, to the way people celebrate God in the happy moments of celebration, to the times when God accompanies us in our journeys, to the way the spirit surrounds us when we pray. I don't believe this process of finding God has changed over the centuries, it's just that the resources have. God is still looked to as a recipient of our thanksgiving. God is still considered a source of healing and benediction. The supernatural is still believed to have the power to cure and to sanctify.

With all this said, the wonders of finding God are to be found in the adventures, the excitement, the joys, the happiness and the testaments of all the explorers and pioneers, the Native Americans and immigrants, the settlers and homesteaders, the outlaws and ranchers, the gamblers and prostitutes, the cattlemen and prairie housewives, the oilfield roustabouts and elderly *abuelos*, the dreamers and businessmen, the women entrepreneurs and rural politicians, the school teachers and sheep ranchers, the *curanderos* and *Iloraderas*, the descendants of Spanish *conquistadors* and Mexican soldiers, and the recent immigrants. All have contributed to the wonders of finding God in this part of the "Land of Enchantment," this "Satan's Paradise."

In the Mid-Pecos Valley of southeastern New Mexico, along US Highway 285 and New Mexico State Route 2, this quest for God had several manifestations for me. These manifestations have roots in the past as well as in present realities, awe-inspiring moments where God's presence is felt, palpable and alive.

The first manifestation is what I call the "Baptismal manifestation", or the Christian encounter with the living God through the new life which we call Baptism. It manifested the wonders of finding God in the sacrament of Baptism, in the profound feelings of joy and pride at having your baby brought into the church family, into the family of God. Like never before, adults were transformed into gushing fonts of piety and spiritual awe at the pouring of the water over their child's forehead as the Trinitarian blessing was bestowed upon that child. It is a way of finding God that brings out the tradition of generations of Christians in these parts, a way of connecting past, present and future. The sacrament of Baptism has not essentially changed over the centuries. It is still the rite of passage for thousands of families and brings with it the support and blessings of the greater church community.

Another manifestation of finding God is in the wonders of music and song, or, as I like to call it, the "lyrical manifestation." I spent some time singing in one of the choirs at one of the parishes I was stationed in in Artesia and discovered the age-old attraction to melodic sound and lyric that has been around in these parts since the early days of Native American chanting and Spanish *guitaristas*. The lure of music encompasses all our senses in some way, whether it is the lilting of soft melodies that take us to other places in our minds and hearts, or whether it is the rhythmic beat of energetic instrument-playing, the wonder of music has a way of bringing God closer to us through our senses and has always been an important part of church life and the spiritual journey. The melodies of non-Christian and Christian tunes have accompanied and continue to accompany generations of native peoples and subsequent generations of immigrant cultures throughout the vast expanse of prairies, deserts, mountains, valleys and river courses of the southeastern New Mexican landscape. You can see in the faces of choir members, of Hispanic, Anglo and Native American descent, the wonder of the musical expression of their faith. It is a wonderful sight to behold and a wonderful sound to listen to.

A third manifestation of this quest of finding God for me was found in the sacrament of Reconciliation, or, Confession, for those who remember it in pre-Vatican Il days. It is the "forgiveness or mercy manifestation." The opportunity to "unload" something that needs to be unloaded, from inside of ourselves, whether it be a serious sin or something that just "bugs" us, is an opportunity to experience God in a way that proves to us that this God is a merciful, compassionate, forgiving and loving God, and not a God of punishment and penance. Indeed, it is a wonder to be experienced by those who really seek forgiveness for their sins.

Time spent in the confessional or in my office hearing confessions was time well spent. It was time that brought out the wonder that is God's mercy, that is God's caring for us. For many people, and I have seen it for myself, it helped them to find God in a way that brought peace to their lives, that brought understanding and acceptance to their lives. In the past, the confessional could be a very scary place, a place of guilt and retribution, a place of sorrow and sin. I have heard horror stories of penitents who have been brought to tears by exacting and incriminating confessors who have squelched the spirit of love and mercy that the sacrament should display. I have also heard stories from confessors who were extremely critical of their penitents, at how wretched and depraved the penitents were.

But, it was the wonder of someone realizing that they were a sinner, then, making the bold move of asking for forgiveness, and finally, realizing the merciful love of God in their lives that makes the sacrament of Reconcilation so awesome and so much a part of finding God. It is a blessing that more people should avail themselves to experience. I have no doubt that, as a confessor, it was my privilege to be a part of such a spiritually enriching experience for many a penitent.

These, then, have been some of my experiences of the 21 st century reality of finding God in this part of America. I have been blessed to have had such experiences and I have found that these experiences have been a continuation of the past in so far as they have been opportunities made available by the presence of church ministers who have and continue to have the courage to pioneer in the southeastern New Mexico landscape of wonder, awe and challenge.

THE SORROWS

It is with a heavy heart that I must relate some of the sorrows I experienced in this part of the country over eleven years, some of the gut-wrenching and soul-searching times spent with individuals and families in life and death situations in their lives. Crosses are sometimes hard to take and accept in our lives. We question God and doubt infiltrates our minds as we wonder why. But, it is just these times when we can find God in our lives, when we have sunk the lowest and we can't sink any lower because of the desolation, pain and suffering.

I remember times when, as a priest, I was called in to bring hope and consolation to a hurting individual or family, or to just be the presence of a minister, as I professed to uphold this responsibility as a Catholic clergy person. There were times at funerals, at the hospital, on sick calls, during prayers of healing over people or in places, during confessions and serving those in need as Director of the St. Vincent de Paul Society, when the sorrow was very apparent, very alive, in the hearts and minds of those I were present with. Memories of human sorrow are the seeds of divine presence in our lives and moments of hope for the future no matter how painful or desolate they are. It has been my privilege to have been present at just such moments in the lives of other human beings. They have blessed me with spiritual depth and fortitude, and helped me to find more of God's presence in the present moment.

I recall one funeral, where, pulling up to the church in my car, I could hear a woman sobbing loudly from inside the church. This continued all the way through the end of the funeral Mass. The young man being buried was a senior at a local high school and was about to graduate when, at a football game, he was found snorting from a chemical can under the stands, and had to be rushed to the hospital. He died in the ambulance on the way to the hospital. The wailings of the young man's mother could barely express the intense grief she felt. And, at the cemetery, in stifling heat, her wailings continued, this time, with other women joining in. The tradition of *lloraderas* continues today, especially in the Hispanic culture.

This was an instance where I was part of a greater scheme of grief that brought with it the cultural tradition of Hispanic grieving into the picture. But, it wasn't just a cultural expression of grief, it was a maternal expression of profound grief. Other funerals I was involved in as a minister involved a man who drank himself to death, a suicide victim, an ex-police chief and the victims of fatal car crashes. No doubt, these experiences were, for all those concerned, instances of looking for and, hopefully, finding God, in difficult and traumatic times.

Other times of God-encounters were visits to the hospital Emergency Room (ER) after a car accident, an attempted suicide, or a 911 episode. One time, while I was ministering to someone in the ER, the ER Director came into the room and asked me if I could stick around, because there had just been an explosion at the local oil refinery and they were bringing two internal burn victims into the ER at that very moment. Other times, there were visits to the Senior Care Unit at the hospital where seniors were more or less quarantined because of Alzheimer's disease or dementia. Psychiatric patients can be very hard to minister to.

Sick calls to the dying, sick or ill were other encounters with God that proved the power of God and the power of faith. At other times, a priest would be needed to exorcise either a place or a person. Normally, in the Catholic Church, each Diocese has a designated exorcist who would be called upon to do exorcisms throughout the diocese. So, I was limited to prayers and exhortations over someone or some place for healing or blessing. Sometimes, someone would call the rectory to ask for a priest to come and dispel evil spirits which they believed existed in their house or within someone. One of the priests I lived with actually answered a call one day that came in from the local movie theater who requested a priest to exorcise the theater itself!

Then, there was the confessional, where penitents would confess grave sins against morality in the privacy of the confessional. Sins against themselves, against others and against God. The motivation for someone coming to the confessional to confess an offense is between that person and God. The guilt that pushes someone to seek forgiveness, no matter how serious the sin, is, in this case, a good thing. It is a sign that that person has a conscience. Despite the sorrowful situations that people may find themselves in, there is the hope of mercy, forgiveness and compassion that the sacrament of Reconciliation brings. It can bring joy out of sorrow.

Another of the sorrows that I experienced in my time in New Mexico involved my ministry with the St. Vincent de Paul Society. To see people struggling with putting food on the table and paying bills, to see people struggling to escape drug or alcohol addiction, to see people who had no place to live, to see people just-released from prison or jail with no money and no place to live, to see victims of domestic abuse, including sexual abuse, to see people who have been abandoned by their families, and to see people who have psychological problems, all coming to St. Vincent de Paul seeking help is a real wake-up call for us ministers and those who have dedicated their lives to helping others. The sorrows and contrition I experienced through social ministry could only be described as revelatory. God was being revealed through the hardships, struggles, and experiences of people caught up in things that sometimes push them over the edge and into depression and hopelessness.

When people would come to the church seeking help with relationships, personal problems, or spiritual dilemmas, I would usually see a note on the bulletin board in the parish office for a priest to call such-and-such a person or persons to set up an appointment. These one-on-one counseling sessions usually addressed the personal struggles of an individual or individuals and would usually involve the spiritual and a person's faith, or lack of faith, in God who became the scapegoat for the persons' dilemma(s). Certainly, the person or persons themselves would also blame themselves, but, in marriage, substance addiction, or spiritual warfare, it seemed that a person's or persons' capacity to cope was being stretched beyond their endurance and ability to handle the situation, and it was affecting the way this person or persons related with themselves, with others and with God.

So, are these present-day realities any different from peoples' struggles with and experiences of finding God in the past along the Pecos River of southeastern New Mexico? I will leave reflections on that for the following pages. But, it is quite obvious to me at least that these experiences are quite revelatory in nature, no matter when they occurred, and help us to find God in our lives.

THE REVELATIONS

In sacred scripture, revelation occurs when God has something to say to us, and, we are willing to listen. God's trans-human presence is validated through human means and it is understood in human terms, but it is still the transcendent God who reveals. It is still the divine that is being revealed, and, we must be ready and willing to receive it. Revelations have occurred throughout the past and continue to this day. God is continually revealing God's self through people, places, and events. It is an ongoing process that will continue into the future. And, the revelations from the present are but a continuation of the past and a precursor of the future. What my experience in the Pecos Valley of New Mexico taught me about revelation is that it is something you don't go looking for, but it is something that just happens. What God revealed to me was very special and precious. Here are just a few of those revelations.

In the area of faith, what has struck me most is the awesome amount of faith people have. Despite sometimes seemingly insurmountable situations, people exhibit a profound faith that keeps them going despite the setbacks. It is this faith that inspires them and it inspires me. When a family is losing a family member to death, praying with the family seems to bring out this faith and I have experienced many such prayer vigils for the dying. Or, when someone in the family does something bad or evil, it is faith that keeps the family together. And, I have seen it with my own eyes. Faith is strong and resilient and can bring one through the tears.

Another revelation was the inherent goodness of people. It is the amazing discovery that, despite what evils people do to one another, and to themselves, they are still good people. Very rarely do you find someone who does not have this goodness, for one reason or another, sometimes, not of their own making. In general, however, people are good. On the outside someone may seem very rude and unforgiving, but deep down they are beautiful people. At times, I would come across people who swore like you wouldn't believe. It seemed that everything that came out of their mouths was a bad word. Yet, these same people would give to a worthy cause, support their church, help someone in need, or donate to charity. As the cliché goes, "you can never tell a book by its cover." Goodness is the God within us trying to come out, to show to others that I am a child of God, that I am created in the image of God and that I am a good person.

Another revelation was hope. It was the sign of hope that I experienced in people that brought me to tears sometimes. Hope does indeed spring eternal, as Alexander Pope once said. And, it is the source of revelation. A big sign of hope for me was on youth retreats, where fifty to a hundred and fifty young people would gather to pray, fellowship and reflect on God, on their lives and on those around them. These were powerful witnesses of hope in a world that can seem to lack such witness. To see the openness of these young people to God seemed almost counter-cultural in that it is generally believed that our youth culture today has lost a sense of morality and the difference between what is right and what is wrong. Lack of hope in the future seemed to be prevalent in many of this generation of the future. So, present signs of hope exist, but there is still a profound need for prayer in the revelatory process.

Prayer played, and continues to play, a vital role in the faith lives of many in the Pecos River Valley of southeastern New Mexico as it did and does in the rest of the world, the mainstay of church worship as it has been for generation upon generation. The times when I prayed with people underscored for me the importance of prayer in their lives. It marked a moment of escaping from this world and all its sorrows into God's world of love, compassion and forgiveness. In prayer groups, in one-to-one encounters, in liturgical settings, in sacramental moments, all these have consoled, inspired, and uplifted those who participated in them. Whether it was with married couples at a group meeting in their homes or with young people on a youth retreat or in the confessional, prayer became a moment of grace that brought a sense of peace into hearts and calm out of chaos.

Another revelation I found was in the love that I saw in others towards others, within families, within communities, in work places, at church and among strangers. To see the concern shown to the poor and needy by families, by the community, by businesses, by schools, by churches, by civic organizations and by individuals, was amazing. People, businesses and organizations would donate food, money and time to help those in need without being asked to. They would just give. This show of love amazed me in its generosity.

This generosity of people spoke to me of the love that is within human beings, it spoke to me of the presence of God manifested in the willingness of people to give of their time, talents and treasures. Generosity is a very human thing, yet, it is a divine thing. It is the giving of ourselves to others, yet, it is a giving of the God within ourselves to others. Generosity comes from a thankfulness for the blessings God has given to me and from a realization that I am a sinner and in need of salvation. Generosity knows no boundaries of time or place. It is still the same over the centuries and within different cultures. It is a presence that transcends our human condition and lets us know that there is a God.

Yet another revelation for me was the fortitude, endurance and strength to survive of those whom I came into contact with on a daily basis. It was their coping with the daily challenges of life that revealed the adaptability and perseverance of the human spirit, just as it had to generations of southeastern New Mexicans before them. The resiliency of the human spirit is a profound reality that can, at times, boggle the mind and heart. It reveals an uncanny knack to adapt and a deep drive to survive that is more powerful than any other human trait. Self-preservation is an innate instinct that says that I don't want to die, that I don't want to give up, that I don't want to give in. Some can seem to have more than others while some who don't seem to have any can have the most. History seems to prove that over the generations, survival is a necessary thing for us human beings, just as it is in the animal world. Survival mode involves a deep desire to say no to the seeming finality of death. It seems to deny resurrection in a way, yet, gives one hope in the resurrection, saying, I can survive, and I will survive. But, just as this will to survive was evident to me in people, there was also a deep desire for repentance that appeared to be just as deep-seeded.

Repentance was revealed, especially, in the confessional. At times, it would seem that some people would be in a continuous state of guilt and repentance. The Spanish and Mexican cultures, especially, seemed to have this profound guilt over their sins and a tremendous need for repentance. Repentance revealed the real-ness of people, that they recognized that they needed to repent of their sins, ala John the Baptist. But, not only, repent of their sins, but it was, I think, in the recognition of the reality of sin in their lives that they recognized God and the mercy of God. To repent was to acknowledge evil and want to overcome it. This takes personal integrity.

This personal integrity was another revelation of the God within. I saw people discovering their own integrity, sometimes, for the very first time. They discovered the quality of their lives and that they were filled with the presence of God in a way that spoke to them of their worth and loveableness in the eyes of God, themselves and others. The integrity that I witnessed, especially the growing integrity among young people, was, in fact, truly revelatory for me. It was a real sign of the ability of people to find God within themselves. Strength and integrity, two more revelations of God in people, and, two more instances of God revealing God's self. But, if revelations aren't remembered, they disappear. And so, my memories, like the memories of generations past, stick with me to remind me of God's presence in the people, places and events I have been privileged to have experienced in my eleven years in the "Land of Enchantment," in "Satan's Paradise."

THE MEMORIES

It is the memories which I carry with me that remind me of God's presence not only in the lives of others, but in my life as well. Those memories are like good books that I can turn to whenever I am having a test of faith in God. The pages of the books are meant to be turned and read. The books are not meant to be closed. This is the purpose of memories, and my memories of eleven years in southeastern New Mexico are meant to be read and interpreted through the eyes of a minister of God, through the eyes of a Catholic priest.

My memories of the times of prayer, of the times of joy, of the times of pain and suffering, of the times of depression and hopelessness, and of the times of revelation are the memories that will live on in my mind and heart. They are the memories of present realities as well as reminders of past times. And, I don't believe for one second that these memories will ever disappear. They have been etched in my psyche like the historical record of the past has been etched in the annals of time in this timeless land. Memories of the faces of those I have encountered continue the legacy of a past history of pioneers, saints, sinners and survivors in a land where encounters with God take on different hues. The lives I have been privileged to have been a part of continue the march of human survival in this Land of Enchantment, this land of *Poco Tiempo*, this land of desert and plain along the course of the Pecos River in what is present-day southeastern New Mexico, between Roswell and Carlsbad, in *Satan's Paradise*.

If memories and historical persons, places and events are made up of encounters with the human face of God, then, these memories can play a part in the future. And, what lies in the future includes changes, changes in how things are done, changes in why things are done, and changes in context. One of these future changes is in the area of ministry. Over the centuries, the practice of one's faith has been inevitably linked with time, place, persons, environment and circumstances. We are essentially no different in human adaptability and temperament now than we were two hundred years ago and we will be two hundred years from now. But, there are challenges for the future. It is hard to predict what will happen in southeastern New Mexico in the years to come, but, it is certain that there will be some changes that occur.

——————— WHAT DOES THE FUTURE HOLD? ———————

Recent national concern over the health and stress level of American Catholic priests, especially as their numbers decline, may be an indicator of changes that need to be made in parish structure because of geographic and socio-economic conditions.

Some see the growth of lay, non-ordained ministry as one means of integrating the sacred and the secular, a spiritual life and a socio-political life. If this is to bring about "an authentic inner response to present realities," that spirituality will have to be based on more than group liturgies or the recitation of private prayers. There will be a consequent need for contemplative prayer, that silence in which the prophetic call to ministry can be heard.

There is no doubt that the changes of Vatican II have been difficult for some American Catholics. Many still cling to passive roles as obedient followers, more concerned about being saved than building the Kingdom. They "still expect their pastor or the bishop to make all the decisions, to do the organizing and to shoulder the responsibility. They do not wish to be shaken out of their apathy." Others, long active in the Church as "volunteers," simply miss "the old-time religion," the old hymns, the ornate high altars, side altars, the solemnity of organ music, and "the statues representing dear old friends who gladdened [them] in joy and consoled [them] in sorrow." Where is the middle ground to be found between a religion of consolation and one of constant challenge? Perhaps, in looking beyond specific changes in parish structure and style and in recovering the prophetic spirit that inspired them, Catholics can (like the Native American and Spanish American cultures) rediscover something old and, in light of current circumstances, make it new. This region's Anglos, Hispanics and Native Americans must call for the kind of exploration that will make diversity and pluralism within the Church once again fruitful. To consider the current statistics on Spanish-speaking immigrants to this country is a step in understanding the history of their invisibility in the American Church, for example.

The so-called "praxis" model recognizes that God is revealed in history. Consequently, history and human stories become the primary theological category. Edward Schillebeeckx once wrote that "grace and salvation, redemption and religion, need not be expressed in strange, supernatural terms; they can be put into ordinary human language, the language of picture and image, testimony and story, never detached from a specific liberating event." These are the events of the past, of the present and of the future. They will continue to forge the act of finding God in a land of barrenness, wind-swept expanse and drought. What the future holds for this region of the United States lies in its past and the lessons learned from that past as well as in the adaptations that will be necessary for changing conditions and populations in the future.

However, it will continue to be formed by its isolation, climate and desperation in the face of the challenges that have always been a part of its story and legacy.

Finding God in the future will require a resourcefulness, ingenuity and imagination that will define future generations in a way that recalls the pioneer histories of the past and the challenges of the present. It will involve asking questions that will be shaped by factors that are present on a more regional, national and international basis. And, in some instances, this search will already have been solved. Sometimes, human beings struggle, or should I say, yearn for what is not familiar to them, unlike the familiarity of the past. The future of discovering new revelations of God depends upon the faith, hope and love that those who will make the journey possess. And, it will be, I hope, a journey not unlike the efforts of those who inhabited these parts in the past, a journey of guts, integrity, passion and understanding that will continue to defy the odds in a land of subsistence and potential, a land of family and independence, a land of enchantment, *una tierra del encanto*!

THE AMENS!

To say Amen to this story invokes a sadness and a joy. To say Amen is to say Yes to all that has transpired, all that continues to transpire and all that will transpire along the southeastern New Mexico Pecos River, in a land called "Little Texas", that was created out of the dust into a living being that has a life that is all its own, a life infused with the trials and tribulations, the joys and celebrations, and the Amens, the *Yes-es*, that continue to echo within it and its places of worship. Nowhere else do these Amens ring out in all their power than here in this still-desolate landscape of tumbleweeds and oil pump-jacks spread out over acres and acres of land that hasn't change much from the time thousands of years ago when indigenous peoples roamed and inhabited these parts.

Putting an exclamation point on these pages is the stark reality of our existence and its relationship with God. If it were not for the lives, passions, foibles and integrity of those who have gone before us, who lived in these parts over the last, more than, two thousand years, this book would not have existed. It would have been a dormant possibility waiting to be opened. Well, now that it has been opened, it is time to echo the Amens of those whose lives spelled out the search for God in a land of ultimate challenges and rewards. And so, I say Amen!

I say Amen to the ingenuity of Native Americans who survived the environment of this land for centuries. I say Amen to the fortitude of a Spanish friar who accompanied the *Conquistadors* who explored this land for Spain. I say Amen to the courage of the Mexican immigrants who fled the persecutions in their native land to settle in this place. I say Amen to the strength of the Negro ex-slaves who left their Civil-War-torn homelands to settle in the expanse of this new land as homesteaders. I say Amen to the perseverance of the pioneer women who kept their families together and taken care of in this hostile land of wind and drought.

I say Amen to the audacity of pioneer preachers who fought against the evils of society with their Bibles in hand. I say Amen to the *parteras* who helped new life come into this land. I say Amen to the cowboys who helped drive cattle herds to feed others. I say Amen to the *curanderos/as* who provided people with natural cures and *remedios* when doctors wouldn't work. Yes, I say Amen to all these and to the thousands of men, women and children who have, continue to have and will have the pioneer spirit it takes to find God in this land of enchantment, in this land of "milk and honey", in this land that is southeast New Mexico.

AFTER-THOUGHTS

I hope that there will be future inquiries into this fascinating part of the world as well as into other just-as-fascinating lands of the earth and their relationship with the quest for God. To find God is to find not just the transcendent presence in all things, no matter who or what they are, but the immanent presence of God in those things. It is the ultimate journey through time, its peoples, places and things, that seeks to provide us with answers to life's questions. My quest in this book has been to relate the past, present and future along the Pecos River of southeastern New Mexico and its environs and how that continuum of people, places and events has been instrumental in how this land has discovered God and found the revelations of that God throughout its history. I hope that I have been able to relate this in a way that honors the past, its people, places and events, respected the present reality of people's faith and faithfully pondered the future of a land of many hues, beliefs and experiences. May God bless this Enchanted Land!

Bibliography/References/Sources

1. Anderson, George B., *History of New Mexico: Its Resources and People*, Volume 2, Pacific States Publishing Company, Los Angeles, CA, 1907.
2. *Artesia Advocate*, "Some Condensed Facts", June 24, 1911.
3. Artesia Chamber of Commerce, "Artesia History and Culture", Artesia, New Mexico, Visitor Information, http://www.artesiachamber.com/vi/his.htm, accessed in 2014.
4. *Artesia Daily Press*, "Methodists Organize Church Here In 1903", Aug. 7, 1955.
5. *Artesia Daily Press*, "Immanuel Lutheran Church Celebrating 50 Years Today", 1965.
6. *Artesia Daily Press*, "Hermosa Church of Christ, Founded March 4, 1956", June 19, 1977.
7. *Artesia Daily Press*, 'Trinity Temple Assembly of God Marks 70th Year", no date.
8. *Artesia Daily Press*, "Lakewood Church is 50 Years Old", August 26, 1990.
9. *Artesia Daily Press*, "First Christian Church - 100th Anniversary Celebration", October, 2004
10. *Artesia Daily Press*, Artesia 'Young Professionals', 2014.
11. *Artesia Enterprise*, "St. Anthony Catholic Church", June 14, 1940.
12. Artesia Historical Museum, "The Catholic Community of Our Lady of Grace"
13. Artesia Historical Museum, "Clark Memorial Methodist Church — Artesia, New Mexico".

14. Artesia Historical Museum, "First Methodist Church —Artesia, New Mexico".

15. Artesia Historical Museum, "First Methodist Church — Dexter, New Mexico".

16. Artesia Historical Museum, "First Methodist Church — Hagerman, New Mexico".

17. Artesia Historical Museum, "First Methodist Church — Lake Arthur, New Mexico".

18. Artesia Historical Museum, "The Growth of Our Lady of Grace From a Mission to Parish".

19. Artesia Historical Museum, "A New Mexico Circuit Rider", John W. Hendrix.

20. Artesia Historical Museum, "Historical Sketch of the Methodist Episcopal Church South — Artesia, New Mexico".

21. Artesia Historical Museum, "Hope Methodist Church — Hope, New Mexico".

22. Artesia Historical Museum, "Incidents Concerning the History of the New Mexico Conference of the Methodist Church".

23. Artesia Historical Museum, "Our Catholic Heritage".

24. Artesia Historical Museum, "Sherman Memorial Methodist Church — Loco Hills, New Mexico".

25. Artesia Historical Society, List of Artesia Churches Foundation Dates, Artesia, New Mexico.

26. Atchison, Topeka & Santa Fe Company, *The Pecos Valley, New Mexico*, January, 1903, reprinted by Leopold Classic Library.

27. Banks, Phyllis Eileen, "Dexter, Hagerman and Lake Arthur", Southern New Mexico Travel and Tourism Information, http://southernnewmexico.com/Articles/Southeast/Chaves/DexterHagermanandLakeArth.html, accessed in 2014.

28. Barrera, Mario, *Race and Class in the Southwest: A Theory of Racial Inequality*, University of Notre Dame Press, Notre Dame, IN, 1979.

29. Beck, Warren A., *New Mexico: A History of Four Centuries*, University of Oklahoma Press, Norman, OK, 1962.

30. Binkovitz, Leah, "Welcome to Blackdom: The Ghost Town That Was New Mexico's First Black Settlement", at the Smithsonian, http://www.smithsonianmag.com/smithsonian-institution/welcome-to-blackdom-the-ghost-town that-was-new-mexico s-first-black-settlement-10750177/?no-ist, accessed in 2014.

31. Birchell, Donna, *Eddy County, Images of America*, Southeastern New Mexico Historical Society, Roswell, NM, 2011.

32. Birchell, Donna Blake & John LeMay, *Hidden History of Southeast New Mexico*, The History Press, Charleston, SC, 2017.

33. Bogener, Stephen, *Ditches Across the Desert: Irrigation in the Lower Pecos Valley*, Texas Tech University Press, Lubbock, TX, 2003.

34. Bureau of Immigration of the Territory of New Mexico, *Eddy County, New Mexico*, J.S. Duncan, Public Printer, 1850, reprinted by Legare Street Press, Creative Media Partners.

35. Burton, Bob, "A Branchline Comes of Age", Part Two, Santa Fe Railway Historical and Modeling Society, http://www.atsfrr.com/resources/burton/branch-2.htm, accessed in 2014.

36. Cabeza de Baca, Fabiola, "We Fed Them Cactus", Albuquerque, NM, 1954, from *The New Mexican Hispano*.

37. Carnett, Daniel R., *Contending for the Faith: Southern Baptists in New Mexico, 1938-1995*, University of New Mexico Press, Albuquerque, NM, 2002.

38. Chaves County Historical Society, *Roundup on the Pecos*, Roswell, NM, 1978.

39. Chavez, Fray Angelico, *My Penitente Land: Reflections on Spanish New Mexico*, University of New Mexico Press, Albuquerque, NM, 1974.

40. City of Albuquerque, "The Town of Blackdom", http://www.cabq.gov/humanrights/public-information-and-education/diversity booklets/black-heritage-in-new-mexico/the-town-of-blackdom/, accessed in 2014.

41. Cremony, John C., *Life Among the Apaches*, A. Roman & Company, New York, NY, 1868.

42. Cortes, Carlos, Editor, *The Mexican American*, "The Penitentes of New Mexico" Arno Press, New York, NY, 1974.

43. Darley, Alex M., "The Passionists of the Southwest or the Holy Brotherhood: A Revelation of the Penitentes", Pueblo, CO, 1893, from Carlos Cortez, Editor, *The Mexican American*, Arno Press, New York, NY, 1974.

44. Dolan, Jay P., Editor, *The American Catholic Parish: A History from 1850 to the Present, Volume Il — Pacific States, Intermountain West, Midwest*, Paulist Press, Mahwah, NJ, 1987.

45. Drive the Old Spanish Trail, "The Ozark Trails, New Mexico — Pecos Valley Route", Old US 90/290/80, St. Augustine, FL to San Diego, CA, http://www.drivetheost.com/pecosvalleyroute.html, accessed in 2014.

46. Drive the Old Spanish Trail, "Pyramids on the Trail", The Ozark Trails, New Mexico — Ozark Trails Marker, Lake Arthur, Old US 90/290/80, St. Augustine, FL to San Diego, CA, http://www.drivetheost.com/pyramidsonthetra.html, accessed in 2014.

47. Dunn, Nancy & Naomi Florez, *Artesia, Images of America*, Artesia Historical Museum & Art Center, Arcadia Publishing, Charleston, South Carolina, 2011.

48. Fails, G.Y., A.B., *A Study of the Development of Town Government in Hagerman, New Mexico, 1905-1948*, Eastern New Mexico University, 1951.

49. Fergusson, Erna, *New Mexico: A Paqeant of Three Peoples*, University of New Mexico Press, Albuquerque, NM, 1973.

50. Fincher, E.B., Ph.D. Dissertation, *Spanish-Americans as a Political Factor in New Mexico: 1912-1950*, Arno Press, New York, NY, 1974.

51. Fleming, Elvis E., *Roundup on the Pecos Il*, iUniverse, Inc., New York, NY, 2005.

52. Foote, Cheryl J., *Women of the New Mexico Frontier, 1846-1912*, University Press of Colorado, 1990.

53. Gamio, Manuel, *Mexican Immigration to the United States: A Study of Human Migration and Adjustment*, Dover Publications, Inc., New York, NY, 1971.

54. Ghosttowns.com, "Alellen – New Mexico Ghost Town", http://ghosttowns.com/states/nm/alellen.html, accessed in 2014.

55. Ghosttowns.com, "Blackdom – New Mexico Ghost Town", http://ghosttowns.com/states/nm/blackdom.html, accessed in 2014.

56. Ghosttowns.com, "Felix – New Mexico Ghost Town", http://ghosttowns.com/states/nm/felix.html, accessed in 2014.

57. Ghosttowns.com, "Greenfield – New Mexico Ghost Town", http://ghosttowns.com/states/nm/greenfield.html, accessed in 2014.

58. Ghosttowns.com, "Lake Van – New Mexico Ghost Town", http://ghosttowns.com/states/nm/lakevan.html, accessed in 2014.

59. Ghosttowns.com, "Orchard Park – New Mexico Ghost Town", http://ghosttowns.com/states/nm/orchardpark.html, accessed in 2014.

60. Ghosttowns.com, "South Spring – New Mexico Ghost Town", http://ghosttowns.com/states/nm/southspring.html, accessed in 2014.

61. Ghosttowns.com, "Vocant – New Mexico Ghost Town", http://ghosttowns.com/states/nm/vocant.html, accessed in 2014.

62. Gonzalez, Nancie L., *The Spanish-Americans of New Mexico: A Heritage of Pride*, University of New Mexico Press, Albuquerque, NM, 1967.

63. Gray, Mary Jane, "Cottonwood Methodist Church Joins Artesia First Methodist Church".

64. Hagerman Historical Society, *Meetinq the Train: Haqerman, New Mexico and Its Pioneers (Facsimile of Oriqinal 1975 Edition)*, Sunstone Press, Santa Fe, 2007.

65. Hagerman, Percy, James John Haqerman: A Sketch of His Life, Colorado Springs, CO, 1932.

66. Henderson, Alice Corbin, "Brothers of Light: The Penitentes of the Southwest", Harcourt, Brace and Company, New York, NY, 1937, from Carlos Cortes, Editor, *The Mexican American*, Arno Press, New York, NY, 1974.

67.   Historical Marker Database, "Blackdom Townsite", http://www. hmdb.org/marker.asp?MarkerID=56143&Print=1, accessed in 2014.

68.   Historical Marker Database, "Civilian Conservation Corps – Lake Arthur Campsite", http://www.hmdb.org/marker.asp?MarkerID=56142&Print=1, accessed in 2014.

69.   Horka-Follick, Lorayne Ann, Ph.D., *Los Hermanos Penitentes: A Vestige of Medievalism in Southwestern United States*, Western Lore Press, Los Angeles, CA, 1969.

70.   Jaramillo, Cleofas M., "Shadow of the Past", Santa Fe, NM, 1941, from *The New Mexican Hispano*.

71.   Jelinek, Arthur J., *A Prehistoric Sequence in the Middle Pecos Valley, New Mexico*, University of Michigan, Ann Arbor, MI, 1967.

72.   Jensen, Joan M. and Darlis A. Miller, *New Mexico Women: Intercultural Perspectives*, "The Women of Lincoln County, 1860-1900", Darlis A. Miller, University of New Mexico Press, Albuquerque, NM, 1986.

73.   Johnson, Rev. Joseph P., S.J., Pastor, *Directory of St. Anthony Catholic Church*, Artesia, NM, 1990.

74.   Lanrath, Fr. John, O.F.M., *Directory of Immaculate Conception Missions of the Pecos Valley: Immaculate Conception Mission in Dexter, St. Catherine Church in Hagerman, Our Lady of Guadalupe in Lake Arthur*, Dexter, New Mexico, 1989.

75.   Larson, Carole, *Forgotten Frontier: The Story of Southeastern New Mexico*, University of New Mexico Press, Albuquerque, NM, 1993.

76.   Lucero, Ruby, *History of the Dexter Parish*, Hagerman, New Mexico.

77.   Lummis, Charles F., *The Land of Poco Tiempo*, University of New Mexico Press, Albuquerque, NM, 1893 (originally), 1969 (3rd printing).

78.   Manson, Craig, "Catholicism in New Mexico", The Catholic Gene, http://catholicgene.wordpress.com/2012/02/13/catholicism-in-new-mexico/, 2012, accessed in 2014.

79. Near Loving's Bend, Chronology of Carlsbad and Eddy County Area from Newspaper Reports, http://nlb.coffeecup.com/files/Download/Chronology, accessed in 2014, 2015 and 2016.

80. New Mexico Farm and Ranch Heritage Museum, "Oral History Program Interview Abstract – Ferdinand Barg", http://www.nmfarmandranchmuseum.org/oralhistory/PDFs/interview_153.pdf, 2001, accessed in 2014.

81. New Mexico Farm and Ranch Heritage Museum, "Oral History Program Interview Abstract – Clarence McKnight 'Bill' Bogle", http://www.nmfarmandranchmuseum.org/oralhistory/detail.php?interview=158, 2000, accessed in 2014.

82. New Mexico Farm and Ranch Heritage Museum, "Oral History Program Interview Abstract – Nick Clemenza", http://www.nmfarmandranchmuseum.org/oralhistory/detail.php?interview=169, 2000, accessed in 2014.

83. New Mexico Farm and Ranch Heritage Museum, "Oral History Program Interview Abstract – Mary E. Dowell", http://www.nmfarmandranchmuseum.org/oralhistory/detail.php?interview=175, 2000, accessed in 2014.

84. New Mexico Farm and Ranch Heritage Museum, "Oral History Program Interview Abstract – Wilfried Gruber", http://www.nmfarmandranchmuseum.org/oralhistory/detail.php?interview=185, 2001, accessed in 2014.

85. New Mexico Farm and Ranch Heritage Museum, "Oral History Program Interview Abstract – Emmett Knight Patterson", http://www.nmfarmandranchmuseum.org/oralhistory/detail.php?interview=166, 2000, accessed in 2014.

86. New Mexico Farm and Ranch Heritage Museum, "Oral History Program Interview Abstract – Walter Schmid/Hans Rudolph Poethig", http://www.nmfarmandranchmuseum.org/oralhistory/detail.php?interview=192, 1999, accessed in 2014.

87. New Mexico Farm and Ranch Heritage Museum, "Oral History Program Interview Abstract – Dwight L. Sharp", http://www.nmfarmandranchmuseum.org/oralhistory/detail.php?interview=197, 2000, accessed in 2014.

88.	New Mexico Farm and Ranch Heritage Museum, "Oral History Program Interview Abstract – Chester/Helen Walker", http://www.nmfarmandranchmuseum.org/oralhistory/detail.php?interview=28, 2000, accessed in 2014.

89.	New Mexico Farm and Ranch Heritage Museum, "Oral History Program Interview Abstract – Farrell L. Watson/Donald W. Watson", http://www.nmfarmandranchmuseum.org/oralhistory/detail.php?interview=33, 2000, accessed in 2014.

90.	New Mexico Geological Society, *Guidebook of Southeastern New Mexico*, Floersheim Printing Company, Roy, NM, 1973.

91.	New Mexico Wanderings, "Blackdom Baptist Church at Blackdom, NM, Southwest United States", http://newmexicowanderings.com/blackdo7.htm, accessed in 2014.

92.	Oakes, Yvonne R., *The Ontiberos Site: A Hispanic Homestead Near Roswell, New Mexico*, Laboratory of Anthropology Note No. 311, Santa Fe, NM, 1983.

93.	Pearce, T.M., Editor, *New Mexico Place Names: A Geographical Dictionary*, University of New Mexico Press, Albuquerque, NM, 1965.

94.	Pritchard, Stu, *Eddy County . . . A Fond Look Back – Memories of Other Years*, Great Western Printing Co., Inc.

95.	Reitenbach, Gail, *How My Neighbor Worships: A Grand Tour of Faith Communities*, Right Hand Communications, Santa Fe, NM, 2006.

96.	Rhodes, Henry K., *A History of the Church of Christ in Artesia, New Mexico*, M.A. Thesis, May, 1958.

97.	Roadside America, "Shrine of the Miracle Tortilla, Lake Arthur, New Mexico", http://www.roadsideamerica.com/story/10166, accessed in 2014.

98.	Robb, John Donald, *Hispanic Folk Music of New Mexico and the Southwest: A Self-Portrait of a People*, University of Oklahoma Press, Norman, OK, 1980.

99.	Robe, Stanley L., *Hispanic Folktales from New Mexico*, Folklore Studies: 30, University of California Press, Berkeley, CA, 1977.

100. Robe, Stanley L., *Hispanic Legends from New Mexico*, Folklore and Mythology Studies: 31, University of California Press, Berkeley, CA, 1980.

101. Scholes, Frances, "Problems in the Early Ecclesiastical History of New Mexico", *New Mexico Historical Review*, January, 1932.

102. Schroeder and Matson, *A Colony on the Move: Gaspar Castano de Sosa's Journal, 1590-1591*, The School of American Research, 1965.

103. Sheridan, Tom, *The Bitter River: A Brief Historical Survey of the Middle Pecos River Basin*, Bureau of Land Management – New Mexico, August, 1975.

104. Simmons, Marc, *New Mexico: A Bicentennial History*, W.H. Norton & Company, Inc., New York, NY, 1977.

105. Southeastern New Mexico Economic Development District, "Town of Dexter History", http://snmedd.com/town-of-dexter-history/, accessed in 2014.

106. Southeastern New Mexico Economic Development District, "Town of Lake Arthur History", http://snmedd.com/town-of-lake-arthur-history/, accessed in 2014.

107. Southeastern New Mexico Historical Society of the Carlsbad, New Mexico Area, http://nearlovingsbend.net, 18,000 historical photographs of the Southeastern New Mexico Historical Society of the Carlsbad, New Mexico Area, 1912-2012: A New Mexico Statehood Centennial Project, Dr. Paul Derby, D.CS., accessed in 2014, 2015 and 2016.

108. Speth, John D. & William J. Parry, *Late Prehistoric Bison Procurement in Southeastern New Mexico*, University of Michigan Department of Anthropology, Ann Arbor, MI, 1980.

109. Stanley, F., *The Seven Rivers, New Mexico Story*, P.O. Box 11, Pep, TX, 1963.

110. Steele, Rhetts and Awalt, *Seeds of Struggle – Harvest of Faith: The History of the Catholic Church in New Mexico*, LPD Press, Albuquerque, NM, 1998.

111. Stone, Cyril, "Personal History with Artesia First Methodist Church".

112. Szasz and Etulain, *Religion in Modern New Mexico*, University of New Mexico Press, Albuquerque, NM, 1997.

113. Twyoniak, Frances Esquibel and Mario T. Garcia, *Migrant Daughter: Coming of Age as a Mexican American Woman*, University of California Press, Berkeley, CA, 2000.

114. U.S. Department of Agriculture, "A Camera Report on El Cerrito: A Typical Spanish-American Community in New Mexico", Washington, D.C., 1942, from *The New Mexican Hispano*.

115. U.S. Department of Agriculture, "Culture of a Contemporary Rural Community: El Cerrito, New Mexico", Washington, D.C., 1941, from *The New Mexican Hispano*.

116. Walker, Henry Pickering, *The Wagonmasters: High Plains Freighting from the Earliest Days of the Santa Fe Trail to 1880*, University of Oklahoma Press, Norman, OK, 1966.

117. Waltrip, Lela and Rufus, *Artesia: Heart of the Pecos*, Staked Plains Press, Canyon, TX, 1979.

118. Weber, David J., *Foreigners in Their Native Land: Historical Roots of the Mexican Americans*, University of New Mexico Press, Albuquerque, NM, 1973.

119. Weigle, Marta, *Brothers of Light, Brothers of Blood: The Penitentes of the Southwest*, University of New Mexico Press, Albuquerque, NM, 1976.

120. Weigle, Marta, Editor, *Telling New Mexico: A New History*, Museum of New Mexico Press, Santa Fe, NM, 2009.

121. Wikipedia, "Blackdom, New Mexico", http://en.wikipedia.org/wiki/Blackdom,_New_Mexico, accessed in 2014.

122. Wiseman, Regge N., *Glimpses of Late Frontier Life in New Mexico's Southern Pecos Valley: Archaeology and History at Blackdom and Seven Rivers*, Museum of New Mexico, Office of Archaeological Studies, Archaeology Notes 233, Santa Fe, NM, 2001.

123. Wiseman, Regge N., *Land of the Relentless Sun: An Examination of Prehistoric Site Structure Along the Lower South Seven Rivers Drainage, Eddy County, New Mexico*, Museum of New Mexico,

Office of Archaeological Studies, Archaeology Notes 284, Santa Fe, NM, 2010.

124. Wiseman, Regge N., *The Roswell South Project: Excavations in the Sacramento Plain and the Northern Chihuahuan Desert of Southeastern New Mexico*, Museum of New Mexico, Office of Archaeological Studies, Archaeology Notes 237, Santa Fe, NM, 2003.

125. Wiseman, Regge N., *U.S. 285 Seven Rivers Project: Plan for Data Recovery at Four Archaeological Sites Along South Seven Rivers, Central Eddy County, New Mexico*, Museum of New Mexico, Office of Archaeological Studies, Archaeology Notes 190, Santa Fe, NM, 1996.

126. Woodward, Dorothy, Ph.D. Dissertation, "The Penitentes of New Mexico", Yale University Graduate School, 1935, from *The Mexican American, The Penitentes of New Mexico*, Carlos Cortes, Editor, Arno Press, New York, NY, 1974.

127. Worthington, Margaret C., "Methodist History", Artesia, NM, 1993.

128. Zeleny, Carolyn, Ph.D. Dissertation, 1944, *Relations Between the Spanish-Americans and Anglo-Americans in New Mexico: A Study of Conflict and Accomodation in a Dual-Ethnic Situation*, Arno Press, New York, NY, 1974.

Prayers

PSALM 95

A Call to Praise and Obedience

I

Come, let us sing joyfully to the Lord;
let us acclaim the Rock of our salvation.
Let us greet him with thanksgiving;
let us joyfully sing psalms to him.
For the Lord is a great God,
and a great king above all gods;
In his hands are the depths of the earth,
and the tops of the mountains are his.
His is the sea, for he has made it,
and the dry land, which his hands have formed.

II

Come, let us bow down in worship;
let us kneel before the Lord who made us.
For he is our God,
and we are the people he shepherds,
the flock he guides.

III

Oh, that today you would hear his voice:
"Harden not your hearts as at Meribah,
as in the day of Massah in the desert.
Where your ancestors tempted me;
they tested me though they had seen my works.
Forty years I loathed that generation,
and I said: They are a people of erring heart,
and they know not my ways.
Therefore I swore in my anger:
They shall not enter into my rest."

(<u>The New American Bible</u>, Thomas Nelson Publishers, New York,
NY, 1971)

PSALM 63

Ardent Longing For God

I

O God, you are my God whom I seek;
for you my flesh pines and my soul thirsts
like the earth, parched, lifeless
and without water.
Thus have I gazed toward you in the sanctuary
to see your power and your glory,
For your kindness is a greater good than life;
my lips shall glorify you.

II

Thus will I bless you while I live;
lifting up my hands, I will call upon your name.
As with the riches of a banquet shall my soul be satisfied,
and with exultant lips my mouth shall praise you.
I will remember you upon my couch,
and through the night watches I will meditate on you:
That you are my help, and in the shadow of your wings I shout for joy.
My soul clings fast to you; your right hand upholds me.

(The New American Bible, Thomas Nelson Publishers, New York,
NY, 1971)

Acknowledgments

Nancy Dunn, Director, Artesia Historical Society and Museum, Artesia, New Mexico

Fr. Augustine Thompson, OP, Professor of Church History, Dominican School of Philosophy and Theology, Berkeley, California

Doe Library, University of California at Berkeley, Berkeley, California

Bancroft Library, University of California at Berkeley, Berkeley, California

Graduate Theological Union Library, Berkeley, California

Matthew Schoonover

WestBow Publishing